SECOND EDITION

Fluid Simulation
for
Computer Graphics

SECOND EDITION

Fluid Simulation
for
Computer Graphics

Robert Bridson

CRC Press
Taylor & Francis Group
Boca Raton London New York

CRC Press is an imprint of the
Taylor & Francis Group, an **informa** business

AN A K PETERS BOOK

CRC Press
Taylor & Francis Group
6000 Broken Sound Parkway NW, Suite 300
Boca Raton, FL 33487-2742

Version Date: 20150810

International Standard Book Number-13: 978-1-4822-3283-7 (Hardback)

Visit the Taylor & Francis Web site at
http://www.taylorandfrancis.com

and the CRC Press Web site at
http://www.crcpress.com

[For my wife, Rowena.]

Contents

Preface

Seven years have now passed since I wrote the first edition of this book. My aim is still not to provide a full survey of the field, but instead a practical introduction to writing fluid solvers. I have tried to distill my knowledge of the research field and my experience in the visual effects industry to hit on what I think now are the most important points, giving enough motivation that hopefully it is clear how and why things work. I hope nobody will be upset if I missed their research: I make no claim to properly overview the field, but am just carving out a path I believe is useful.

Compared to the first edition there is plenty of new material, for example new chapters on level sets and vortex methods. The ordering of topics has changed to make more sense when read the first time through, and I have upgraded several parts according to my experience. I still assume the reader has no background in fluid dynamics, and not much in the way of numerical methods, but a comfort with vector calculus, ordinary differential equations, and the standard graphics mix of linear algebra and geometry is necessary.

Previously I thanked Ron Fedkiw, who introduced me to graphics and fluids; my coauthors and students (many more now!); Marcus Nordenstam with whom I wrote several important fluid solvers including Naiad and now Bifrost; Jim Hourihan, Matthia Müller-Fischer, Eran Guendelman, and Alice Peters (of A K Peters) who all helped in the process of turning ideas and enthusiasm into the first edition. To these I would also add Wei-Pai Tang who got me started in numerical methods; the University of British Columbia Computer Science Department; Michael Nielsen; and the staff at Taylor and Francis who have made this second edition possible. Above all I would like to thank my family, especially my wife, for supporting me through the late nights, stress, one-sided conversations, and all the rest that accompany writing a book.

Robert Bridson
April 2015

Part I

The Basics

1

The Equations of Fluids

Fluids surround us, from the air we breathe to the oceans covering two thirds of the Earth, and are at the heart of some of the most beautiful and impressive phenomena we know. From water splashing, to fire and smoke swirling, fluids have become an important part of computer graphics. This book aims to cover the basics of simulating these effects for animation. So let's jump right in with the fundamental equations governing their motion.

Most fluid flow of interest in animation is governed by the famous *incompressible Navier-Stokes equations*, a set of partial differential equations that are supposed to hold throughout the fluid. The equations are usually written as

$$\frac{\partial \vec{u}}{\partial t} + \vec{u} \cdot \nabla \vec{u} + \frac{1}{\rho} \nabla p = \vec{g} + \nu \nabla \cdot \nabla \vec{u}, \qquad (1.1)$$

$$\nabla \cdot \vec{u} = 0. \qquad (1.2)$$

These may appear pretty complicated at first glance! We'll soon break them down into easy-to-understand parts (and in Appendix B provide a more rigorous explanation), but first let's begin by defining what each symbol means.

1.1 Symbols

The letter $\vec{u}$ is traditionally used in fluid mechanics for the velocity of the fluid. Why not $\vec{v}$? It's hard to say, but it fits another useful convention to call the three components of 3D velocity (u, v, w), just as the three components of position $\vec{x}$ are often taken to be (x, y, z).

The Greek letter ρ stands for the density of the fluid. For water, this is roughly 1000 kg/m^3, and for air in usual sea-level conditions this is roughly 1.3 kg/m^3, a ratio of about $700 : 1$.

It's worth emphasizing right away my insistence on using real units (meters, kilograms, etc.): long experience has shown me that it is well worth keeping all quantities in a solver implicitly in SI units, rather than just set to arbitrary values. It is tempting when starting to program a new solver to just fill in unit-less values like 1 for physical quantities such as density or to drop them altogether from expressions, whether you're operating from a quick-and-dirty just-make-it-work point of view or a more mathematically founded non-dimensionalization rationale[1]. However, this often comes back to haunt you when simulations don't quite look right, or need to be resized, or adjusted in other ways where it's not clear which of a plethora of nonphysical parameters need to be tweaked. We'll discuss the ramifications of this in algorithm design as well throughout the book.

The letter p stands for **pressure**, the force per unit area that the fluid exerts on anything.

The letter $\vec{g}$ is the familiar acceleration due to gravity, usually $(0, -9.81, 0)$ m/s^2. Now is a good time to mention that in this book we'll take as a convention that the y-axis is pointing vertically upwards, and the x- and z-axes are horizontal. We should add that in animation, additional control accelerations (to make the fluid behave in some desired way) might be added on top of gravity — we'll lump all of these into the one symbol $\vec{g}$. More generally, people call these **body forces**, because they are applied throughout the whole body of fluid, not just on the surfaces.

The Greek letter ν is technically called the **kinematic viscosity**. It measures how viscous the fluid is. Fluids like molasses have high viscosity, and fluids like mercury have low viscosity: it measures how much the fluid resists deforming while it flows (or more intuitively, how difficult it is to stir).

1.2 The Momentum Equation

The first differential equation (1.1), which is actually three in one wrapped up as a vector equation, is called the **momentum equation**. This really is good old Newton's equation $\vec{F} = m\vec{a}$ in disguise. It tells us how the fluid accelerates due to the forces acting on it. We'll try to break this down before moving onto the second differential equation (1.2), which is called the **incompressibility condition**.

Let's first imagine we are simulating a fluid using a particle system (later in the book we will actually use this as a practical method, but for now let's just use it as a thought experiment). Each particle might represent a little blob of fluid. It would have a mass m, a volume V, and a velocity $\vec{u}$. To integrate the system forward in time all we need is to

---

[1]Non-dimensionalization is a strategy for mathematically simplifying physical equations by rewriting all quantities as ratios to characteristic values of the problem at the hand, like the usual density of the fluid and the width of the container, rather than using SI units. This can reduce the number of constants that appear in the equations to the minimal set that matter, making some analysis much easier.

figure out what the forces acting on each particle are: $\vec{F} = m\vec{a}$ then tells us how the particle accelerates, from which we get its motion. We'll write the acceleration of the particle in slightly odd notation (which we'll later relate to the momentum equation above):

$$\vec{a} \equiv \frac{D\vec{u}}{Dt}.$$

The big D derivative notation is called the **material derivative** (more on this later). Newton's law is now

$$m\frac{D\vec{u}}{Dt} = \vec{F}.$$

So what are the forces acting on the particle? The simplest is of course gravity: $m\vec{g}$. However, it gets interesting when we consider how the rest of the fluid also exerts force: how the particle interacts with other particles nearby.

The first of the fluid forces is pressure. High-pressure regions push on lower-pressure regions. Note that what we really care about is the net force on the particle: for example, if the pressure is equal in every direction there's going to be a net force of zero and no acceleration due to pressure. We only see an effect on the fluid particle when there is an imbalance, i.e. higher pressure on one side of the particle than on the other side, resulting in a force pointing away from the high pressure and toward the low pressure. In the appendices we show how to rigorously derive this, but for now let's just point out that the simplest way to measure the imbalance in pressure at the position of the particle is simply to take the negative gradient of pressure: $-\nabla p$. (Recall from calculus that the gradient is in the direction of "steepest ascent," thus the negative gradient points away from high-pressure regions toward low-pressure regions.) We'll need to integrate this over the volume of our blob of fluid to get the pressure force. As a simple approximation, we'll just multiply by the volume V. You might be asking yourself, but what is the pressure? We'll skip over this until later, when we talk about incompressibility, but for now you can think of it being whatever it takes to keep the fluid at constant volume.

The other fluid force is due to viscosity. A viscous fluid tries to resist deforming. Later we will derive this in more depth, but for now let's intuitively develop this as a force that tries to make our particle move at the average velocity of the nearby particles, i.e., that tries to minimize differences in velocity between nearby bits of fluid. You may remember from image processing, digital geometry processing, the physics of diffusion or heat dissipation, or many other domains, that the differential operator that measures how far a quantity is from the average around it is the

Laplacian $\nabla \cdot \nabla$. (Now is a good time to mention that there is a quick review of vector calculus in the appendices, including differential operators like the Laplacian.) This will provide our viscous force then, once we've integrated it over the volume of the blob. We'll use the **dynamic viscosity coefficient**, which is denoted with the Greek letter μ (dynamic means we're getting a *force* out of it; the kinematic viscosity from before is used to get an *acceleration* instead). I'll note here that near the surface of a liquid (where there isn't a complete neighborhood around the blob) and for fluids with variable viscosity, this term ends up being a little more complicated; see Chapter 10 for more details.

Putting it all together, here's how a blob of fluid moves:

$$m\frac{D\vec{u}}{Dt} = m\vec{g} - V\nabla p + V\mu\nabla \cdot \nabla\vec{u}.$$

Obviously we're making errors when we approximate a fluid with a small finite number of particles. We will take the limit then as our number of particles goes to infinity and the size of each blob goes to zero. Of course, this clearly makes a different sort of error, as real fluids are in fact composed of a (very large) finite number of molecules! But this limit, which we call the **continuum model**, has the advantages of mathematical conciseness and independence from the exact number of blobs, and has been shown experimentally to be in extraordinarily close agreement with reality in a vast range of scenarios. However, taking the continuum limit does pose a problem in our particle equation, because the mass m and volume V of the particle must then go to zero, and we are left with nothing meaningful. We can fix this by first dividing the equation by the volume, and then taking the limit. Remembering m/V is just the fluid density ρ, we get

$$\rho\frac{D\vec{u}}{Dt} = \rho\vec{g} - \nabla p + \mu\nabla \cdot \nabla\vec{u}.$$

Looking familiar? We'll divide by the density and rearrange the terms a bit to get

$$\frac{D\vec{u}}{Dt} + \frac{1}{\rho}\nabla p = \vec{g} + \frac{\mu}{\rho}\nabla \cdot \nabla\vec{u}.$$

To simplify things even a little more, we'll define the kinematic viscosity as $\nu = \mu/\rho$ to get

$$\frac{D\vec{u}}{Dt} + \frac{1}{\rho}\nabla p = \vec{g} + \nu\nabla \cdot \nabla\vec{u}.$$

We've almost made it back to the momentum equation! In fact this form, using the material derivative D/Dt, is actually more important to us in computer graphics and will guide us in solving the equation numerically. But we still will want to understand what the material derivative is and how it relates back to the traditional form of the momentum equation. For that, we'll need to understand the difference between the **Lagrangian** and **Eulerian** viewpoints.

1.3   Lagrangian and Eulerian Viewpoints

When we think about a continuum (like a fluid or a deformable solid) moving, there are two approaches to tracking this motion: the Lagrangian viewpoint and the Eulerian viewpoint.

The Lagrangian approach, named after the French mathematician Lagrange, is what you're probably most familiar with. It treats the continuum just like a particle system. Each point in the fluid or solid is labeled as a separate particle, with a position $\vec{x}$ and a velocity $\vec{u}$. You could even think of each particle as being one molecule of the fluid. Nothing too special here! Solids are almost always simulated in a Lagrangian way, with a discrete set of particles usually connected up in a mesh.

The Eulerian approach, named after the Swiss mathematician Euler, takes a different tactic that's usually used for fluids. Instead of tracking each particle, we instead look at fixed points in space and see how measurements of fluid quantities, such as density, velocity, temperature, etc., at those points change in time. The fluid is probably flowing past those points, contributing one sort of change: for example, as a warm fluid moves past followed by a cold fluid, the temperature at the fixed point in space will decrease—even though the temperature of any individual particle in the fluid is not changing! In addition the fluid variables can be changing in the fluid, contributing the other sort of change that might be measured at a fixed point: for example, the temperature measured at a fixed point in space will decrease as the fluid everywhere cools off.

One way to think of the two viewpoints is in doing a weather report. In the Lagrangian viewpoint you're in a balloon floating along with the wind, measuring the pressure and temperature and humidity, etc., of the air that's flowing alongside you. In the Eulerian viewpoint you're stuck on the ground, measuring the pressure and temperature and humidity, etc., of the air that's flowing past. Both measurements can create a graph of how conditions are changing, but the graphs can be completely different as they are measuring the rate of change in fundamentally different ways.

Numerically, the Lagrangian viewpoint corresponds to a particle system, with or without a mesh connecting up the particles, and the Eulerian viewpoint corresponds to using a fixed grid that doesn't change in space even as the fluid flows through it.

It might seem the Eulerian approach is unnecessarily complicated: why not just stick with Lagrangian particle systems? Indeed, there are schemes, such as vortex methods (see, e.g., [YUM86, GLG95, AN05, PK05]) and smoothed particle hydrodynamics (SPH) (see, e.g., [DC96,MCG03,PTB$^+$03]) that do this. However, even these rely on the Eulerian-derived equations for forces in the fluid, and in this book we will largely stick with Eulerian methods for a few reasons:

- It's easier to analytically work with the spatial derivatives like the pressure gradient and viscosity term in the Eulerian viewpoint.

- It's much easier to numerically approximate those spatial derivatives on a fixed Eulerian mesh than on a cloud of arbitrarily moving particles.

The key to connecting the two viewpoints is the material derivative. We'll start with a Lagrangian description: there are particles with positions $\vec{x}$ and velocities $\vec{u}$. Let's look at a generic quantity we'll call q: each particle has a value for q. (Quantity q might be density, or velocity, or temperature, or many other things.) In particular, the function $q(t, \vec{x})$ tells us the value of q at time t for the particle that happens to be at position $\vec{x}$: this is an Eulerian variable since it's a function of space, not of particles. So how fast is q changing for the particle whose position is given by $\vec{x}(t)$ as a function of time, i.e., the Lagrangian question? Just take the total derivative (a.k.a. the Chain Rule):

$$\frac{d}{dt}q(t, \vec{x}(t)) = \frac{\partial q}{\partial t} + \nabla q \cdot \frac{d\vec{x}}{dt}$$

$$= \frac{\partial q}{\partial t} + \nabla q \cdot \vec{u}$$

$$\equiv \frac{Dq}{Dt}.$$

This is the material derivative!

Let's review the two terms that go into the material derivative. The first is $\partial q/\partial t$, which is just how fast q is changing at that fixed point in space, an Eulerian measurement. The second term, $\nabla q \cdot \vec{u}$, is correcting for how much of that change is due just to differences in the fluid flowing past (e.g., the temperature changing because hot air is being replaced by cold air, not because the temperature of any molecule is changing).

Just for completeness, let's write out the material derivative in full, with all the partial derivatives:

$$\frac{Dq}{Dt} = \frac{\partial q}{\partial t} + u\frac{\partial q}{\partial x} + v\frac{\partial q}{\partial y} + w\frac{\partial q}{\partial z}.$$

Obviously in 2D, we can just get rid of the w- and z-term.

Note that I keep talking about how the quantity, or molecules, or particles, move with the velocity field $\vec{u}$. This is called **advection** (or sometimes **convection** or **transport**; they all mean the same thing). An **advection equation** is just one that uses the material derivative, at its simplest setting it to zero:

$$\frac{Dq}{Dt} = 0,$$

$$\text{i.e.,} \quad \frac{\partial q}{\partial t} + \vec{u} \cdot \nabla q = 0.$$

This just means the quantity is moving around but isn't changing in the Lagrangian viewpoint.

1.3.1 An Example

Hopefully to lay the issue to rest, let's work through an example in one dimension. Instead of q we'll use T for temperature. We'll say that at one instant in time, the temperature profile is

$$T(x) = 10x;$$

that is, it's freezing at the origin and gets warmer as we look further to the right, to a temperature of 100 at $x = 10$. Now let's say there's a steady wind of speed c blowing, i.e., the fluid velocity is c everywhere:

$$\vec{u} = c.$$

We'll assume that the temperature of each particle of air isn't changing — they're just moving. So the material derivative, measuring things in the Lagrangian viewpoint says the change is zero:

$$\frac{DT}{Dt} = 0.$$

If we expand this out, we have

$$\frac{\partial T}{\partial t} + \nabla T \cdot \vec{u} = 0,$$

$$\frac{\partial T}{\partial t} + 10 \cdot c = 0$$

$$\Rightarrow \quad \frac{\partial T}{\partial t} = -10c;$$

that is, at a fixed point in space, the temperature is changing at a rate of $-10c$. If the wind has stopped, $c = 0$, nothing changes. If the wind is blowing to the right at speed $c = 1$, the temperature at a fixed point will drop at a rate of -10. If the wind is blowing faster to the left at speed $c = -2$, the temperature at a fixed point will increase at a rate of 20. So even though the Lagrangian derivative is zero, in this case the Eulerian derivative can be anything depending on how fast and in what direction the flow is moving.

1.3.2 Advecting Vector Quantities

One point of common confusion is what the material derivative means when applied to vector quantities, like RGB colors, or most confusing of all, the velocity field $\vec{u}$ itself. The simple answer is: treat each component separately. Let's write out the material derivative for the color vector $\vec{C} = (R, G, B)$:

$$\frac{D\vec{C}}{Dt} = \begin{bmatrix} DR/Dt \\ DG/Dt \\ DB/Dt \end{bmatrix} = \begin{bmatrix} \partial R/\partial t + \vec{u} \cdot \nabla R \\ \partial G/\partial t + \vec{u} \cdot \nabla G \\ \partial B/\partial t + \vec{u} \cdot \nabla B \end{bmatrix} = \frac{\partial \vec{C}}{\partial t} + \vec{u} \cdot \nabla \vec{C}.$$

So although the notation $\vec{u} \cdot \nabla \vec{C}$ might not strictly make sense (is the gradient of a vector a matrix? what is the dot-product of a vector with a matrix?[2]) it's not hard to figure out if we split up the vector into scalar components.

Let's do the same thing for velocity itself, which really is no different except $\vec{u}$ appears in two places, as the velocity field in which the fluid is moving and as the fluid quantity that is getting advected. People sometimes call this **self-advection** to highlight that velocity is appearing in two different roles, but the formulas work exactly the same as for color. So just by copying and pasting, here is the advection of velocity $\vec{u} = (u, v, w)$ spelled out:

$$\frac{D\vec{u}}{Dt} = \begin{bmatrix} Du/Dt \\ Dv/Dt \\ Dw/Dt \end{bmatrix} = \begin{bmatrix} \partial u/\partial t + \vec{u} \cdot \nabla u \\ \partial v/\partial t + \vec{u} \cdot \nabla v \\ \partial w/\partial t + \vec{u} \cdot \nabla w \end{bmatrix} = \frac{\partial \vec{u}}{\partial t} + \vec{u} \cdot \nabla \vec{u},$$

or if you want to get right down to the nuts and bolts of partial derivatives,

$$\frac{D\vec{u}}{Dt} = \begin{bmatrix} \frac{\partial u}{\partial t} + u\frac{\partial u}{\partial x} + v\frac{\partial u}{\partial y} + w\frac{\partial u}{\partial z} \\ \frac{\partial v}{\partial t} + u\frac{\partial v}{\partial x} + v\frac{\partial v}{\partial y} + w\frac{\partial v}{\partial z} \\ \frac{\partial w}{\partial t} + u\frac{\partial w}{\partial x} + v\frac{\partial w}{\partial y} + w\frac{\partial w}{\partial z} \end{bmatrix}.$$

If you want to go even further, advecting matrix quantities around, it's no different: just treat each component separately.

---

[2] With slightly more sophisticated tensor notation, this can be put on a firm footing, but traditionally people stick with the dot-product.

1.4   Incompressibility

Real fluids, even liquids like water, change their volume. In fact, that's just what sound waves are: perturbations in the volume, and thus density and pressure, of the fluid. You may once have been taught that the difference between liquids and gases is that gases change their volume but liquids don't, but that's not really true: otherwise you wouldn't be able to hear underwater!

However, the crucial thing is that usually fluids don't change their volume very much. It's next to impossible, even with an incredibly powerful pump, to change the volume of water much at all. Even air won't change its volume much unless you stick it in a pump, or are dealing with really extreme situations like sonic booms and blast waves. The study of how fluids behave in these situations is generally called **compressible flow**. It's complicated and expensive to simulate, and apart from acoustics doesn't enter that visibly into everyday life — and even sound waves are such tiny perturbations in the volume and have so small of an effect on how fluids move at a macroscopic level (water sloshing, smoke billowing, etc.) that they're practically irrelevant for animation.

What this means is that in animation we can generally treat all fluids, both liquids and gases, as **incompressible**, which means their volume doesn't change.[3] What does this mean mathematically? There's a more rigorous explanation in Appendix B again, but we can sketch out a quick argument now.

Pick an arbitrary chunk of fluid to look at for some instant in time. We'll call this volume Ω and its boundary surface $\partial\Omega$ (these are the traditional symbols). We can measure how fast the volume of this chunk of fluid is changing by integrating the normal component of its velocity around the boundary:

$$\frac{d}{dt}\text{volume}(\Omega) = \iint_{\partial\Omega} \vec{u} \cdot \hat{n}.$$

If the surface is moving tangentially, that doesn't affect the volume; if it's moving in the outward/inward direction, volume increases/decreases proportionally. For an incompressible fluid, the volume had better stay constant, i.e., this rate of change must be zero:

$$\iint_{\partial\Omega} \vec{u} \cdot \hat{n} = 0.$$

Now we can use the divergence theorem to change this to a volume integral. Basically, this is a multi-dimensional version of the Fundamental Theorem

---

[3]Even if we need to somehow animate sonic booms and blast waves, they're basically invisible and extremely fast moving, thus most audiences have no idea really how they behave. It's probably a much better idea, from an artistic/perceptual/economic viewpoint, to hack together something that looks cool than try to simulate them accurately.

of Calculus: if you integrate the derivative of a function, you get the original function evaluated at the bounds of your integration (see Appendix A for a review if you need to brush up on your vector calculus). In this case, we get

$$\iiint_\Omega \nabla \cdot \vec{u} = 0.$$

Now, here's the magical part: this equation should be true for any choice of Ω, any region of fluid. The only continuous function that integrates to zero independent of the region of integration is zero itself. Thus the integrand has to be zero everywhere:

$$\nabla \cdot \vec{u} = 0.$$

This is the *incompressibility condition*, the other part of the incompressible Navier-Stokes equations.

A vector field that satisfies the incompressibility condition is called **divergence-free** for obvious reasons. One of the tricky parts of simulating incompressible fluids is making sure that the velocity field stays divergence-free. This is where the pressure comes in.

One way to think about pressure is that it's precisely the force needed to keep the velocity divergence-free. If you're familiar with constrained dynamics, you can think of the incompressibility condition as a constraint and the pressure field as the Lagrange multiplier needed to satisfy that constraint subject to the principle of zero virtual work. If you're not, don't worry. Let's derive exactly what the pressure has to be.

The pressure only shows up in the momentum equation, and we want to somehow relate it to the divergence of the velocity. Therefore, let's take the divergence of both sides of the momentum equation:

$$\nabla \cdot \frac{\partial \vec{u}}{\partial t} + \nabla \cdot (\vec{u} \cdot \nabla \vec{u}) + \nabla \cdot \frac{1}{\rho} \nabla p = \nabla \cdot (\vec{g} + \nu \nabla \cdot \nabla \vec{u}). \qquad (1.3)$$

We can change the order of differentiation in the first term to the time derivative of divergence:

$$\frac{\partial}{\partial t} \nabla \cdot \vec{u}.$$

If the incompressibility condition always holds, this had better be zero. Subsequently, rearranging Equation (1.3) gives us an equation for pressure:

$$\nabla \cdot \frac{1}{\rho} \nabla p = \nabla \cdot (-\vec{u} \cdot \nabla \vec{u} + \vec{g} + \nu \nabla \cdot \nabla \vec{u})$$

This isn't exactly relevant for our numerical simulation, but it's worth seeing because we'll go through almost exactly the same steps, from looking at how fast a volume is changing to an equation for pressure, when we discretize.

1.5 Dropping Viscosity

In some situations, viscosity forces are extremely important: e.g., simulating honey or very small-scale fluid flows. But in most other cases that we wish to animate, viscosity plays a minor role, and thus we often drop it: the simpler the equations are, the better. In fact, most numerical methods for simulating fluids unavoidably introduce errors that can be physically reinterpreted as viscosity (more on this later) — so even if we drop viscosity in the equations, we will still get something that looks like it. In fact, one of the big challenges in computational fluid dynamics is avoiding this spurious viscous error as much as possible. Thus for the rest of this book, apart from Chapter 10 that focuses on high or even varying viscosity fluids, we will assume viscosity has been dropped.

The Navier-Stokes equations without viscosity are called the **Euler equations** and such an ideal fluid with no viscosity is called **inviscid**. Just to make it clear what has been dropped, here are the incompressible Euler equations using the material derivative to emphasize the simplicity:

$$\frac{D\vec{u}}{Dt} + \frac{1}{\rho}\nabla p = \vec{g},$$

$$\nabla \cdot \vec{u} = 0.$$

It is these equations that we'll mostly be using. Do not forget they are a further approximation, and it's not that water and air are actually ideal inviscid fluids — it's just that the contribution of their viscosity to a numerical simulation is usually dwarfed by other errors in the simulation and thus not worth modeling.

1.6 Boundary Conditions

Most of the, ahem, "fun" in numerically simulating fluids is in getting the boundary conditions correct. So far, we've only talked about what's happening in the interior of the fluid: so what goes on at the boundary?

For now, let's focus on just two boundary conditions, **solid walls** and **free surfaces**.

A solid wall boundary is where the fluid is in contact with a solid. It's simplest to phrase this in terms of velocity: the fluid had better not be flowing into the solid or out of it, thus the normal component of velocity has to be zero:

$$\vec{u} \cdot \hat{n} = 0.$$

Things are a little more complicated if the solid itself is moving too. In general, we need the normal component of the fluid velocity to match the normal component of the solid's velocity, so that the *relative* velocity has zero normal component:

$$\vec{u} \cdot \hat{n} = \vec{u}_{\text{solid}} \cdot \hat{n}.$$

In both these equations, $\hat{n}$ is of course the normal to the solid boundary. This is sometimes called the **no-stick** condition, since we're only restricting the normal component of velocity, allowing the fluid to freely slip past in the tangential direction. This is an important point to remember: the tangential velocity of the fluid might have no relation at all to the tangential velocity of the solid.

So that's what the velocity does: how about the pressure at a solid wall? We again go back to the idea that pressure is "whatever it takes to make the fluid incompressible." We'll add to that, "and enforce the solid wall boundary conditions." The $\nabla p / \rho$ term in the momentum equation applies even on the boundary, so for the pressure to control $\vec{u} \cdot \hat{n}$ at a solid wall, obviously that's saying something about $\nabla p \cdot \hat{n}$, otherwise known as the normal derivative of pressure: $\partial p / \partial \hat{n}$. We'll wait until we get into numerically handling the boundary conditions before we get more precise.

That's all there is to a solid wall boundary for an **inviscid** fluid. If we do have viscosity, life gets a little more complicated. In that case, the stickiness of the solid generally influences the tangential component of the fluid's velocity, forcing it to match. This is called the **no-slip** boundary condition, where we simply say

$$\vec{u} = 0,$$

or if the solid is moving,

$$\vec{u} = \vec{u}_{\text{solid}}.$$

For fluids with very low but nonzero viscosity, this is actually more accurate than the no-stick condition when looking in microscopic detail at the flow next to the solid, but typically the effect of viscosity and the no-stick condition are only seen in a vanishingly thin **boundary layer** around the solid, and elsewhere in the fluid it's as if we had a no-stick boundary. Boundary layers are a difficult area of research, but since they usually are far thinner than what we can resolve in an animation simulation, we won't worry about them and just use no-stick except for high viscosity goop. Again, we'll avoid a discussion of exact details until we get into numerical implementation.

You may be puzzled if you think about these boundary conditions in the context of a drop of liquid falling off a solid: how can it actually separate from the solid if its normal component of velocity is zero at the surface of the solid? At some level the answer is that separation isn't really properly treated by the continuum model: it's a molecular-scale process and can't be abstracted away. Generally we either get plausible separation for free from the numerical errors in a simulation method, or we hack it in if it doesn't look plausible. Batty et al. [BBB07] introduced a more principled "macroscopic" model of separation into graphics with an inequality condition allowing the fluid to move away from the wall but not into it:

$$\vec{u} \cdot \hat{n} \geq \vec{u}_{\text{solid}} \cdot \hat{n}.$$

The ramifications of this condition, both physical and algorithmic, are still quite unclear so we will not follow up further in this book though it is a prime direction of research.

As a side note, sometimes the solid wall actually is a vent or a drain that fluid *can* move through: in that case, we obviously want $\vec{u} \cdot \hat{n}$ to be different from the wall velocity. It should rather be the velocity at which fluid is being pumped in or out of the simulation at that point.

The other boundary condition that we're interested in is at a free surface. This is where we stop modeling the fluid. For example, if we simulate water splashing around, then the water surfaces that are *not* in contact with a solid wall are free surfaces. In this case there really is another fluid, air, but we may not want the hassle of simulating the air as well. And since air is 700 times lighter than water, it's not able to have that big of an effect on the water anyhow (with a few notable exceptions like bubbles!). So instead we make the modeling simplification that the air can be represented as a region with constant atmospheric pressure. In actual fact, since only *differences* in pressure matter (in incompressible flow), we can set the air pressure to be any arbitrary constant: zero is the most convenient. Thus a free surface is one where $p = 0$, and we don't control the velocity in any particular way.

The other case in which free surfaces arise is where we are trying to simulate a bit of fluid that is part of a much larger domain: for example, simulating smoke in the open air. We obviously can't afford to simulate the entire atmosphere of the Earth, so we will just make a grid that covers the region we expect to be "interesting." (I'll preemptively state here that to simulate smoke, you *need* to simulate the smoke-free air nearby as well, not just the smoky region itself — however, we can get away with not simulating the air distant enough from all the action.) Past the boundaries of the simulated region the fluid continues on, but we're not tracking it; we allow fluid to enter and exit the region as it wants, so it's natural to consider this a free surface, $p = 0$, even though there's not actually a visible surface.[4]

---

[4]Technically this assumes there is no gravitational acceleration $\vec{g}$ included in the equations. If there is, we would take the hydrostatic pressure $p = \rho\vec{g} \cdot \vec{x}$ as the open boundary condition. To avoid having to do this, we can write the momentum equation

One final note on free surfaces: for smaller-scale liquids, surface tension can be very important. At the underlying molecular level, surface tension exists because of varying strengths of attraction between molecules of different types. For example, water molecules are more strongly attracted to other water molecules than they are to air molecules: therefore, the water molecules at the surface separating water and air try to move to be as surrounded by water as much as possible. From a geometric perspective, physical chemists have modeled this as a force that tries to minimize the surface area or, equivalently, tries to reduce the mean curvature of the surface. You can interpret the first idea (minimizing surface area) as a tension that constantly tries to shrink the surface, hence the name surface tension; it can be a little more convenient to work with the second approach using mean curvature. (Later, in Chapter 8 we'll talk about how to actually measure mean curvature and exactly what it means.) In short, the model is that there is actually a jump in pressure between the two fluids, proportional to the mean curvature:

$$[p] = \gamma \kappa.$$

The $[p]$ notation means the jump in pressure, i.e., the difference in pressure measured on the water side and measured on the air side, γ is the surface tension coefficient that you can look up (for water and air at room temperature it is approximately $\gamma \approx 0.073 N/m$), and κ is the mean curvature, measured in $1/m$. What this means for a free surface with surface tension is that the pressure at the surface of the water is the air pressure (which we assume to be zero) plus the pressure jump:

$$p = \gamma \kappa. \tag{1.4}$$

Free surfaces do have one major problem: air bubbles immediately collapse (there's no pressure inside to stop them losing their volume). While air is much lighter than water, and so usually might not be able to transfer much momentum to water, it still has the incompressibility constraint: an air bubble inside water largely keeps its volume. Modeling the air bubble with a free surface will let the bubble collapse and vanish. To handle this kind of situation, you need either hacks based on adding bubble particles to a free surface flow, or more generally a simulation of both air and water (called **two-phase** flow, because there are two phases or types of fluid involved).

---

in terms of the pressure perturbation from hydrostatic rest: $p = \rho \vec{g} \cdot \vec{x} + p'$. Substituting this into the pressure gradient cancels out $\vec{g}$ on the other side, and we can use the simpler open boundary condition $p' = 0$.

2

Overview of Numerical Simulation

Now that we know and understand the basic equations, how do we discretize them to numerically simulate fluids using the computer? There are an awful lot of choices for how to do this, and people are continuing to invent new ways; we won't be able to cover even a fraction of the field but will instead focus on some well-established approaches for graphics.

2.1 Splitting

The first choice we take is something called **splitting**: we split up a complicated equation into its component parts to be solved separately in turn. If we say that the rate of change of one quantity is the sum of several terms, we can numerically update it by computing each term and including their effect one after the other.

Let's make that clearer with an incredibly simple "toy" example, a single ordinary differential equation:

$$\frac{dq}{dt} = 1 + 2.$$

You of course already know that the answer is $q(t) = 3t + q(0)$, but let's work out a numerical method based on splitting. We'll split it into two steps, each one of which looks like a simple forward Euler update (if you want to remind yourself what forward Euler is, refer to Appendix A):

$$\tilde{q} = q^n + 1\Delta t, \tag{2.1}$$
$$q^{n+1} = \tilde{q} + 2\Delta t. \tag{2.2}$$

The notation used here is that q^n is the value of q computed at time step n, and Δt is the amount of time between consecutive time steps.[1] What we have done is split the equation up into two steps: after the first step (2.1), we get an intermediate quantity $\tilde{q}$ that includes the contribution of the first term ($= 1$) but not the second ($= 2$), and then the second step (2.2) goes from the intermediate value to the end by adding in the missing term's contribution. In this example, obviously, we get exactly the right answer, and splitting didn't buy us anything.

Let's upgrade our example to something more interesting:

$$\frac{dq}{dt} = f(q) + g(q). \tag{2.3}$$

Here $f()$ and $g()$ are some black box functions representing separate software modules. We could do splitting with forward Euler again:

$$\tilde{q} = q^n + \Delta t f(q^n), \tag{2.4}$$
$$q^{n+1} = \tilde{q} + \Delta t g(\tilde{q}). \tag{2.5}$$

A simple Taylor series analysis shows that this is still a first-order–accurate algorithm if you're worried. If you're not, ignore this:

$$\begin{aligned}
q^{n+1} &= (q^n + \Delta t f(q^n)) + \Delta t g(q^n + \Delta t f(q^n)) \\
&= q^n + \Delta t f(q^n) + \Delta t \left(g(q^n) + O(\Delta t)\right) \\
&= q^n + \Delta t (f(q^n) + g(q^n)) + O(\Delta t^2) \\
&= q^n + \frac{dq}{dt} \Delta t + O(\Delta t^2).
\end{aligned}$$

Wait, you say, that hasn't bought you anything beyond what simple old forward Euler *without* splitting gives you. Aha! Here's where we get a little more sophisticated. Let's assume that the reason we've split $f()$ and $g()$ into separate software modules is that we have special numerical methods that are really good at solving the simpler equations

$$\frac{dr}{dt} = f(r),$$
$$\frac{ds}{dt} = g(s).$$

This is precisely the motivation for splitting: we may not be able to easily deal with the complexity of the whole equation, but it's built out of separate

---

[1]In particular, do not get confused with raising q to the power of n or $n + 1$: this is an abuse of notation, but it is so convenient when we add in subscripts for grid indices that it's consistently used in fluid simulation. On the rare occasion that we do raise a quantity to some exponent, we'll very clearly state that: otherwise assume the superscript indicates at what time step the quantity is.

terms that we *do* have good methods for. I'll call the special integration algorithms $F(\Delta t, r)$ and $G(\Delta t, s)$. Our splitting method is then

$$\tilde{q} = F(\Delta t, q^n), \tag{2.6}$$

$$q^{n+1} = G(\Delta t, \tilde{q}). \tag{2.7}$$

If $F()$ and $G()$ were just forward Euler, then this is exactly the same as Equations (2.4) and (2.5), but again the idea is that they're something better. If you do the Taylor series analysis, you can show we still have a first-order–accurate method[2] but I'll leave that as an exercise.

Splitting really is just the principle of divide-and-conquer applied to differential equations: solving the whole problem may be too hard, but you can split it into pieces that are easier to solve and then combine the solutions.

If you're on the ball, you might have thought of a different way of combining the separate parts: instead of sequentially taking the solution from $F()$ and then plugging it into $G()$, you could run $F()$ and $G()$ in parallel and add their contributions together. The reason we're *not* going to do this but will stick to sequentially working through the steps, is that our special algorithms (the integrators $F()$ and $G()$ in this example) will guarantee special things about their output that are needed as preconditions for the input of other algorithms. Doing it in the *right* sequence will make everything work, but doing it in parallel will mess up those guarantees. We'll talk more about what those guarantees and preconditions are in the next section.

2.2   Splitting the Fluid Equations

We're going to use splitting on the incompressible fluid equations. In particular, we'll separate out the advection part, the body forces (gravity) part, and the pressure/incompressibility part. If viscosity is important, we can also elect to separate it out: see Chapter 10.

---

[2]There are more complicated ways of doing splitting in fluid dynamics, which can get higher-order accuracy, but for now we won't bother with them. At the time of writing this book, this has remained a sadly overlooked area for improvement within graphics: the first-order time-splitting error can be very significant indeed.

That is, we'll work out methods for solving these simpler equations:

$$\frac{Dq}{Dt} = 0 \qquad \text{(advection)}, \tag{2.8}$$

$$\frac{\partial \vec{u}}{\partial t} = \vec{g} \qquad \text{(body forces)}, \tag{2.9}$$

$$\frac{\partial \vec{u}}{\partial t} + \frac{1}{\rho}\nabla p = 0$$

such that $\quad \nabla \cdot \vec{u} = 0. \qquad$ (pressure/incompressibility) $\qquad$ (2.10)

We used the generic quantity q in the advection equation because we may be interested in advecting other things, not just velocity $\vec{v}$.

Let's call our algorithm for solving the advection, Equation (2.8), $\texttt{advect}(\vec{u}, \Delta t, q)$: it advects quantity q through the velocity field $\vec{u}$ for a time interval Δt. Chapter 3 will cover some good approaches to do this.

For the body force, Equation (2.9), forward Euler $\vec{u} \leftarrow \vec{u} + \Delta t \vec{g}$ is fine.

For the pressure/incompressibility part, Equation (2.10), we'll develop an algorithm called $\texttt{project}(\Delta t, \vec{u})$ that calculates and applies just the right pressure to make $\vec{u}$ divergence-free and also enforces the solid wall boundary conditions. Chapter 5 deals with this part (and explains the odd choice of word, "project").

The important precondition/guarantee issue we mentioned in the previous section is that advection should only be done in a divergence-free velocity field. When we move fluid around and want it to conserve volume, the velocity field we are moving it in must be divergence-free: we covered that already in Chapter 1. So we want to make sure we only run $\texttt{advect}()$ with the output of $\texttt{project}()$: the sequence of our splitting matters a lot!

Putting it together, here is our basic fluid algorithm:

- Start with an initial divergence-free velocity field $\vec{u}^0$.
- For time step $n = 0, 1, 2, \ldots$
  - Determine a good time step Δt to go from time t_n to time t_{n+1}.
  - Set $\vec{u}^A = \texttt{advect}(\vec{u}^n, \Delta t, \vec{u}^n)$.
  - Add $\vec{u}^B = \vec{u}^A + \Delta t \vec{g}$.
  - Set $\vec{u}^{n+1} = \texttt{project}(\Delta t, \vec{u}^B)$.

2.3   Time Steps

Determining a good time-step size is the first step of the algorithm. One obvious concern is that we don't want to go past the duration of the current animation frame: if we pick a candidate Δt but find $t_n + \Delta t > t_{\text{frame}}$, then we should clamp it to $\Delta t = t_{\text{frame}} - t_n$ and set a flag that alerts us to the fact that we've hit the end of the frame. (Note that checking if $t_{n+1} = t_{\text{frame}}$ may be a bad idea, since inexact floating-point arithmetic may mean t_{n+1} isn't exactly equal to t_{frame} if compilers have taken any liberties.) At the end of each frame we'll presumably do something special like save the state of the fluid animation to disk, or render it on the screen.

Subject to that clamping, we should select a Δt that satisfies any requirements made by the separate steps of the simulation: advection, body forces, etc. We'll discuss these in the chapters that follow. Selecting the minimum of these suggested time steps is generally safe (but not guaranteed in all instances!).

Finally, for the quality desired of the simulation, we may need to take even smaller time steps to adequately resolve the fluid phenomena. Often this is based around on calculating how fast things are moving in the simulation, and limiting how far they can go in one step by adjusting the time stamp accordingly. For example, overly large time steps might mean that the position of a fast-moving solid is only sampled before and after it travels through a smoky region, and this undersampling will result in the smoke not being properly disturbed. Limiting the time step size so that the solid will definitely be sampled at intermediate times in the smoky region will give much better quality results.

However, in some situations we may have a performance requirement that won't let us take lots of small time steps every frame. If we only have time for, say, three time steps per frame, we had better make sure Δt is at least a third of the frame time. This might be larger than the suggested time-step sizes from each step, so we will make sure in this book that all the methods we use can tolerate the use of larger-than-desired time steps—they should generate plausible results in this case, even if they're quantitatively inaccurate.

2.4 Grids

In this numerical section, so far we have only talked about discretizing in time, not in space. While we will go into more detail about this in the subsequent chapters, we'll introduce the basic grid structure here.

In the early days of computational fluid dynamics, Harlow and Welch introduced the marker-and-cell (MAC) method [HW65] method for solving incompressible flow problems. One of the fundamental innovations of this paper was a new grid structure that (as we will see later) makes for a very effective algorithm for enforcing incompressibility, though it may seem inconvenient for everything else.

The so-called **MAC grid** is a **staggered** grid, i.e., a grid where the different variables are stored at different locations. Let's look at it in two

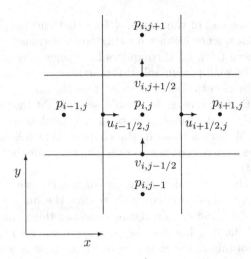

Figure 2.1. The two-dimensional MAC grid.

dimensions first, illustrated in Figure 2.1. The pressure in grid cell (i, j) is sampled at the center of the cell, indicated by $p_{i,j}$. The velocity is split into its two Cartesian components. The horizontal u-component is sampled at the centers of the vertical cell faces, for example indicated by $u_{i+1/2,j}$ for the horizontal velocity between cells (i, j) and $(i + 1, j)$. The vertical v-component is sampled at the centers of the horizontal cell faces, for example indicated by $v_{i,j+1/2}$ for the vertical velocity between cells (i, j) and $(i, j + 1)$. Note that this means we aren't storing a velocity vector anywhere: the different components of velocity are sampled at different locations, and can't simply be combined into a vector. Also note that for grid cell (i, j) we have sampled the *normal* component of the velocity at the center of each of its faces: this will very naturally allow us to estimate the amount of fluid flowing into and out of the cell.

In three dimensions, the MAC grid is set up the same way, with pressure at the grid cell centers and the three different components of velocity split up so that we have the normal component of velocity sampled at the center of each cell face (see Figure 2.2).

We'll go into more detail about why we use this staggered arrangement in Chapter 5, but briefly put it's so that we can use accurate **central differences** for the pressure gradient and for the divergence of the velocity field without the usual disadvantages of central differences. Consider just a one-dimensional example: estimating the derivative of a quantity q sampled at grid locations $\ldots, q_{i-1}, q_i, q_{i+1}, \ldots$. To estimate $\partial q / \partial x$ at grid point i

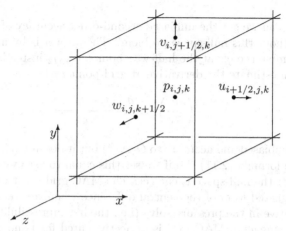

Figure 2.2. One cell from the three-dimensional MAC grid.

without any bias, the natural formula is the first central difference:

$$\left(\frac{\partial q}{\partial x}\right)_i \approx \frac{q_{i+1} - q_{i-1}}{2\Delta x}. \tag{2.11}$$

This is unbiased and accurate to $O(\Delta x^2)$, as opposed to a forward or backward difference, such as

$$\left(\frac{\partial q}{\partial x}\right)_i \approx \frac{q_{i+1} - q_i}{\Delta x}, \tag{2.12}$$

which is biased to the right and only accurate to $O(\Delta x)$. However, formula (2.11) has a major problem in that the derivative estimate at grid point i completely ignores the value q_i sampled there! To see why this is so terrible, recall that a constant function can be defined as one whose first derivative is zero. If we require that the finite difference (2.11) is zero, we are allowing q's that aren't necessarily constant—q_i could be quite different from q_{i-1} and q_{i+1} and still the central difference will report that the derivative is zero as long as $q_{i-1} = q_{i+1}$. In fact, a very jagged function like $q_i = (-1)^i$ (here we are using an exponent) which is far from constant, will register as having zero derivative according to formula (2.11). On the other hand, only truly constant functions satisfy the forward difference (2.12) equal to zero. The problem with formula (2.11) is technically known as having a non-trivial **null-space**: the set of functions where the formula evaluates to zero contains more than just the constant functions to which it should be restricted.

How can we get the unbiased second-order accuracy of a central difference without this null-space problem? The answer is by using a staggered
grid: sample the q's at the half-way points, $q_{i+1/2}$ instead. Then we naturally can estimate the derivative at grid point i as

$$\left(\frac{\partial q}{\partial x}\right)_i \approx \frac{q_{i+1/2} - q_{i-1/2}}{\Delta x}. \tag{2.13}$$

This is unbiased and accurate to $O(\Delta x^2)$ but it doesn't skip over any values
of q like formula (2.11). So if we set this equal to zero we can only have q
constant: the null-space is correct. The MAC grid is set up so that we use
this staggered form of the central difference wherever we need to estimate
a derivative in the pressure solve (i.e., the incompressibility condition).

The staggered MAC grid is perfectly suited for handling pressure and
incompressibility, but it's frankly a pain for other uses. For example, if
we actually want to evaluate the full velocity vector somewhere, we will
always need to use some kind of interpolation even if we're looking at a
grid point! At an arbitrary location in space, we'll do separate bilinear
or trilinear interpolation for each component of velocity, but since those
components are offset from each other we will need to compute a different
set of interpolation weights for each component. At the grid locations
themselves, this boils down to some simple averaging. In two dimensions
these averages are

$$\vec{u}_{i,j} = \left(\frac{u_{i-1/2,j} + u_{i+1/2,j}}{2}, \quad \frac{v_{i,j-1/2} + v_{i,j+1/2}}{2}\right),$$

$$\vec{u}_{i+1/2,j} = \left(u_{i+1/2,j}, \quad \frac{v_{i,j-1/2} + v_{i,j+1/2} + v_{i+1,j-1/2} + v_{i+1,j+1/2}}{4}\right),$$

$$\vec{u}_{i,j+1/2} = \left(\frac{u_{i-1/2,j} + u_{i+1/2,j} + u_{i-1/2,j+1} + u_{i+1/2,j+1}}{4}, \quad v_{i,j+1/2}\right).$$

In three dimensions the formulas are similar:

$$\vec{u}_{i,j,k} = \left(\frac{u_{i-1/2,j,k} + u_{i+1/2,j,k}}{2}, \quad \frac{v_{i,j-1/2,k} + v_{i,j+1/2,k}}{2}, \quad \frac{w_{i,j,k-1/2} + w_{i,j,k+1/2}}{2}\right)$$

$$\vec{u}_{i+1/2,j,k} = \left(u_{i+1/2,j,k}, \quad \frac{\begin{matrix}v_{i,j-1/2,k} + v_{i,j+1/2,k}\\ +v_{i+1,j-1/2,k} + v_{i+1,j+1/2,k}\end{matrix}}{4}, \quad \frac{\begin{matrix}w_{i,j,k-1/2} + w_{i,j,k+1/2}\\ +w_{i+1,j,k-1/2} + w_{i+1,j,k+1/2}\end{matrix}}{4}\right)$$

$$\vec{u}_{i,j+1/2,k} = \left(\frac{\begin{aligned}u_{i-1/2,j,k} + u_{i+1/2,j,k}\\ +u_{i-1/2,j+1,k} + u_{i+1/2,j+1,k}\end{aligned}}{4}, \; v_{i,j+1/2,k}, \; \frac{\begin{aligned}w_{i,j,k-1/2} + w_{i,j,k+1/2}\\ +w_{i,j+1,k-1/2} + w_{i,j+1,k+1/2}\end{aligned}}{4} \right)$$

$$\vec{u}_{i,j,k+1/2} = \left(\frac{\begin{aligned}u_{i-1/2,j,k} + u_{i+1/2,j,k}\\ +u_{i-1/2,j,k+1} + u_{i+1/2,j,k+1}\end{aligned}}{4}, \; \frac{\begin{aligned}v_{i,j-1/2,k} + v_{i,j+1/2,k}\\ +v_{i,j-1/2,k+1} + v_{i,j+1/2,k+1}\end{aligned}}{4}, \; w_{i,j,k+1/2} \right)$$

Finally, a word is in order about the curious half indices, such as $i+1/2$. These are convenient theoretically and conceptually, fixing the location of the sample points with respect to the grid. However, an implementation obviously should use integer indices. A standard convention is needed, for example:

$$\texttt{p(i,j,k)} = p_{i,j,k}, \tag{2.14}$$
$$\texttt{u(i,j,k)} = u_{i-1/2,j,k}, \tag{2.15}$$
$$\texttt{v(i,j,k)} = v_{i,j-1/2,k}, \tag{2.16}$$
$$\texttt{w(i,j,k)} = w_{i,j,k-1/2}. \tag{2.17}$$

Then for an $\texttt{nx} \times \texttt{ny} \times \texttt{nz}$ grid, the pressure is stored in an $\texttt{nx} \times \texttt{ny} \times \texttt{nz}$ array, the u component in a $(\texttt{nx+1}) \times \texttt{ny} \times \texttt{nz}$ array, the v component in a $\texttt{nx} \times (\texttt{ny+1}) \times \texttt{nz}$ array, and the w component in a $\texttt{nx} \times \texttt{ny} \times (\texttt{nz+1})$ array.

2.5 Dynamic Sparse Grids

For a basic fluid solver, especially if the fluid fills most of its bounding box, the basic 3D grid above works fine, and is the simplest structure to implement and use. However there are three problems in general.

The first is the easiest to deal with: if the region the fluid occupies changes significantly throughout the simulation (for example, water flooding through an initially dry scene) then taking a single static grid that covers the entire region that may ever see fluid can be enormously wasteful. The obvious solution is to dynamically adjust the grid dimensions and where it lies in space at every time step, just to cover the region of interest. For a liquid, this is probably just the bounding box of the liquid's previous state, adjusted by the fluid velocity field times the time step as an estimate of where it could move, plus at least a few grid cells' worth of padding for safety (and to avoid awkward edge-of-grid boundary conditions affecting the water). For smoke it may be trickier as the fluid being simulated, the air, extends off into the atmosphere as a whole: in that case, criteria such as a minimum padding distance around the region where smoke concentration is visibly nonzero can work well.

The second problem is just efficiency on modern hardware. Points (i, j, k) and $(i, j, k + 1)$ will be nx×ny elements distant from each other in memory, so most of our common operations on grids will not have as good data locality as would like—we can expect more page faults and cache misses than strictly necessary.

The third and most severe problem is how much memory and processing is wasted when the fluid occupies only a small fraction of the volume of its bounding box. Examples of this abound: a sinuous river, liquid splashing from a tipped-over glass, a waterfall above a pool, a thin smoke trail from the curving trajectory of an aircraft, small flames on a non-flat surface.

The solution to these last two, and which subsumes the first, is to use sparse blocked grids [Bri03, LKHW03, MCZ07, Mus11, Mus13]. We conceptually begin with an extraordinarily large virtual grid, say 2^{32} along each dimension and indexed by signed 32-bit integers in each coordinate (so that negative indices as well as positive may be used for convenience). This virtual grid is large enough to cover any fluid simulation we undertake, without having to adjust its origin or dimensions. We then partition the grid into fixed size blocks or tiles, say of dimensions $6 \times 6 \times 6$ each, which are stored as tiny contiguous 3D arrays. Finally, we only allocate and store the blocks we need for a given time step, in an associative data structure that maps from indices to the stored blocks. Since we only store the blocks of the grid we care about, this is a sparse structure and nicely addresses the first and third problems: we don't waste storage or processing on voxels far from the action. Because we map blocks of voxels rather than individual voxels, the overhead of the associative data structure can be minimized; meanwhile operations inside a block have extremely good data locality which resolves the second problem.

My original implementation of sparse blocked grids [Bri02] used a simple two-level hierarchy, a 3D "coarse" array of pointers to the fine blocks, but later work showed that extending this to a three or four level tree is much more effective [Bri03, Mus13]. Alternatively, to avoid some tree structure overheads and potentially allow an even larger index space, you can use a hash table to store references to the fine blocks [Bri03], but with the disadvantage that parallel updates to hash tables are much trickier.

Writing code around sparse blocked grids is somewhat trickier than for dense grids: instead of just three nested loops for the entire domain with simple indexing, you also need an outer loop over the blocks and a bit more logic in accessing neighboring voxels (which may be in a different block, or not there at all). Another subtle difficulty is the staggering of the MAC-grid: a block for the u component must have the same dimensions as any other component, for example, so there is the risk of slightly breaking symmetry in a smoke simulation by including an extra degree of freedom for u on the negative side of the blocks than on the positive side. The remedy is to ignore (despite storing) the extra layer of u-samples on the negative side of any block with no negative-in-x neighboring block and so forth. Due to complications like these, I would highly recommend sticking to dense 3D arrays for your first fluid solver, and (**as with everything in this book!**) to prototype a sparse grid simulation in 2D before doing it in 3D.

2.6 Two Dimensional Simulations

That last point bears repeating, and emphasizing, redundantly and multiple times as necessary. Always prototype a 3D solver in 2D first. Always prototype a 3D solver in 2D first. Even once you get to a working 3D solver, keep your 2D prototype around and up-to-date so that you can easily jump back to it when working out new features or old bugs. In fact, if it's at all meaningful (which for incompressible flow is not always the case) prototype in 1D before 2D.

Even though ultimately we almost always care just about the results from 3D simulations, not 2D, so it may seem like a bit of a waste of time to implement algorithms in 2D—and sometimes a little awkward since content creation tools for 3D graphics typically don't have a 2D mode—my experience over a decade, with many code bases, projects, institutions and companies, is that this gives you a huge boost in productivity. Fluid solvers rarely work at all the first time you write them, and even after they get to the point of giving acceptable results, infrequent and subtle bugs that occasionally ruin your simulations may persist for a long time. We are going up against some really hard unsolved problems after all. Expect to spend a large amount of time chasing down strange artifacts, NaN's, iterations that don't converge, etc., and think about optimizing your development time around that reality.

Solvers in 2D need somewhat less code than 3D, run at least an order of magnitude faster, scale up to high resolution far more gracefully, occasionally avoid the "curse of dimensionality" that hits some geometric algorithms (e.g. *robustly* finding if a point is inside a 2D polygon is much simpler than finding if a point is inside a 3D mesh), and generally involve fewer indices and simpler mathematical formulas—all of which make programming and debugging far more efficient. Above all else, visualizing and analyzing results in 2D is far easier than in 3D: one image or even a spreadsheet of numbers can instantly tell you exactly what's happening in a 2D velocity field, but trying to see the same thing in 3D is a major problem in its own right for scientific visualization. At the same time, most of the lessons learned in 2D carry over to 3D, so the time and effort spent making a solver work in 2D is invariably recovered many times over when jumping to 3D.

Having said that, it is worth warning about one particularly common bug due to porting a 2D code to 3D: incomplete copy-and-paste. Beginning with 2D code like this,

```
u(i,j) = (phi(i,j) - phi(i-1,j)) / dx;
v(i,j) = (phi(i,j) - phi(i,j-1)) / dx;
```

one might easily copy and paste the last line and add k indices to extend it to 3D,

```
u(i,j,k) = (phi(i,j,k) - phi(i-1,j,k)) / dx;
v(i,j,k) = (phi(i,j,k) - phi(i,j-1,k)) / dx;
w(i,j,k) = (phi(i,j,k) - phi(i,j-1,k)) / dx;
```

but forget to change the copied v formula to be correct for w:

```
w(i,j,k) = (phi(i,j,k) - phi(i,j,k-1)) / dx;
```

This kind of bug is particularly difficult to spot when reading over code, and may be quite mysterious in terms of interpreting the output. While many standard debugging practices help here, such as unit tests to check small sections of your code against analytic test cases or assertions guarding array indexing etc., it's also good to be forewarned about the likelihood of such bugs so you can specifically look for them, and know to spend a bit of extra care when copying and pasting.

Advection Algorithms

In the previous chapter we saw that a crucial step of the fluid simulation is solving the advection equation

$$Dq/Dt = 0.$$

We will encapsulate this in a numerical routine

$$q^{n+1} = \texttt{advect}(\vec{u}, \Delta t, q^n),$$

which given a velocity field $\vec{u}$ (discretized on a MAC grid), a time step size Δt, and the current field quantity q^n returns an approximation to the result of advecting q through the velocity field over that duration of time.

It bears repeating here: advection should only be called with a divergence-free velocity field $\vec{u}$, i.e., one meeting the incompressibility constraint, which also satisfies the required boundary conditions. Failure to do so can result in peculiar artifacts, such as gain or loss of fluid and its momentum.

3.1   Semi-Lagrangian Advection

The obvious approach to solving Dq/Dt for a time step is to simply write out the PDE, e.g., in one dimension:

$$\frac{\partial q}{\partial t} + u \frac{\partial q}{\partial x} = 0$$

and then replace the derivatives with finite differences. For example, if we use forward Euler for the time derivative and an accurate central difference for the spatial derivative we get

$$\frac{q_i^{n+1} - q_i^n}{\Delta t} + u_i^n \frac{q_{i+1}^n - q_{i-1}^n}{2\Delta x} = 0,$$

which can be arranged into an explicit formula for the new values of q:

$$q_i^{n+1} = q_i^n - \Delta t\, u_i^n \frac{q_{i+1}^n - q_{i-1}^n}{2\Delta x}.$$

At first glance this seems just fine. But there are disastrous problems lurking here!

First off, it turns out that forward Euler is unconditionally *unstable* for this discretization of the spatial derivative: no matter how small we make Δt, it will always eventually blow up! (If you know about the stability region of forward Euler, what's happening is that the eigenvalues of the Jacobian generated by the central difference are pure imaginary, thus always outside the region of stability. If you don't, don't worry: we'll get to a method that works soon enough!)

Even if we replace forward Euler with a more stable time integration technique, in fact even if we were to somehow *exactly* solve the time part of the PDE, the spatial discretization will give us major troubles. At first glance it's not clear why: this is a pretty accurate estimate of the derivative, after all, and some fancy analysis can show that such a scheme will exactly conserve properties like the "energy" (the 2-norm) of the problem, just as the exact solution does. However, trying it out on a simple 1D problem will immediately show the problems lurking here. Remember from the last chapter that discussion of the problem null-space of standard central differences? Well, it raises its ugly head here too: **high-frequency**[1] jagged components of the solution, like $(-1)^i$, erroneously register as having zero or near-zero spatial derivative, and so don't get evolved forward in time—or at least move much more slowly than the velocity u they should move at. Meanwhile the low frequency components are handled accurately and move at almost exactly the right speed u. Thus the low frequency components end up separating out from the high-frequency components, and you are left with all sorts of strange high-frequency wiggles and oscillations appearing and persisting that *shouldn't be there*!

We won't go into a more rigorous analysis of the problems of simple central differences, but rest assured there is plenty of high-powered numerical analysis, which not only carefully identifies the disease but also supplies a cure with more sophisticated finite difference formulas for the spatial derivative.

We will instead first take a different, simpler, and physically-motivated approach called the **semi-Lagrangian** method. The word Lagrangian should remind you that the advection equation $Dq/Dt = 0$ is utterly trivial in the Lagrangian framework, and if we were using particle system methods it's solved automatically when we move our particles through the velocity field. That is, to get the new value of q at some point $\vec{x}$ in space, we could

---

[1]By frequency in this context, we mean frequency in space, as if you performed a Fourier transform of the function, expressing it as a sum of sine or cosine waves of different spatial frequencies. The high frequency components correspond to sharp features that vary over a small distance, and the low frequency components correspond to the smooth large-scale features.

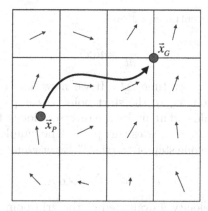

Figure 3.1. To find a fluid value at grid point $\vec{x}_G$ at the new time step, we need to know where the fluid at $\vec{x}_G$ was one time step ago, position $\vec{x}_P$, following the velocity field.

conceptually just find the particle that ends up at $\vec{x}$ and look up its value of q.

We can apply that reasoning on our grid to get the semi-Lagrangian method introduced to graphics by Stam [Sta99]. We want to figure out the new value of q at a grid point, and to do that in a Lagrangian way we need to figure out the old value of q that the particle that ends up at the grid point possesses. The particle is moving through the velocity field $\vec{u}$, and we know where it ends up—so to find where it started we simply run backwards through the velocity field from the grid point. We can grab the old value of q from this start point, which will be the new value of q at the grid point! But wait, you say, what if that start point wasn't on the grid? In that case we simply interpolate the old value of q from the old values on the grid, and we're done.

Let's go through that again, slowly and with formulas. We'll say that the location in space of the grid point we're looking at is $\vec{x}_G$. We want to find the new value of q at that point, which we'll call q_G^{n+1}. We know from our understanding of advection that if a hypothetical particle with old value q_P^n ends up at $\vec{x}_G$, when it moves through the velocity field for the time step Δt, then $q_G^{n+1} = q_P^n$. So the question is, how do we figure out q_P^n?

The first step is figuring out where this imaginary particle would have started from, a position we'll call $\vec{x}_P$. The particle moves according to the simple ordinary differential equation

$$\frac{d\vec{x}}{dt} = \vec{u}(\vec{x})$$

and ends up at $\vec{x}_G$ after time Δt. If we now run time backwards, we can go in reverse from $\vec{x}_G$ to the start point of the particle—i.e., finding where a particle would end up under the reverse velocity field $-\vec{u}$ "starting" from $\vec{x}_G$. Figure (3.1) illustrates this path. The simplest possible way to estimate $\vec{x}_P$ is to use one step of "forward" Euler going backwards in time:

$$\vec{x}_P = \vec{x}_G - \Delta t\, \vec{u}(\vec{x}_G),$$

where we use the velocity $\vec{u}$ evaluated at the grid point to take a Δt-step backwards through the flow field. It turns out forward Euler is sometimes adequate, but significantly better results can be obtained using a slightly more sophisticated technique such as a higher-order Runge-Kutta method. See Appendix A to review time integration methods. In particular, at least a second-order Runge-Kutta method is recommended as a bare minimum, such as

$$\vec{x}_{\text{mid}} = \vec{x}_G - \frac{1}{2}\Delta t\, \vec{u}(\vec{x_G}),$$

$$\vec{x}_P = \vec{x}_G - \Delta t\, \vec{u}(\vec{x}_{\text{mid}}).$$

Here a half-step is taken to get an intermediate position $\vec{x}_{\text{mid}}$ approximating the particle's position halfway along the trajectory. The velocity field is interpolated from the grid at this intermediate location, and that velocity value is used to finally get to $\vec{x}_P$. Even better results, particularly around swirls and other rotational flow elements, can be had with a third order method; the RK3 scheme given in the appendix is the best default to use. Depending on how large Δt is—see later in this chapter—it may even be wise to split the trajectory tracing into smaller substeps for better accuracy.

We now know the position where the imaginary particle started; next we have to figure out what old value of q it had. Most likely $\vec{x}_P$ is not on the grid, so we don't have the exact value, but we can get a good approximation by interpolating from q^n at nearby grid points. Trilinear (bilinear in two dimensions) interpolation is often used, though this comes with a serious penalty which we will fix at the end of the chapter.

Putting this together into a formula, our basic semi-Lagrangian formula, assuming the particle-tracing algorithm has tracked back to location $\vec{x}_P$ (typically with RK2 above), is

$$q_G^{n+1} = \texttt{interpolate}(q^n, \vec{x}_P). \tag{3.1}$$

Note that the particle I've described is purely hypothetical. No particle is actually created in the computer: we simply use Lagrangian particles to conceptually figure out the update formula for the Eulerian advection step. Because we are almost using a Lagrangian approach to do an Eulerian calculation, this is called the semi-Lagrangian method.

Just for completeness, let's illustrate this in one dimension again, using linear interpolation for the semi-Lagrangian operations. For grid point x_i, the particle is traced back to $x_P = x_i - \Delta t u$. Assuming this lies in the interval $[x_j, x_{j+1}]$, and letting $\alpha = (x_P - x_j)/\Delta x$ be the fraction of the interval the point lands in, the linear interpolation is $q_P^n = (1-\alpha)q_j^n + \alpha q_{j+1}^n$. So our update is

$$q_i^{n+1} = (1 - \alpha)q_j^n + \alpha q_{j+1}^n.$$

In practice we will need to advect the velocity field, and perhaps additional variables such as smoke density or temperature. Usually the additional variables are stored at the grid cell centers, but the velocity components are stored at the staggered grid locations discussed in the previous chapter. In each case, we will need to use the appropriate averaged velocity, given at the end of the previous chapter, to estimate the particle trajectory.

3.2   Boundary Conditions

If the starting point of the imaginary particle is in the interior of the fluid, then doing the interpolation is no problem. What happens though if the estimated starting point happens to end up outside of the fluid boundaries? This could happen because fluid is flowing in from outside the domain (and the particle is "new" fluid), or it could happen due to numerical error (the true trajectory of the particle actually stayed inside the fluid, but our forward Euler or Runge-Kutta step introduced error that put us outside).

This is really the question of boundary conditions. In the first case, where we have fluid flowing in from the outside, we should know what the quantity is that's flowing in: that's part of stating the problem correctly. For example, if we say that fluid is flowing in through a grating on one side of the domain at a particular velocity $\vec{U}$ and temperature T, then any particle whose starting point ends up past that side of the domain should get velocity $\vec{U}$ and temperature T.

In the second case, where we simply have a particle trajectory that strayed outside the fluid boundaries due to numerical error, the appropriate strategy is to extrapolate the quantity from the nearest point on the boundary—this is our best bet as to the quantity that the true trajectory (which should have stayed inside the fluid) would pick up. Sometimes that extrapolation can be easy: if the boundary we're closest to has a specified fluid velocity we simply use that. For example, for simulating smoke in the open air we could assume a constant wind velocity $\vec{U}$ (perhaps zero) outside of the simulation domain.

The trickier case is when the quantity isn't known *a priori* but has to be numerically extrapolated from the fluid region where it is known. We will go into more detail on this extrapolation soon, in Chapter 4. For now, let's just stick with finding the closest point that is on the boundary of the fluid region and interpolating the quantity from the fluid values stored on the grid near there. In particular, this is what we will need to do for finding velocity values when our starting point ends up inside a solid object or for free surface flows (water) if we end up in the free space.

Taking the fluid velocity at a solid boundary is *not* the same as the solid's velocity in general. As we discussed earlier, the normal component of the fluid velocity had better be equal to the normal component of the solid's velocity, but apart from in viscous flows, the tangential component can be completely different. Thus we usually interpolate the fluid velocity at the boundary and don't simply take the solid velocity. However, for the particular case of viscous flows (or at least, a fluid-solid interaction that we want to appear viscous and sticky), we can indeed take the shortcut of just using the solid's velocity.

3.3   Time Step Size

A primary concern for any numerical method is whether it is stable: will it (or any of the numerical errors we make) blow up? Happily the semi-Lagrangian approach above is **unconditionally stable**: no matter how big Δt is, we never blow up. It's easy to see why: wherever the particle starting point ends up, we interpolate from old values of q to get the new values for q. Linear/bilinear/trilinear interpolation always produces values that lie between the values we're interpolating from: we can't create larger or smaller values of q than were already present in the previous time step. So q stays bounded. This is really very attractive: we can select the time step based purely on the accuracy versus speed trade-off curve. If we want to run at real-time rates regardless of the accuracy of the simulation, we can pick Δt equal to the frame duration for example.

In practice, the method can produce some strange results if we are too aggressive with the time step size. A good rule of thumb from Foster and Fekiw [FF01] is to limit Δt so that the furthest a particle trajectory is traced is at most some constant number of grid cell widths, such as five:

$$\Delta t \leq \frac{5\Delta x}{u_{\max}}, \tag{3.2}$$

where u_{max} is an estimate of the maximum velocity in the fluid. This could be as simple as the maximum velocity currently stored on the grid. A more robust estimate takes into account velocities that might be induced due to acceleration g from gravity (or other body forces like buoyancy) over the time step. In that case,

$$u_{max} = \max(|u^n|) + \Delta t\,|g|.$$

Unfortunately this estimate depends on Δt (which we're trying to find), but if we replace Δt with the upper bound from inequality (3.2) we get

$$u_{max} = \max(|u^n|) + \frac{5\Delta x}{u_{max}}|g|.$$

Solving for u_{max} and taking a simple upper bound gives

$$u_{max} = \max(|u^n|) + \sqrt{5\Delta x\,g}.$$

This has the advantage of always being positive, even when the initial velocities are zero, so we avoid a divide-by-zero in inequality (3.2).

In some cases artifacts will still be present with a time step of this size; one possible remedy that avoids the expense of running the entire simulation at a smaller time step is to just trace the trajectories used in semi-Lagrangian advection with several small substeps. If each substep is limited to $|\vec{u}(\vec{x})|\Delta t < \Delta x$, i.e., so that each substep only traverses roughly one grid cell, there is little opportunity for problems to arise. Note that this substep restriction can be taken locally: in fast-moving regions of the fluid more substeps might be used than in slow-moving regions.

3.3.1 The CFL Condition

Before leaving the subject of time-step sizes, let's take a closer look at something called the **CFL condition**. There is some confusion in the literature about exactly what this condition is, so in this section I'll try to set the story straight. This section can be safely skipped if you're not interested in some of the more technical aspects of numerical analysis.

The CFL condition, named for applied mathematicians R. Courant, K. Friedrichs, and H. Lewy, is a simple and very intuitive necessary condition for convergence. Convergence means that if you repeat a simulation with smaller and smaller Δt and Δx, in the limit going to zero, then your numerical solutions should approach the exact solution.[2]

---

[2] As an aside, this is a sticky point for the three-dimensional incompressible Navier-Stokes equations, and at the time of this writing nobody has managed to prove that they do in fact have a unique solution for all time. It has already been proven in two dimensions, and in three dimensions up to some finite time; a million-dollar prize has been offered from the Clay Institute for the first person to finish the proof in three dimensions.

The solution $q(\vec{x}^\star, t^\star)$ of a time-dependent partial differential equation, such as the advection equation, at a particular point in space $\vec{x}^\star$ and time $t^\star$ depends on some or all of the initial conditions. That is, if we modify the initial conditions at some locations and solve the problem again, it will change $q(\vec{x}^\star, t^\star)$; at other locations the modifications may have no effect. In the case of the constant-velocity advection equation, the value $q(\vec{x}^\star, t^\star)$ is exactly equal to $q(\vec{x}^\star - t^\star \vec{u}, 0)$, so it only depends on a single point in the initial conditions. For other PDEs, such as the heat-diffusion equation $\partial q/\partial t = \nabla \cdot \nabla q$, each point of the solution depends on *all* points in the initial conditions. The **domain of dependence** for a point is precisely the set of locations that have an effect on the value of the solution at that point.

Each point of a numerical solution also has a domain of dependence: again, the set of locations in the initial conditions that have an effect on the value of the solution at that point. It should be intuitively obvious that the numerical domain of dependence, at least in the limit, must contain the true domain of dependence if we want to get the correct answer. This is, in fact, the CFL condition: convergence is only possible in general if, in the limit as $\Delta x \to 0$ and $\Delta t \to 0$, the numerical domain of dependence for each point contains the true domain of dependence.

For semi-Lagrangian methods the CFL condition is satisfied if, in the limit, the particle trajectories we trace are close enough to the true trajectories— close enough that we interpolate from the correct grid cells and get the correct dependence. This should hold, since unless we do something terribly wrong, in the limit the particle tracing should converge to the correct trajectories.

That said, for standard explicit finite difference methods for the advection equation, where the new value of a grid point q_i^{n+1} is calculated from a few of the old values at neighboring grid points, i.e., from points only $C\Delta x$ away for a small integer constant C, there is a much more apparent CFL condition. In particular, the true solution is moving at speed $|\vec{u}|$, so the speed at which numerical information is transmitted, i.e., $C\Delta x/\Delta t$, must be at least as fast. That is, for convergence we will require

$$\frac{C\Delta x}{\Delta t} \geq |\vec{u}|,$$

which turns into a condition on the time step:

$$\Delta t \leq \frac{C\Delta x}{|\vec{u}|}. \tag{3.3}$$

Here is where most of the confusion arises. This is often the same, up to a small constant factor, as the maximum stable time step for the method— and in particular, in the original paper by Courant et al. [CFL28], these were identical. Thus sometimes the CFL condition is confused with a stability condition. In fact, there are methods that are unstable no matter what the time-step size is, such as the forward Euler and central difference scheme that began this chapter.[3] There are also explicit methods that are stable for arbitrary time-step sizes—however, they can't converge to the correct answer unless the CFL condition is met.

To further muddy the waters, there is a related quantity called the **CFL number**, often denoted α. If c is the maximum speed of information propagation in the problem—assuming this concept makes sense, for example in the advection equation we're studying (where $c = \max |\vec{u}|$) or in certain wave equations where it might be termed the "speed of sound"—then the CFL number α of a given discretization is defined from

$$\Delta t = \alpha \frac{\Delta x}{c}. \tag{3.4}$$

Thus the time step we talked about above, inequality (3.2), could be expressed as taking a CFL number of five. The CFL condition for explicit finite difference schemes can be expressed as a limit on the CFL number; similarly the stability of some, though not all, explicit finite difference schemes can be conveniently expressed as another limit on the CFL number. The CFL number by itself is just a useful parameter, not a condition on anything.

3.4 Diffusion

Notice that in the interpolation step of semi-Lagrangian advection we are taking a weighted average of values from the previous time step. That is, with each advection step, we are doing an averaging operation. Averaging tends to smooth out or blur sharp features, **diffusing** or **dissipating** them. In signal-processing terminology, we have a low-pass filter. A single blurring step is pretty harmless, but if we repeatedly blur every time step, you can imagine there are going to be problems.

Let's try to understand this smoothing behavior more physically. We'll use a technique called **modified PDEs**. The common way of looking at numerical error in solving equations is that our solution gets perturbed from the true solution by some amount: we're only approximately solving

---

[3]Interestingly, despite being unconditionally unstable, this method will still converge to the correct solution at a fixed end time T if the initial conditions are adequately smooth and in the limit $\Delta x \to 0$ the time step is reduced as $O(\Delta x^2)$. Taking the time step much smaller than the grid spacing reduces the rate of exponential blow-up to zero in the limit, though of course this is not an efficient method. Naturally it satisfies the CFL condition since it converges.

the problem. The approach that we'll now use, sometimes also called **back-wards error analysis**, instead takes the perspective that we *are* solving a problem exactly—it's just the problem we solved isn't quite the same as the one we started out with, i.e., the problem has been perturbed in some way. Often interpreting the error this way, and understanding the perturbation to the problem being solved, is extremely useful.

To make our analysis as simple as possible, we'll solve the advection problem in one dimension with a constant velocity $u > 0$:

$$\frac{\partial q}{\partial t} + u\frac{\partial q}{\partial x} = 0.$$

We'll assume $\Delta t < \Delta x/u$, i.e., that the particle trajectories span less than a grid cell—the analysis easily extends to larger time steps too, but nothing significant changes. In that case, the starting point of the trajectory that ends on grid point i is in the interval $[x_{i-1}, x_i]$. Doing the linear interpolation between q_{i-1}^n and q_i^n at point $x_i - \Delta t u$ gives

$$q_i^{n+1} = \frac{\Delta t\, u}{\Delta x}\, q_{i-1}^n + \left(1 - \frac{\Delta t\, u}{\Delta x}\right) q_i^n.$$

We can rearrange this to get

$$q_i^{n+1} = q_i^n - \Delta t\, u\, \frac{q_i^n - q_{i-1}^n}{\Delta x}, \tag{3.5}$$

which is in fact exactly the Eulerian scheme of forward Euler in time and a one-sided finite difference in space.[4] Now recall the Taylor series for q_{i-1}^n:

$$q_{i-1}^n = q_i^n - \left(\frac{\partial q}{\partial x}\right)_i^n \Delta x + \left(\frac{\partial^2 q}{\partial x^2}\right)_i^n \frac{\Delta x^2}{2} + O(\Delta x^3).$$

Substituting this into Equation (3.5) and doing the cancellation gives

$$q_i^{n+1} = q_i^n - \Delta t\, u\, \frac{1}{\Delta x}\left(\left(\frac{\partial q}{\partial x}\right)_i^n \Delta x - \left(\frac{\partial^2 q}{\partial x^2}\right)_i^n \frac{\Delta x^2}{2} + O(\Delta x^3)\right)$$

$$= q_i^n - \Delta t\, u\, \left(\frac{\partial q}{\partial x}\right)_i^n + \Delta t\, u\Delta x \left(\frac{\partial^2 q}{\partial x^2}\right)_i^n + O(\Delta x^2).$$

---

[4]If you're interested, note that the side to which the finite difference is biased is the side from which the fluid is flowing. This is no coincidence and makes perfect physical sense—in the real physical world, you get information from upwind, not downwind, directions in advection. In general, biasing a finite difference to the direction that flow is coming from is called **upwinding**. Most advanced Eulerian schemes are upwind-biased schemes that do this with more accurate finite difference formulas.

Up to a second-order truncation error, we can see this is forward Euler in time applied to the *modified PDE*:

$$\frac{\partial q}{\partial t} + u\frac{\partial q}{\partial x} = u\Delta x \frac{\partial^2 q}{\partial x^2}.$$

This is the advection equation with an additional viscosity-like term with coefficient $u\Delta x$! (Recall from the momentum equation of Navier-Stokes that viscosity appears as the Laplacian of velocity, which in one dimension is simply the second derivative.) That is, when we use the simple semi-Lagrangian method to try to solve the advection equation *without* viscosity, our results look like we are simulating a fluid *with* viscosity. It's called **numerical diffusion** (or numerical viscosity, or numerical dissipation—they all mean the same thing in this context).

Fortunately the coefficient of this numerical dissipation goes to zero as $\Delta x \to 0$, so we get the right answer in the limit. However, in computer graphics we don't have the patience or supercomputing resources to take Δx extremely small: we want to see good-looking results with Δx as large as possible!

So how bad is it? It depends on what we're trying to simulate. If we're trying to simulate a viscous fluid, which has plenty of natural dissipation already, then the extra numerical dissipation will hardly be noticed—and more importantly, looks plausibly like real dissipation. But, most often we're trying to simulate nearly inviscid fluids, and this is a serious annoyance which keeps smoothing the interesting features like small vortices from our flow. As bad as this is for velocity, in Chapter 8 we'll see it can be much much worse for other fluid variables.

3.5   Reducing Numerical Diffusion

There are many approaches to fixing the numerical diffusion problem. We'll outline one particularly simple but effective strategy for fixing the semi-Lagrangian method presented so far. As we saw in the last section, the problem mainly lies with the excessive averaging induced by linear interpolation (of the quantity being advected; linearly interpolating the velocity field in which we trace is not the main culprit and can be used as is). Thus, the natural next step is to use sharper interpolation. For example, Fedkiw et al. [FSJ01] proposed using a specially limited form of Catmull-Rom interpolation; we will go even further with a more accurate and significantly less diffusive interpolant.

Tracing back through the velocity field is the expensive part of semi-Lagrangian advection, particularly with all its mixing of floating-point calculations with integer arithmetic and dependent memory look-ups (finding grid points) and irregular memory reads (actually looking up velocity and the fields to be interpolated). Once we have done all that, we may as well do just a little more computation with an extra layer of values (which were probably also fetched in cache anyhow) to get a much better result.

In one dimension, we do this with a cubic interpolant. If we are estimating the value of q at fraction s between grid points x_i and x_{i+1}, the linear interpolant is

$$q \approx (1 - s)x_i + s\, x_{i+1}.$$

This is the value of the linear polynomial which passes through (x_i, q_i) and (x_{i+1}, q_{i+1}). The interpolant is exact for linear polynomials, obviously; it also matches smooth functions up to the first term of their Taylor series, but leaves a quadratic remainder term. We instead can use the *cubic* polynomial which passes through (x_{i-1}, q_{i-1}), (x_i, q_i), (x_{i+1}, q_{i+1}), and (x_{i+2}, q_{i+2}), including an additional data point on either side, with this formula:

$$
\begin{aligned}
q \approx \quad & \left[-\tfrac{1}{3}s + \tfrac{1}{2}s^2 - \tfrac{1}{6}s^3 \right] q_{i-1} \\
+ & \left[1 - s^2 + \tfrac{1}{2}(s^3 - s) \right] q_i \\
+ & \left[s + \tfrac{1}{2}(s^2 - s^3) \right] q_{i+1} \\
+ & \left[\tfrac{1}{6}(s^3 - s) \right] q_{i+1}.
\end{aligned}
\tag{3.6}
$$

You can double-check this is exact if q is really any cubic polynomial; it also matches smooth functions up to the third term of their Taylor series, leaving a much tinier quartic remainder term. This is two orders of magnitude more accurate than linear interpolation.

Figure (3.2) shows the difference cubic interpolation can make. This is a pure advection example with a constant velocity, so the original profile of the function should ideally be translated unchanged. However, on the left linear interpolation quickly diffuses an initial sharp triangular pulse down to a smooth hump; the cubic interpolation on the right does gradually smooth out the shape as well, but keeps it much sharper and higher for much longer.

In two or three dimensions, we can extend cubic interpolation to bicubic or tricubic just the same way we do with linear interpolation, doing it dimension by dimension. For example, in two dimensions we can interpolate data along the x-axis first (using w_{-1}, w_0, ... for the weighting coefficients shown in equation (3.6) above):

$$q_{j-1} = w_{-1}(s)q_{i-1,j-1} + w_0(s)q_{i,j-1} + w_1(s)q_{i+1,j-1} + w_2(s)q_{i+2,j-1},$$
$$q_j = w_{-1}(s)q_{i-1,j} + w_0(s)q_{i,j} + w_1(s)q_{i+1,j} + w_2(s)q_{i+2,j},$$
$$q_{j+1} = w_{-1}(s)q_{i-1,j+1} + w_0(s)q_{i,j+1} + w_1(s)q_{i+1,j+1} + w_2(s)q_{i+2,j+1},$$
$$q_{j+2} = w_{-1}(s)q_{i-1,j+2} + w_0(s)q_{i,j+2} + w_1(s)q_{i+1,j+2} + w_2(s)q_{i+2,j+2}.$$

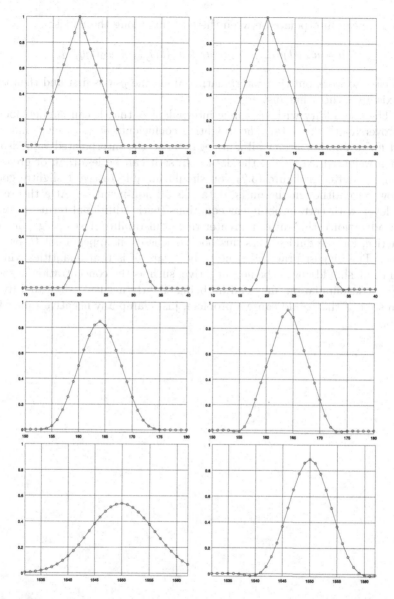

Figure 3.2. Numerical diffusion illustrated in semi-Lagrangian advection of a triangular signal transported at constant velocity. From top to bottom, we see the initial signal, after one time step, after ten time steps, and after a hundred time steps. The left side shows plain linear interpolation; the right side shows cubic interpolation. The correct behaviour is for the triangle to translate unchanged.

Then we can interpolate between these results along the y-axis:

$$q = w_{-1}(t)q_{j-1} + w_0(t)q_j + w_1(t)q_{j+1} + w_2(t)q_{j+2}.$$

It's easy to work out that interpolating along the y-axis first and then the x-axis gives the same answer.

The one oddity with the cubic interpolant is that it can "undershoot" or "overshoot" the data. The weighting coefficients w_{-1}, w_0, w_1, and w_2 add up to one but aren't all non-negative, so the interpolated value isn't just a weighted average of the data points: it can be less than or greater than the data. In figure (3.2) you should be able to see it slightly goes below zero, although the initial data was all non-negative. At a theoretical level, with certain nonlinear equations (with additional terms beyond just advection), this raises a greater risk of instability developing—but in practice, for the fluid solvers this book discusses, it appears not to be an issue. The biggest practical issue to be aware of is that quantities which you think should always be non-negative, such as the concentration of soot in a smoke simulation, may end up being slightly negative after an advection step: if that could cause a problem, just clamp any negative values to zero.

4

Level Set Geometry

Before continuing on to the heart of our basic fluid solver, the pressure projection step to make the fluid incompressible and satisfy its boundary conditions, we need to take a diversion into geometry. In the previous chapter we already ran up against boundary conditions and related geometric problems:

- when is a point inside a solid? (the point may be where we traced back to during semi-Lagrangian)

- what is the closest point on the surface of some geometry?

- how do we extrapolate values from one region into another?

The first two queries are extremely common in fluid solvers. We also more generally want representations of geometry which play well with equations discretized on grids, and one of the most practical answers is the **level set** method.

In this book we'll touch on just the basics we need; readers might look at the book by Osher and Fedkiw [OF02], for example, for a more detailed study of the numerics and applications of level sets.

The first query above suggests the right approach is **implicit surfaces**. While there are potentially a lot of ways to generalize this, we will focus on the case where we have a continuous scalar function $\phi(x, y, z)$ which defines the geometry as follows:

- a point $\vec{x}$ is outside the geometry when $\phi(\vec{x}) > 0$,

- it's inside the geometry when $\phi(\vec{x}) < 0$, and

- a point $\vec{x}$ is on the surface when $\phi(\vec{x}) = 0$.

In some other contexts within computer graphics, the convention may be reversed (the "outside" is the negative region) or a threshold value other than zero could be used, but this is usually the way we do it in fluid simulation.

The surface can also be referred to as the **zero isocontour** of $\phi(\vec{x})$, "isocontour" referring to a contour where the value is everywhere the same ("iso") and "zero" indicating that special value. The term "level set" is also used for this in calculus (the set of points where $\phi(\vec{x})$ is at a certain level) but in numerical methods and computer graphics it has come to mean a lot more, which we'll get to in this chapter.

If $phi(\vec{x})$ can be differentiated at a point on the surface, vector calculus also tells us that the gradient vector, $\nabla\phi(\vec{x})$, must point in a direction normal to the surface. Since ϕ is negative on the inside and increase to positive on the outside, the gradient in fact has to be an outward-pointing vector normal to the surface. This is often convenient information to have.

What if we were to ask that the gradient be exactly the unit-length normal on the surface? In other words, demand that

$$\|\nabla\phi(\vec{x})\| = 1,$$

at least near the surface? Since the gradient has to be parallel to the normal, this would imply the directional derivative of ϕ in the normal direction $\hat{n}$ is exactly one,

$$\frac{\partial\phi(\vec{x})}{\partial\hat{n}} = 1,$$

which means for a small number d and a point $\vec{x}$ on the surface,

$$\frac{\left(\phi(\vec{x} + d\,\hat{n}) - \phi(\vec{x})\right)}{d} \approx 1$$
$$\Rightarrow \quad \phi(\vec{x} + d\,\hat{n}) - 0 \approx d.$$

In this case d is literally the distance away from the surface we are evaluating ϕ in the outward direction, and this tells us that the value of ϕ must approximately be that distance itself. More precisely, we are looking at **signed distance**, where the value d is the negative of distance when inside the geometry: it is the distance in the outward direction, which is negative when we go inwards.

In fact, we can turn this around: given any geometric representation, *define* $\phi(\vec{x})$ as the signed distance function, sometimes abbreviated SDF. The resulting ϕ will then serve as an excellent implicit surface description.

4.1 Signed Distance

Given any closed set S of points, the **distance function** for the set is

$$\text{distance}_S(\vec{x}) = \min_{\vec{p} \in S} \|\vec{x} - \vec{p}\|;$$

that is, it's the distance to the closest point in S. If S divides space into a well-defined inside and outside, then the **signed distance function** is

$$\phi_S(\vec{x}) = \begin{cases} \text{distance}_S(\vec{x}) : \vec{x} \text{ is outside,} \\ -\text{distance}_S(\vec{x}) : \vec{x} \text{ is inside.} \end{cases}$$

Signed distance has many useful properties in addition to the gradient being equal to the unit-length outward-pointing normal at the surface. For example, at some point $\vec{x}$ **outside** the geometry, let $\vec{p}$ be the closest point to $\vec{x}$ on the surface. Clearly the distance function ϕ will increase fastest if we move directly away from the closest point on the surface, and vector calculus tells us that the gradient $\nabla\phi$ must point in the direction of "steepest ascent." In other words, outside the geometry, $-\nabla\phi(\vec{x})$ always points towards the closest point on the surface. Similar reasoning shows that inside the geometry, $\nabla\phi$ points toward the closest point on the surface.

Now let $\hat{c}$ be the direction to the closest point:

$$\hat{c} = \frac{\vec{p} - \vec{x}}{\|\vec{p} - \vec{x}\|}.$$

Clearly if we move a small distance ϵ in this direction, to $\vec{x}^* = \vec{x} + \epsilon\hat{c}$, the closest point to $\vec{x}^*$ is still $\vec{p}$: the closest point on the surface doesn't change as you move directly closer to it! Therefore the distance function at the new point, $\phi(\vec{x}^*)$, must be equal to $\phi(\vec{x}) - \epsilon$. This gives us the directional derivative:

$$\begin{aligned} \frac{\partial\phi(\vec{x})}{\partial\hat{c}} &= \lim_{\epsilon\to 0} \frac{\phi(\vec{x} + \epsilon\hat{c}) - \phi(\vec{x})}{\epsilon} \\ &= \lim_{\epsilon\to 0} \frac{\phi(\vec{x}) - \epsilon - \phi(\vec{x})}{\epsilon} \\ &= \lim_{\epsilon\to 0} \frac{-\epsilon}{\epsilon} \\ &= -1. \end{aligned}$$

We already know that the gradient outside the geometry is pointing in the opposite direction from $\hat{c}$, and the directional derivative is just the dot-product of the gradient with the direction, $\partial\phi/\partial\hat{c} = \nabla\phi \cdot \hat{c}$, therefore we can work out the gradient is just $-\hat{c}$ outside the geometry. Again, similar reasoning shows it is $\hat{c}$ inside the geometry. In summary:

- outside the geometry, $-\nabla\phi$ is the unit-length vector pointing towards the closest point on the surface,

- inside the geometry, $\nabla\phi$ is the unit-length vector pointing towards the closest point on the surface,

- and on the surface, $\nabla\phi$ is the unit-length outward-pointing normal.

If we combine this with the fact that the value of ϕ is the distance (or negative distance inside) to the closest point, we get another useful fact: for any point $\vec{x}$,

$$\vec{x} - \phi(\vec{x})\nabla\phi(\vec{x})$$

is the closest point to $\vec{x}$ on the surface. Signed distance functions easily give us answers to the first two queries listed at the start of this chapter!

Another beautiful consequence is that $\nabla\phi(\vec{x})$ is the unit-length outward-pointing normal to the surface at the closest point to $\vec{x}$ on the surface. In other words, it gives us a sensible extension of the concept of "normal" to points that aren't even on the surface. For example, for fluid flow near but not exactly on a solid surface, we can easily break the velocity $\vec{u}$ into a component that is normal to the surface, $\vec{u} \cdot \hat{n}$, and the remainder which is tangential to the surface, $\vec{u} - (\vec{u} \cdot \hat{n})\hat{n}$, using $\hat{n} = \nabla\phi$.

Diving deeper into the mathematical side of level sets, the fact that the gradient is always unit-length can be expressed as a nonlinear PDE called the **Eikonal equation**:

$$\|\nabla\phi\| = 1$$

It turns out that with the appropriate boundary conditions (namely that $\phi = 0$ at the surface of the geometry) and a technical condition on the information flow in the problem, this is enough to define signed distance as well. Some papers and algorithms work from this perspective, but we will mostly stick with geometrical reasoning in this book.

It can be shown that in fact signed distance is smooth (i.e., $\nabla\phi$ and higher derivatives exist) everywhere except on the **medial axis**, consisting of points that are equidistant to different parts of the surface. The medial axis is exactly where there isn't a *unique* closest point, such as the center of a sphere and the middle plane inside a flat slab. It stretches out to touch edges and corners of sharp geometry. Around concave geometry, there are parts of the medial axis outside the geometry.

For typical surfaces the medial axis is a small, lower-dimensional set which we don't often have to worry about—and even on the medial axis, ϕ is still continuous, just with a kink. In particular, where the surface itself is smooth, signed distance is smooth on and near the surface. However, it's important to keep in mind that all of the above discussion about the gradient $\nabla\phi$ breaks down on the medial axis: the function isn't even differentiable there, so the gradient doesn't exist. Numerical approximations to the gradient, which we will discuss soon, will typically still give a vector, but it may be much less than unit-length, perhaps even zero.

Higher derivatives of the signed distance function, where it's smooth, also can have geometric meaning. For example, the signed distance function of a sphere of radius r centered at the origin is

$$\phi(\vec{x}) = \|\vec{x}\| - r.$$

The gradient is

$$\nabla \phi(\vec{x}) = \frac{\vec{x}}{\|\vec{x}\|},$$

and the divergence of this, the Laplacian of the original signed distance function, in three dimensions is (after a lot of tedious differentiation I am not going to drag you through)

$$\nabla \cdot \nabla \phi(\vec{x}) = \frac{2}{\|x\|}.$$

In particular, on the surface where $\|x\| = r$, the Laplacian is exactly the mean curvature $2/r$ of the sphere. This is no accident: it can be shown in general for any smooth curved surface, the Laplacian of the signed distance function evaluated at the surface is the mean curvature.

4.2   Discretizing Signed Distance Functions

So far we have worked with the exact signed distance function. For a few geometric objects, this is easy enough to write out analytically. A sphere of radius r centered at $\vec{c}$ has signed distance

$$\phi_{\text{sphere}}(\vec{x}) = \|\vec{x} - \vec{c}\| - r.$$

The infinite plane going through point $\vec{p}$ with outward-pointing normal $\hat{n}$ has signed distance

$$\phi_{\text{plane}}(\vec{x}) = (\vec{x} - \vec{p}) \cdot \hat{n}.$$

The signed distance function for an axis-aligned box defined as $[x_0, x_1] \times [y_0, y_1] \times [z_0, z_1]$ can be computed by checking first if the point is inside or outside, then using the distance to the closest face on the inside but directly finding the closest point if on the outside: see Figure 4.1 for details. Cylinders and cones are also fairly simple, but thats about it for easy formulas.

We will cover how to compute the signed distance to a triangle mesh below, but it is significantly more complicated, and without optimized acceleration structures, can be very slow. Clearly we're not doing ourselves a favor by rephrasing the inside/outside geometric query as just evaluating a signed distance function, if the signed distance function evaluation is even more expensive than simply computing inside/outside directly from a mesh. We also haven't really changed the underlying geometric representation: we've just hidden it.

This is where the **level set method** comes into play. Instead of computing signed distance analytically from some other geometric information,

- If $x_0 < x < x_1$ and $y_0 < y < y_1$ and $z_0 < z < z_1$ (inside)
  - Return $\phi = \max(x_0 - x,\ x - x_1,\ y_0 - y,\ y - y_1,\ z_0 - z,\ z - z_1)$
- Else (outside)
  - (Find the closest point (p, q, r) on the surface of the box)
  - If $x < x_0$ set $p = x_0$; else if $x > x_1$ set $p = x_1$; else set $p = x$.
  - If $y < y_0$ set $q = y_0$; else if $y > y_1$ set $q = y_1$; else set $q = y$.
  - If $z < z_0$ set $r = z_0$; else if $z > z_1$ set $r = z_1$; else set $r = z$.
  - Return $\phi = \sqrt{(x - p)^2 + (y - q)^2 + (z - r)^2}$.

Figure 4.1. How to compute the signed distance function of an axis-aligned box

we will instead store values of signed distance directly on a grid, just like any other fluid variable. Then when we need to evaluate $\phi(\vec{x})$, we **interpolate** an approximate value from the surrounding grid points. The answer will not be exact in general, but is often good enough: all of fluid simulation deals with approximate answers, in any case, so some approximation in the geometry is admissible too. This is the core of what people more conventionally understand by the term "level set": a signed distance function that has been sampled on a grid.

Once we're dealing with just grid values, evaluating ϕ is fast and easy through interpolation. Approximating the gradient is also easy enough, using finite differences. For example, an accurate finite difference estimate of $\partial\phi/\partial x$ is available halfway along the x-axis between any two grid points:

$$\left(\frac{\partial\phi}{\partial x}\right)_{i+1/2,j,k} \approx \frac{\phi_{i+1,j,k} - \phi_{i,j,k}}{\Delta x}.$$

Likewise we can get estimates for the y-derivative and z-derivative at other midpoints between grid values; we can then interpolate between these to get an approximate gradient vector at any point in the grid. Usually this is preferable to directly differentiating the interpolant of ϕ, since the interpolants we usually use (piecewise trilinear or piecewise tricubic) have jump discontinuities in their derivative between grid cells.

Moreover, we can do many interesting geometric operations simply by directly manipulating the values stored of ϕ stored on the grid. We'll return to this later in the chapter.

4.3   Computing Signed Distance

If we don't have a simple analytic formula for a given piece of geometry, but we want to produce a level set of it, we need an algorithm to compute signed distance on the grid. One particularly helpful footnote is that the algorithm needn't be exact: when we interpolate, we already introduce errors, so small errors in the grid values themselves can be tolerated, especially away from the surface itself.

There are two main approaches to computing level sets: from geometry (finding closest points and measuring the distance to them) or from PDEs (solving the Eikonal equation $\|\nabla \phi\| = 1$). Both have their uses: the geometric approach is typically more accurate, and easier to understand, but the PDE approach applies in cases where the geometry isn't explicitly known (it is described implicitly as the zero contour of a function that is *not* signed distance, and we want signed distance instead).

4.3.1   Distance to Points

We'll begin with a special case that is nonetheless a common operation: finding the distance to a finite set of points, computed with the geometric approach. Note that there is no "inside" so whether this distance is signed or not is moot. The algorithm is given in Figure 4.2, with one key ingredient left unspecified: the order in which we loop over the grid to propagate distance information. It is based on algorithm 4 in Tsai's article [Tsa02]. For a review of many other algorithms, see the paper by Jones et al. [JBS06].

In the first stage we compute exact distance and closest point information directly in the grid cells immediately surrounding the input points, without needing any fancy geometric data structures. The second stage can efficiently propagate that from neighbor to neighbor through the grid, again without need for extra data structures. However, it is not exact: the point closest to a given grid cell may not be the same as the points closest to any of its neighbors. That being said, the distance to the true closest point can never be very different from the distance to the almost closest point calculated by this method: in practice, this works extremely well.

4.3.2   Loop Order

There are two suggestions for the loop order given by Tsai et al. [Tsa02], one based on the fast marching method [Set96, Tsi95] and one based on the fast sweeping method [Zha05].

The fast marching method is based on the realization that grid points should get information about the distance to the geometry from points that are closer, not the other way around. We thus want to loop over the grid points going from the closest to the furthest. This can be facilitated by

---

- Begin with a 3D array of distances $\phi_{i,j,k}$ set to ∞ (or some finite upper bound on all possible distances), and a 3D array of integer indices for the closest point $t_{i,j,k}$ set to -1 to indicate unknown.
- (Initialize the arrays near the input geometry)
- Loop over the input points $\vec{p}_e$ for $e = 0, 1, \ldots, n - 1$:
  - Locate point $\vec{p}_e = (p, q, r)$ in the grid, so that $x_i \leq p \leq x_{i+1}$, $y_j \leq q \leq y_{j+1}$, and $z_k \leq r \leq z_{k+1}$.
  - If the distance $d = \|\vec{x}_{i,j,k} - \vec{p}_e\|$ between the grid point and $\vec{p}_e$ is less than $\phi_{i,j,k}$:
    - Set $\phi_{i,j,k} = d$ and $t_{i,j,k} = e$.
- (Propagate closest point and distance estimates to the rest of the grid)
- Loop over the grid points (i, j, k) in a chosen order:
  - For each neighboring grid point (i', j', k') worth considering, if $e = t_{i',j',k'} \neq -1$:
    - If the distance $d = \|\vec{x}_{i,j,k} - \vec{p}_e\|$ between the grid point and $\vec{p}_e$ is less than $\phi_{i,j,k}$:
      - Set $\phi_{i,j,k} = d$ and $t_{i,j,k} = e$.

Figure 4.2. Computing distance on a grid to a set of points.

storing unknown grid points in a priority queue (typically implemented as a heap) keyed by the current estimate of their distance. We initialize the heap with the neighbors of the known grid points, with their distance values and closest points estimated from those known grid points. We select the minimum and remove it from the priority queue, set it as known, and then update the distance and closest-point information of its unknown neighbors (possibly adding them to or moving them up in the priority queue). And then do that again, and again, until the priority queue is empty. This runs in $O(n \log n)$ time for n unknown grid points.

The fast sweeping method approach draws a different tactic from the fact that information propagates out from closer points to farther points. For any grid point, in the end its closest point information is going to come to it from one particular direction in the grid—e.g., from $(i + 1, j, k)$, or maybe from $(i, j - 1, k)$, and so on. To ensure that the information can propagate in the right direction, we thus sweep through the grid points in all possible loop orders: i ascending or descending, j ascending or descending, k ascending or descending. There are eight combinations in three dimensions, four in two dimensions. For more accuracy, we can repeat the sweeps again; in practice two times through the sweep gives excellent results, though more iterations are possible.

The benefit of fast sweeping over fast marching is that it is $O(n)$, requires no extra data structures beyond grids, and thus is extremely simple to implement. When computing distance across a full grid, fast sweeping is probably the best bet.

However, as mentioned earlier, a modern fluid solver will probably use sparse tiled grids, which complicates sweeping. In this case, a hybrid approach is possible. We can run fast sweeping efficiently inside a tile to update distances based on information in the tile and its neighbors, but we can choose the order in which to solve tiles (and re-solve them when neighbors are updated) in a fast marching style. Begin with the tiles containing input points as the set to "redistance". Whenever a tile has been redistanced with fast sweeping, check to see if the distance value in any face neighbor is more than Δx larger than the distance stored in this tile: if so, add the neighboring tile to the set needing redistancing.

4.3.3 Finding Signed Distance for a Triangle Mesh

Let's tackle more interesting geometry next: a closed triangle mesh. We'll take the same general approach, but instead of keeping track of closest points, we'll track closest triangles for better accuracy. We'll also take an additional stage to figure out inside/outside information, first computing raw absolute distance and fixing the signs in the last loop. Figure 4.3 gives the pseudo-code. Again the loop order for distance propagation is left unspecified: fast sweeping, fast marching, or a hybrid tiled combination applies equally well here.

Computing the distance between a point and a triangle is a core operation in this algorithm. Jones provides details on two possible techniques in technical report worth reading [Jon95]. The more direct but potentially slower approach first solves for the barycentric coordinates α, β, γ of the closest point to x_0 on the plane through triangle vertices $\vec{x}_1$, $\vec{x}_2$, and $\vec{x}_3$, with the following 2×2 linear system:

$$\begin{bmatrix} \vec{x}_{21} \cdot \vec{x}_{21} & \vec{x}_{21} \cdot \vec{x}_{31} \\ \vec{x}_{21} \cdot \vec{x}_{31} & \vec{x}_{31} \cdot \vec{x}_{31} \end{bmatrix} \begin{bmatrix} \beta \\ \gamma \end{bmatrix} = \begin{bmatrix} \vec{x}_{21} \cdot \vec{x}_{01} \\ \vec{x}_{31} \cdot \vec{x}_{01} \end{bmatrix}$$
$$\alpha = 1 - \beta - \gamma,$$

where $\vec{x}_{21}$ is short for $\vec{x}_2 - \vec{x}_1$ and so forth. If the barycentric coordinates are all non-negative, the closest point in the plane is inside the triangle, and you can use the distance between $\vec{x}_0$ and $\alpha\vec{x}_1 + \beta\vec{x}_2 + \gamma\vec{x}_3$. Otherwise, the closest point must lie on one of the triangle's edges. If a barycentric coordinate is positive, the opposite edge needn't be checked (α is opposite

- Begin with a 3D array of distances $\phi_{i,j,k}$ set to ∞ (or some finite upper bound on all possible distances), and a 3D array of integer indices for the closest triangle $t_{i,j,k}$ set to -1 to indicate unknown, and a 3D array of integers $c_{i,j,k}$ to keep intersection counts along grid edges.
- (Initialize the arrays near the input geometry)
- Loop over the input triangles T_e for $e = 0, 1, \ldots, n-1$:
  - Loop over the grid edges $(i, j, k) - (i+1, j, k)$ which exactly intersect triangle T_e (consistently breaking ties at endpoints):
    - Increment $c_{i,j,k}$.
    - If the distance d between grid point $\vec{x}_{i,j,k}$ and triangle T_e is less than $\phi_{i,j,k}$:
      - Set $\phi_{i,j,k} = d$ and $t_{i,j,k} = e$.
- (Propagate closest triangle and distance estimates to the rest of the grid)
- Loop over the grid points (i, j, k) in a chosen order:
  - For each neighboring grid point (i', j', k') worth considering, if $e = t_{i',j',k'} \neq -1$:
    - If the distance d between grid point $\vec{x}_{i,j,k}$ and triangle T_e is less than $\phi_{i,j,k}$:
      - Set $\phi_{i,j,k} = d$ and $t_{i,j,k} = e$.
- (Determine signs for inside/outside)
- For each horizontal grid line (j, k):
  - Set the cumulative intersection count $C = 0$ at the minimum i coordinate.
  - Loop over i to maximum grid coordinate:
    - If C is odd, set $\phi_{i,j,k} = -\phi_{i,j,k}$ (grid point is inside).
    - Set $C = C + c_{i,j,k}$.

Figure 4.3. Computing distance on a grid to a closed, watertight triangle mesh.

to $\vec{x}_2 - \vec{x}_3$ etc.), but in some cases two edges must both be considered, and the minimum distance from the two taken.

Computing the distance between a point $\vec{x}_0$ and an edge $\vec{x}_1 - \vec{x}_2$ follows a similar procedure. First compute the barycentric coordinate θ of the closest point along the infinite line containing the edge:

$$\theta = \frac{(\vec{x}_2 - \vec{x}_1) \cdot (\vec{x}_0 - \vec{x}_1)}{\|\vec{x}_2 - \vec{x}_1\|^2}.$$

If $\theta < 0$ the closest point is $\vec{x}_1$, if $\theta > 1$ the closest point is $\vec{x}_2$, and otherwise the closest point is $(1 - \theta)\vec{x}_1 + \theta\vec{x}_2$:

The other tricky point, in fact a much trickier point, in the algorithm is the determination of inside/outside. It essentially determines whether a grid point is inside the mesh by casting a ray along the negative x-axis to minus infinity, counting the number of intersections with triangles, and deciding on "inside" if the intersection count is odd. This assumes that at minus infinity, we are outside the mesh, and that if we were to move back along the axis, every time we cross a triangle we must be switching from inside to outside or vice versa. This is indeed true for closed, "watertight" triangle meshes.

For this algorithm to be robust, the intersection routine has to be very carefully written. If an intersection is missed, the count will be off and the results wrong. If two triangles meet exactly along an x-aligned grid line, and we count zero or two intersections, the count will be off and the results wrong: we can count one and only one intersection in this case. If a triangle lies parallel to the x-axis and exactly on a grid line, which frequently happens if the geometry happens to include an axis aligned plane, we should be sure not to count any intersections. Getting all these cases correct every time goes beyond the scope of this book; my code relies on Shewchuk's robust predicates for computing sign-exact orientation determinants [She97], along with careful symbolic perturbations to consistently "break ties" when triangles line up with the grid exactly, following the strategy of Simulation Of Simplicity (SOS) [EM90].

Sometimes, of course, input triangle meshes are not perfect watertight structures. They might have cracks, or overlapping parts that don't quite meet, for example, or only one side has been specified (for example, the top surface of an ocean without the bottom given). We can still compute a distance field for the triangles with the algorithm above, but the intersection counts and inside/outside signs are unreliable.

If the input triangles all have consistent outward-pointing normals, one possibility is to set the sign (inside/outside) of nearby grid points in the initial loop according to the dot-product of $(\vec{x}_T - \vec{x}_{i,j,k}) \cdot \hat{n}_T$ between the vector from the grid point $\vec{x}_{i,j,k}$ to the closest point $\vec{x}_T$ on the triangle and the triangle's normal. Then in the distance propagation loop, we use $|\phi_{i,j,k}|$ instead of $\phi_{i,j,k}$ to compare distances, and we take the sign (inside/outside) from the neighbor.

With even rougher models, more complicated schemes to estimate inside/outside (which may not be at all clear) are necessary. The most thorough recent example is Jacobson et al. [JKSH13], who essentially compute the probability that a random ray fired in any direction will cross an odd number of triangles to decide on a "raw" estimate of inside/outside, and then further process the results at all points to get a clean segmentation.

4.4   Recomputing Signed Distance

The previous section used geometrically-based algorithms to compute signed distance directly from explicitly given geometry. Another common case we encounter is where we have a level set defined by values on a grid which are far from being signed distance, and we want to recompute the signed distance accurately, or **redistance**, the level set. This commonly happens as the result of geometric processing algorithms which don't preserve distance exactly.

Here we don't have explicit geometry available to provide convenient closest points, so instead we take the PDE approach and solve the Eikonal equation directly. This follows the original fast marching method [Set96, Tsi95] and fast sweeping method [Zha05].

Our first step is to estimate distance accurately immediately next to the surface, i.e. in grid cells where there is a sign change (some corners are negative, others are positive). If we are confident these are close enough to distance already, we can leave them untouched. Otherwise we need to estimate where in the grid cell the zero isocontour lies, and use signed distance to that. Suppose the old function is F, and at grid point (i, j, k) we find that $F_{i,j,k}$ has a different sign from $F_{i+1,j,k}$. We can linearly interpolate F along the edge between those two points, and solve for the fraction along the edge where the linear interpolant is zero:

$$\theta = \frac{F_{i,j,k}}{F_{i,j,k} - F_{i+1,j,k}}.$$

We can provisionally set $\phi_{i,j,k} = \text{sign}(F_{i,j,k}) \theta \Delta x$, i.e. the distance to that intersection point inheriting the sign (inside/outside) from F. Of course, we should do the same calculation for all neighbors with a different sign in F, and take the signed distance value closest to zero. For a slightly more accurate result, we can even fit a segment or triangle through collections of these intersection points (in fact, locally producing a Marching Cubes [WMW86, LC87] style of mesh) and take the closest point to that.

After settling ϕ for the grid points immediately adjacent to the surface, we set the remainder to $\pm\infty$, or otherwise an upper bound for all possible distances with sign positive or negative according to the input F. We then loop through the grid propagating distance as before, with sweeping or marching or a hybrid. However, instead of using geometric calculations to determine distance values, we directly solve the Eikonal equation. Recall again this is just the statement that the gradient of the signed distance function should have unit length:

$$\left(\frac{\partial \phi}{\partial x}\right)^2 + \left(\frac{\partial \phi}{\partial y}\right)^2 + \left(\frac{\partial \phi}{\partial z}\right)^2 = 1$$

To estimate signed distance $\phi_{i,j,k}$ at a grid point from some known neighboring values, we substitute in finite differences for the partial derivatives and solve the resulting quadratic equation for the unknown value. The critical principle at play, however, is that we can only compute distance at a grid point from points that are closer to the surface (that have smaller absolute distance values).

Suppose, for example, we are estimating $\phi_{i,j,k}$ from neighbors $\phi_{i-1,j,k}$, $\phi_{i,j+1,k}$, and $\phi_{i,j,k-1}$. Discretizing the equation above, if we actually can use all three, would give something like:

$$\left(\frac{\phi_{i,j,k} - \phi_{i-1,j,k}}{\Delta x}\right)^2 + \left(\frac{\phi_{i,j+1,k} - \phi_{i,j,k}}{\Delta x}\right)^2 + \left(\frac{\phi_{i,j,k} - \phi_{i,j,k-1}}{\Delta x}\right)^2 = 1$$

For simplicity, assume all values are positive (just flip the signs if not, compute the new value, and then flip the sign again). Let those three neighboring values be $\phi_0 \leq \phi_1 \leq \phi_2$ in sorted order. We then try using one, two, or three neighboring values to estimate the distance, taking the smallest computed distance only if it's smaller than our existing estimate for $\phi_{i,j,k}$. See Figure 4.4.

4.5 Operations on Level Sets

The level set approach to geometry pays extra dividends when it comes to what you can do efficiently with them. First let us take a look at geometric queries. We already saw that determining inside versus outside is a simple matter of interpolating ϕ from nearby grid points and checking its sign; estimating the normal or the direction to the closest point on the surface is as simple as taking some finite differences to approximate $\nabla \phi$.

Actually finding the closest point $\vec{p}$ on the surface from a given point $\vec{x}$ is not quite as simple as we made it out to be initially. With an exact signed distance function, $\vec{p} = \vec{x} - \phi(\vec{x})\nabla \phi(\vec{x})$. However, if we have errors in the values of ϕ and errors from interpolation and finite differences, this formula isn't guaranteed to give a point exactly on the surface. A simple iterative procedure can be used to give more reliable results, taking steps along the gradient as long as the value of ϕ keeps getting closer to zero: see Figure 4.5.

- (Try just the closest neighbor)
- Set $d = \phi_0 + \Delta x$.
- If $d > \phi_1$:
  - (Try the two closest neighbors)
  - Set $d = \frac{1}{2}(\phi_0 + \phi_1 + \sqrt{2\Delta x^2 - (\phi_1 - \phi_0)^2})$.
  - If $d > \phi_2$:
    - (Use all three neighbors)
    - Set

$$d = \frac{1}{3}\Big(\phi_0 + \phi_1 + \phi_2 + $$
$$\sqrt{\max(0, (\phi_0 + \phi_1 + \phi_2)^2 - 3(\phi_0^2 + \phi_1^2 + \phi_2^2 - \Delta x^2))}\Big).$$

- If $d < \phi_{i,j,k}$ set $\phi_{i,j,k} = d$.

Figure 4.4. Updating distance $\phi_{i,j,k}$ from the Eikonal equation on a grid, given neighboring distance values $\phi_0 \leq \phi_1 \leq \phi_2$ along the three axes.

- Set $\vec{p} = \vec{x}$, $\phi_p = \phi(\vec{p})$, $\vec{d} = \nabla\phi(\vec{p})$.
- For up to N iterations:
  - Set $\alpha = 1$.
  - For up to M iterations:
    - Set $\vec{q} = \vec{p} - \alpha\phi_p\vec{d}$.
    - If $|\phi(\vec{q})| < |\phi_p|$:
      - Set $\vec{p} = \vec{q}$, $\phi_p = \phi(\vec{q})$, $\vec{d} = \nabla\phi(\vec{q})$.
      - If $|\phi_p| < \epsilon$ for some tolerance ϵ, return with $\vec{p}$.
    - Else set $\alpha = 0.7\alpha$ (scale back the step by some conservative amount)
- Return $\vec{p}$ as best guess seen.

Figure 4.5. Finding from $\vec{x}$ the closest point $\vec{p}$ on the level set surface.

Level sets can be ray-traced directly for rendering, and intersecting a ray against a level set may also be of use elsewhere. One possibility is to march through the grid treating it as a regular ray-tracing acceleration structure: you can skip through a grid cell if all the values of ϕ at the corners have the same sign (so the zero isocontour does not pass through the grid cell). This can be further accelerated with octrees or coarse grids. Another possibility to speed up tracing is to use the signed distance values themselves: if they are accurate enough, they provide a conservative lower bound on how far along the ray you can travel without touching the surface (since the distance to the closest point on the surface is a lower bound on the distance along the ray to the surface). Once close enough to the surface, and in particular once two points on the ray have been found with differing signs, numerical root-finding algorithms like bisection search or secant search can be used to get the intersection.

It should be noted that the interpolation method used for the level set plays a big role in what it will look like when ray-traced. Simple piecewise trilinear interpolation gives smooth trilinear patches within grid cells, but the normal to the surface can discontinuously jump from one grid cell to the next: this can be very obvious even with a diffuse shader. Smoother C^1 approaches are usually necessary, such as using quadratic B-splines.

Level sets, like any other field, can be advected by a velocity field. We will return to this in Chapter 8 where this is an important component of simulating liquids like water. In particular, if we want to move a surface around with a velocity field $\vec{u}$, the points where $\phi(\vec{x}) = 0$ should follow $d\vec{x}/dt = \vec{u}$ while keeping their value of ϕ at zero. More generally we could say every point in the domain should move with the velocity field and keep its value of ϕ as it goes, giving the equation:

$$\frac{D\phi}{Dt} = 0. \tag{4.1}$$

This will move the surface as desired, up to numerical errors, producing a new level set. Usually the new level set will no longer be exactly signed distance, so we decide to recompute distance each frame, but in most cases the values directly next to the surface will be "good enough" and do not require recomputing (which could cause artifacts). Level set advection is very sensitive to numerical diffusion, so it's essential to at least use the sharp cubic interpolation we discussed at the end of Chapter 3. Even so, over time, sharp features are bound to be smoothed away and even disappear: small holes can fill in, thin structures can vanish. How to better handle this will be left to later in the book.

Advection can also be used to apply displacement textures or freeform deformations to level sets, thinking of the volumetric displacement field as basically integrating one step of velocity to deform the original level set geometry. Alternatively, carefully designed "bump map" fields can just be directly added to the level set values to perturb the geometry slightly in the normal direction, though this can be an unreliable way to texture geometry if taken too far.

Adding a constant to a level set will grow or shrink the geometry. Consider again the level set of a sphere of radius r:

$$\phi(\vec{x}) = \|\vec{x}\| - r.$$

If we add d to the values, $\phi = \phi + d$, it's obvious we get a sphere of radius $r - d$. This applies generally: if we add a positive value d to the level set, it shrinks the level set inwards along the normal by a distance d, and if we add a negative value d it grows or "dilates" the level set outwards along the normal by a distance $|d|$. However, a cautionary note: except in very simple cases like the sphere, the resulting level set might not be true signed distance anymore. Following an operation like this, it may be necessary to recompute distance.

Smoothing and sharpening filters can also be applied to level sets directly, as if they were any other 3D data. These generally have the expected results, except where the filter kernel overlaps the medial axis (the "halfway point" between two or more different parts of the surface): in this case, information from another part of the surface starts to contaminate the calculation. A smoothing filter whose radius is wider than the thickness of one part of the surface can cause that part of the surface to completely vanish. Two disjoint surface components can affect each other if they are closer than the filter kernel's radius.

Boolean or Constructive Solid Geometry (CSG) operations can be computed very easily, at least approximately, with level sets. The complement of an object (turning inside to outside and vice versa) can be accomplished simply by reversing the sign to $-\phi$. The union of two objects with level sets ϕ_1 and ϕ_2 can be computed as

$$\phi = \min(\phi_1, \phi_2),$$

and the intersection as

$$\phi = \max(\phi_1, \phi_2).$$

In the former, a point is in the union (has a negative value) if and only if the point is in at least one of the objects (the minimum of the two values is negative), with similar logic for the latter. Note that taking the minimum of two interpolated values can be very different from interpolating the minimums: if you compute a new level set sampled on the grid by taking minimums or maximums between other level sets, and then work with the new level set with standard interpolation, you will find the "seam" where the earlier geometry intersects has been smoothed away. This can be a good thing or a bad thing, depending on what you want. The result of Boolean operations like union and intersection also locally still satisfies the Eikonal equation, but may be very far from true signed distance: again, redistancing may be required.

4.6   Contouring

One last common operation for level sets is to reconstruct a mesh of the zero isocontour. Although level sets make some operations easy or even trivial, others are far easier or faster with a mesh, like accurately estimating surface integrals or rendering with rasterizing GPU hardware. Some software libraries only accept meshes as input geometry, not level sets.

The standard approach is the Marching Cubes algorithm, invented first by Wyvill et al. [WMW86] and then independently by Lorensen and Cline [LC87]. The essential idea is to put a mesh vertex wherever the zero isosurface crosses an edge of the 3D grid, and then connect up the vertices with faces inside each grid cell which will naturally approximate the zero isosurface.

Finding if and where the zero isosurface crosses an edge of the grid is easy enough, assuming linear interpolation of the level set function between values stored at grid cell corners. For example, there is a zero crossing on the edge between (i, j, k) and $(i + 1, j, k)$ if and only if the sign of $\phi_{i,j,k}$ is opposite the sign of $\phi_{i+1,j,k}$, and the zero of the linear interpolant between those two points happens at fraction

$$\theta = \frac{\phi_{i,j,k}}{\phi_{i,j,k} - \phi_{i+1,j,k}},$$

i.e. at location $((i + \theta)\Delta x, j\Delta x, k\Delta x)$.

If one or more of the level set values on the grid is exactly zero, $\phi_{i,j,k} = 0$, it can be really hard to make a robust algorithm which will produce a watertight mesh. The simplest solution is to replace any exact zeros with an extremely small nonzero instead, like 10^{-36} for single-precision floating point numbers. A number this small will not in general have any effect on the location of mesh vertices, due to rounding errors, but it will avoid the need for any special cases in the mesh generation code which is a huge advantage.

In a grid cell which contains the zero isosurface, i.e. which has differing signs for ϕ at its corners, figuring out how to connect up the mesh vertices generated on the appropriate edges is not trivial. There are 254 different cases to consider, and even with look-up tables to help control the complexity, Lorensen and Cline's original method still on occasion produces holes in the final mesh due to topological ambiguities [Dür88]. There are several possibilities to solve this, but the one I prefer is Marching Tetrahedra [MW99], where we first decompose each grid cell into a set of smaller tetrahedra (which themselves line up at shared grid faces to form a valid tetrahedral mesh of all space), construct zero crossing vertices on the edges of those tetrahedra, and connect up the vertices to form mesh faces within each tetrahedron independently.

The great advantage of working in a tetrahedron instead of a cube is that the linear interpolation of ϕ from the corners of the tetrahedron has a flat (planar) zero isocontour which can be unambiguously meshed: in a cube, with trilinear interpolation, the zero isosurface is typically curved and can have more complicated topology (such as splitting into multiple disconnected components). In fact, the zero isocontour cutting through a tetrahedron can only be single triangle or a quadrilateral, which can be split along either diagonal to give two triangles. There are also only 16 cases of signs to consider, reducing the code complexity. The only downside to using tetrahedra instead of cubes is that, on average, somewhat more triangles will be emitted than are strictly necessary.

The one slightly tricky point in making Marching Tetrahedra work is in coming up with the set of tetrahedra. The minimal subdivision of the cube is into five tetrahedra, with an equilateral tetrahedron in the middle and four surrounding it. In fact, there are two ways to do this. For the unit cube we can use the following tetrahedra, listed as consistently-oriented 4-tuples of vertex coordinates:

- $(0, 1, 1) - (1, 0, 1) - (0, 0, 0) - (0, 0, 1)$

- $(0, 0, 0) - (0, 1, 1) - (0, 1, 0) - (1, 1, 0)$

- $(1, 0, 1) - (0, 1, 1) - (0, 0, 0) - (1, 1, 0)$ (equilateral)

- $(1, 0, 0) - (1, 0, 1) - (0, 0, 0) - (1, 1, 0)$

- $(1, 1, 1) - (0, 1, 1) - (1, 0, 1) - (1, 1, 0)$

or the mirror image (geometrically reflected but with the same orientation):

- $(0, 0, 1) - (1, 1, 1) - (1, 0, 0) - (1, 0, 1)$

- $(1, 1, 1) - (1, 0, 0) - (1, 1, 0) - (0, 1, 0)$

- $(1, 1, 1) - (0, 0, 1) - (1, 0, 0) - (0, 1, 0)$ (equilateral)

- $(0, 0, 1) - (0, 0, 0) - (1, 0, 0) - (0, 1, 0)$

- $(1, 1, 1) - (0, 1, 1) - (0, 0, 1) - (0, 1, 0)$

For grid cell (i, j, k), simply add i, j, k to the coordinates listed above. It turns out we need to use both to get a valid tetrahedralization of all space. Just using one or other leads to a mismatch between tetrahedra across a common face in the grid; instead we have to alternate between the two in a "checkerboard" pattern. For example, you can use the first set for the grid cell with least corner (i, j, k) if $i + j + k$ is odd, and use the second set if $i + j + k$ is even.

The triangle meshes generated from marching typically aren't of great quality. If the isosurface just barely includes a grid point, then the triangles generated nearby will often be "slivers," with one or more very short edges. In most scenarios some further mesh smoothing is required: move each vertex towards the average of its neighbor vertices, then project it back to the zero isosurface using the underlying level set. This tends to produce much better shaped triangles of more uniform size, while staying faithful to the level set.

Williams' thesis on constructing high quality meshes to wrap around fluid particles takes us a step further [Wil08]. The first observation is that regular Marching Cubes and Marching Tetrahedra using the above decomposition, or many others, typically generates triangle meshes with many degree four vertices, i.e. vertices incident on only four triangles. Such vertices can cause problems for further mesh processing (e.g. the simple mesh smoothing doesn't work as well near them, and subdivision surfaces tend to have curvature problems there). Degree four vertices only can occur where only four tetrahedra in the underlying tetrahedral mesh share an edge. However, in an *acute* tetrahedralization of space, where every dihedral angle is strictly less than 90°, at least five tetrahedra must meet at every edge (since the sum of dihedral angles around an edge is 360°). Therefore, if we march on acute tetrahedra, the output mesh cannot have a vertex with degree less than five: this gives much better connectivity, which leads to much better mesh improvement, subdivision, and other post-processing.

Williams used a fairly convenient acute tetrahedralization earlier identified by Üngör [Ü01]. Unfortunately, while it tiles space in a grid-like way, the tetrahedra don't neatly decompose cubic grid cells: the repeating tile resembles a "dented" cube. However, we don't actually care so much about the geometry of the tetrahedra: the important point is their connectivity, that at least five meet at every shared edge. It turns out we can warp this tetrahedralization back to line up perfectly with a regular grid, where we use a carefully selected decomposition of each grid cell into five or six tetrahedra depending on the parity of the coordinates taken individually.

If $i \equiv 0, j \equiv 0, k \equiv 0 \pmod 2$:

- $(0,1,1) - (1,0,1) - (0,0,0) - (0,0,1)$
- $(0,0,0) - (0,1,1) - (0,1,0) - (1,1,0)$
- $(1,0,1) - (0,1,1) - (0,0,0) - (1,1,0)$
- $(1,0,0) - (1,0,1) - (0,0,0) - (1,1,0)$
- $(1,1,1) - (0,1,1) - (1,0,1) - (1,1,0)$

If $i \equiv 1, j \equiv 0, k \equiv 0 \pmod 2$:

- $(1,1,1) - (0,0,0) - (1,0,0) - (1,1,0)$
- $(0,0,0) - (1,1,1) - (0,0,1) - (0,1,0)$
- $(1,1,1) - (0,0,0) - (0,0,1) - (1,0,1)$
- $(1,1,1) - (0,1,1) - (0,0,1) - (0,1,0)$
- $(0,0,0) - (1,1,1) - (1,0,0) - (1,0,1)$
- $(0,0,0) - (1,1,0) - (1,1,1) - (0,1,0)$

If $i \equiv 0, j \equiv 0, k \equiv 1 \pmod 2$:

- $(0,0,1) - (1,0,1) - (1,1,1) - (1,0,0)$
- $(0,0,1) - (1,0,0) - (0,1,1) - (0,0,0)$
- $(0,1,1) - (1,0,0) - (0,1,0) - (0,0,0)$
- $(0,1,0) - (1,1,0) - (1,0,0) - (0,1,1)$
- $(1,1,1) - (0,1,1) - (0,0,1) - (1,0,0)$
- $(1,1,0) - (0,1,1) - (1,1,1) - (1,0,0)$

If $i \equiv 1, j \equiv 0, k \equiv 1 \pmod 2$:

- $(0,0,0) - (1,1,1) - (0,0,1) - (0,1,1)$
- $(1,1,1) - (0,0,0) - (0,0,1) - (1,0,0)$
- $(1,1,1) - (0,1,0) - (0,1,1) - (0,0,0)$
- $(0,0,0) - (1,1,0) - (1,0,0) - (1,1,1)$
- $(1,0,1) - (1,0,0) - (1,1,1) - (0,0,1)$
- $(0,1,0) - (1,1,1) - (1,1,0) - (0,0,0)$

If $i \equiv 0, j \equiv 1, k \equiv 0 (\mathrm{mod}2)$:

- $(1,1,1) - (1,1,0) - (0,1,0) - (1,0,1)$
- $(0,1,0) - (0,0,1) - (1,0,0) - (0,0,0)$
- $(1,0,1) - (1,1,0) - (0,1,0) - (1,0,0)$
- $(1,0,1) - (0,0,1) - (0,1,0) - (0,1,1)$
- $(0,0,1) - (1,0,1) - (0,1,0) - (1,0,0)$
- $(0,1,0) - (1,1,1) - (1,0,1) - (0,1,1)$

If $i \equiv 1, j \equiv 1, k \equiv 0 (\mathrm{mod}2)$:

- $(0,1,0) - (0,0,1) - (1,0,1) - (0,0,0)$
- $(0,1,0) - (1,0,0) - (0,0,0) - (1,0,1)$
- $(1,0,0) - (0,1,0) - (1,1,0) - (1,0,1)$
- $(1,0,1) - (0,1,0) - (1,1,0) - (1,1,1)$
- $(0,1,0) - (0,1,1) - (1,1,1) - (0,0,1)$
- $(0,0,1) - (0,1,0) - (1,0,1) - (1,1,1)$

If $i \equiv 0, j \equiv 1, k \equiv 1 (\mathrm{mod}2)$:

- $(1,0,0) - (0,0,0) - (0,1,0) - (0,0,1)$
- $(0,1,1) - (1,1,0) - (0,1,0) - (1,0,0)$
- $(0,0,1) - (0,1,1) - (1,0,0) - (1,0,1)$
- $(0,1,1) - (0,0,1) - (1,0,0) - (0,1,0)$
- $(0,1,1) - (1,1,1) - (1,1,0) - (1,0,0)$
- $(1,1,1) - (0,1,1) - (1,0,1) - (1,0,0)$

If $i \equiv 1, j \equiv 1, k \equiv 1 (\mathrm{mod}2)$:

- $(0,1,1) - (0,1,0) - (0,0,0) - (1,1,0)$
- $(0,0,0) - (1,0,1) - (0,0,1) - (0,1,1)$
- $(0,1,1) - (0,0,0) - (1,0,1) - (1,1,0)$
- $(0,0,0) - (1,0,0) - (1,0,1) - (1,1,0)$
- $(1,1,0) - (1,1,1) - (1,0,1) - (0,1,1)$

4.7   Limitations of Level Sets

Level sets are a very powerful tool, but they are not a panacea. They can only reliably represent non-intersecting geometry with a well-defined inside and outside, obviously enough. The surface is defined where ϕ interpolates to zero, and most interpolation schemes can't reliably produce a zero unless some of the values are negative and others positive. A thin piece of cloth without an interior has a well-defined positive distance field, but its surface simply won't show up in a level set algorithm unless you first dilate it, thickening it up by some amount.

In fact, a level set on a grid with spacing Δx cannot reliably represent any features that are less than Δx thick. For anything thinner than that, whether or not it shows up in a grid sample at all will depend on how the grid lines up: shift the grid a small amount and it may fall between grid samples and disappear. Indeed, taking into account that strange things can happen across the medial axis (poor gradient estimates for normals, etc.), a better rule of thumb is that only features at least $2\Delta x$ thick can reliably be handled. It may, in some cases, be appropriate to use a finer grid for the level sets in a solver. Exploiting modern sparse tiled grid technology and storing values only near the surface can make this quite practical.

Sharp features also cannot be reliably represented with a level set. Standard interpolants, even the piecewise cubic we used at the end of Chapter 3, inevitably produce smooth variations in between grid cells. Nonstandard interpolants which try to estimate where sharp features may occur inside a grid cell are a possibility, but there is no standard method out there yet.

4.8   Extrapolating Data

We close the chapter with one particularly important operation commonly associated with level sets, extrapolation. This is where we have known values at some grid points, and we want to extend or extrapolate those values to the rest of the grid. For example, we will commonly do this in a fluid solve where we compute velocity in the fluid region, and then extrapolate that velocity to the rest of the domain (inside solids, for example), so we can apply advection without any worries near boundaries.

The simplest and in some cases the best choice for extrapolation is to use a simple breadth-first search. Say we begin with a 3D array containing the known values F, an auxiliary integer array d initialized to zero for the known values and the maximum integer (at least larger than the sum of the array dimensions) for the unknown values, the algorithm in Figure 4.6 extends the data to the rest of the grid.

However, this approach doesn't always give the most convincing ex-

- Begin with a 3D array of values $F_{i,j,k}$, an integer marker array $m_{i,j,k}$ set to 0 for known values and the maximum integer for unknown values, and an empty array W of grid indices in the "wavefront."
- (Initialize the first wavefront)
- Loop over the entire grid with (i, j, k):
  - If $d_{i,j,k} \neq 0$ but at least one neighbor has $d = 0$:
    - Set $d_{i,j,k} = 1$.
    - Push (i, j, k) onto W.
- Set $t = 0$.
- While $t < \text{length}(W)$:
  - Let $(i, j, k) = W[t]$.
  - Set $F_{i,j,k}$ equal to the average of neighbors (i', j', k') of (i, j, k) where $d_{i',j',k'} < d_{i,j,k}$.
  - For any neighbor (i', j', k') with $d_{i',j',k'}$ equal to the maximum integer:
    - Set $d_{i',j',k'} = d_{i,j,k} + 1$, and push (i', j', k') onto W.
  - Set $t = t + 1$.

Figure 4.6. Extrapolating data in F using a breadth-first search.

trapolation. Values close to the surface are quite reasonable, and if that's all that's needed, it's hard to do better. However, farther away, grid artifacts show up, with values extending through space along axis lines a little unnaturally.

If a signed distance function is being computed geometrically, with auxiliary closest point information computed at each grid point along the way, then the closest point field can be used to directly extrapolate data everywhere: simply set the value at a grid point equal to the value on the input geometry at that closest point. This is very useful in the common case where you want to turn input geometry into a level set, but also want to voxelize other data stored on the geometry (like a velocity field, or texture information).

Finally, if we have data sampled at the same grid points as a signed distance field (not staggered, like a MAC-grid velocity field might be), with known values where $\phi \leq 0$ and unknown values where $\phi > 0$, we can also directly use the level set itself in guiding extrapolation. If we want the value $F(\vec{x})$ at a point $\vec{x}$ to be the same as the value $F(\vec{p})$ at the closest point $\vec{p}$ on the surface, then that value will be taken at every point along the straight line back to the closest point on the surface. That is, the value F should be constant moving along the direction $-\nabla\phi$, and in particular its directional derivative should be zero:

$$\frac{\partial F}{\partial \nabla \phi} = \nabla F \cdot \nabla \phi = 0.$$

We can discretize this simple PDE similar to how we treated the Eikonal equation, and sweep or march through the grid setting values. However, I will leave the details of this algorithm unspecified, as in practice the previous two algorithms (breadth-first search and closest point) are much more important.

5

Making Fluids Incompressible

In this chapter we'll look at the heart of a fluid simulation, making the fluid incompressible and simultaneously enforcing boundary conditions: implementation of the routine $\texttt{project}(\Delta t, \vec{u})$ we mentioned earlier in Chapter 2.

The $\texttt{project}$ routine will subtract the pressure gradient from the intermediate velocity field $\vec{u}$,

$$\vec{u}^{n+1} = \vec{u} - \Delta t \frac{1}{\rho} \nabla p,$$

so that the result satisfies incompressibility inside the fluid,

$$\nabla \cdot \vec{u}^{n+1} = 0,$$

and satisfies the solid wall boundary conditions

$$\vec{u}^{n+1} \cdot \hat{n} = \vec{u}_{\text{solid}} \cdot \hat{n} \quad \text{at solid boundaries,}$$

while also respecting the free surface boundary condition that pressure be zero there:

$$p = 0 \quad \text{at free surfaces.}$$

Before we jump into discretization of these equations, and methods to solve them numerically, we need to model the fluid domain discretely. We will begin the chapter with a "voxelized" model, where each voxel is discretely labeled as fluid, solid, or empty. The fluid voxels contain fluid, the solid voxels are solid, and the empty voxels (if there are any) contain nothing at all—in a free surface liquid simulation they represent the un-modeled air. The voxel faces between solid and fluid voxels will be where we impose the solid boundary condition, and the voxel faces between fluid and empty voxels are our free surface. See Figure (5.1) for an illustration. We will forego a full discussion of determining the discrete labeling, as later in the chapter we will switch to a more accurate geometric model using level sets, but this is not a difficult proposition: checking if the center of each voxel is inside a solid or inside the fluid, or neither, is trivial if you have level set geometry available.

E	E	E	E	E	E	E	E
E	F	E	E	E	E	E	E
S	E	E	F	F	E	E	S
S	E	E	E	F	F	F	S
S	E	F	F	F	F	F	S
S	F	F	F	F	F	S	S
S	F	F	F	S	S	S	S
S	S	S	S	S	S	S	S

Figure 5.1. A two-dimensional example of a voxelized fluid domain. **F** stands for fluid, **S** for solid, and **E** for empty.

With this model in mind, we will first write down the discretization of the pressure update: how do we approximate the pressure gradient on the MAC grid (assuming we know the pressure)? After that we'll look at defining the discrete divergence on the MAC grid and, putting the two together, come up with a system of linear equations to solve to find the pressure. We'll cover both the system and some effective ways to solve it.

5.1   The Discrete Pressure Gradient

The raison d'être of the MAC grid, as we briefly discussed before, is that the staggering makes accurate central differences robust. For example, where we need to subtract the $\partial/\partial x$-component of the pressure gradient from the u-component of velocity, there are two pressure values lined up perfectly on either side of the u-component just waiting to be differenced. You might want to refer back to Figure 2.1 to see how this works.

So without further ado, here are the formulas for the pressure update in two dimensions, using the central difference approximations for $\partial p/\partial x$ and $\partial p/\partial y$:

$$u^{n+1}_{i+1/2,j} = u_{i+1/2,j} - \Delta t \frac{1}{\rho} \frac{p_{i+1,j} - p_{i,j}}{\Delta x},$$

$$v^{n+1}_{i,j+1/2} = v_{i,j+1/2} - \Delta t \frac{1}{\rho} \frac{p_{i,j+1} - p_{i,j}}{\Delta x},$$

$$(5.1)$$

and in three dimensions, including $\partial p/\partial z$ too:

$$u^{n+1}_{i+1/2,j,k} = u_{i+1/2,j,k} - \Delta t \frac{1}{\rho} \frac{p_{i+1,j,k} - p_{i,j,k}}{\Delta x},$$

$$v^{n+1}_{i,j+1/2,k} = v_{i,j+1/2,k} - \Delta t \frac{1}{\rho} \frac{p_{i,j+1,k} - p_{i,j,k}}{\Delta x},$$

$$(5.2)$$

$$w^{n+1}_{i,j,k+1/2} = w_{i,j,k+1/2} - \Delta t \frac{1}{\rho} \frac{p_{i,j,k+1} - p_{i,j,k}}{\Delta x}.$$

These pressure updates apply to every velocity component that has a valid fluid pressure on either side, and actually borders some fluid. One of the trickiest parts of writing a correct pressure solve is keeping track of which velocity and pressure samples are "active," so it's good to keep this in mind or perhaps refer to a diagram near you while you program. For the voxelized fluid model, fluid-containing voxels have an unknown pressure to be solved for (at which point it is valid), solid voxels do not have a valid pressure, and empty voxels have a valid pressure that's already fixed at zero. The active velocity components we will update with Equation (5.1) or (5.2) are those adjacent to at least one fluid voxel, zero or one empty voxels, and no solid voxels.

Focus on the empty voxels again: because the free surface boundary condition specifies pressure is zero, we set the pressures in empty voxels to zero. This is called a **Dirichlet** boundary condition if you're interested in the technical lingo: Dirichlet means we're directly specifying the value of the quantity at the boundary. This is usually the simpler sort of boundary condition to handle in a numerical solve.

The more difficult pressure boundary condition is at solid walls, though it's still not too troublesome when dealing with the voxelized geometry approximation, where the staggered velocity components exactly line up with the solid surfaces, both in position and normal. We can go one step beyond the pressure gradient update above and directly set the fluid velocity components on solid voxel faces adjacent to fluid equal to the solid velocity there. We will do this as a post-process, part of the pressure gradient update. We can even think of this as an extension of the pressure gradient update by conceptually including a **ghost** value for pressure inside the solid voxel. For example, if the u-component of velocity at $(i + 1/2, j, k)$ is between a solid voxel at (i, j, k) and a fluid voxel at $(i + 1, j, k)$, then setting

$$u_{i+1/2,j,k}^{n+1} = u_{i+1/2,j,k}^{\text{solid}}$$

is compatible with the usual pressure gradient update

$$u_{i+1/2,j,k}^{n+1} = u_{i+1/2,j,k} - \Delta t \frac{1}{\rho} \frac{p_{i+1,j,k} - p_{i,j,k}^{\text{ghost}}}{\Delta x}$$

as long as the ghost pressure in (i, j, k) satisfies

$$p_{i,j,k}^{\text{ghost}} = p_{i+1,j,k} - \frac{\rho \Delta x}{\Delta t} \left(u_{i+1/2,j,k} - u_{i+1/2,j,k}^{\text{solid}} \right). \tag{5.3}$$

This isn't important for programming, but it is a worthwhile concept to wrap your head around: we can extend a fluid quantity, pressure, into the solid to make the usual equations we use in the interior of the fluid also handle the boundary condition.

In fact, with just a little rewriting, the pressure condition at this solid boundary is

$$\frac{\Delta t}{\rho} \frac{p_{i+1,j,k} - p_{i,j,k}^{\text{ghost}}}{\Delta x} = u_{i+1/2,j,k} - u_{i+1/2,j,k}^{\text{solid}}.$$

We can see this as a finite difference approximation to

$$\frac{\Delta t}{\rho} \frac{\partial p}{\partial x} = u - u^{\text{solid}}.$$

Going back to the continuum equations, if we likewise substitute the pressure gradient update into the solid boundary condition we get, more generally,

$$\frac{\Delta t}{\rho} \nabla p \cdot \hat{n} = (\vec{u} - \vec{u}^{\text{solid}}) \cdot \hat{n}.$$

When solving for pressure, the solid boundary condition amounts to specifying the normal derivative of pressure, $\partial p / \partial \hat{n} = \nabla p \cdot \hat{n}$, rather than the value of pressure. This is technically known as a **Neumann** boundary condition in the study of PDEs.

Using the same convention for storage from Chapter 2, Equations (2.14)–(2.17), the pressure update can be translated into code similar to Figure 5.2. We use the trick of directly setting solid wall velocities instead of working it out as a pressure update. The terms such as `usolid(i,j,k)`

```
scale = dt / (density*dx);
loop over i,j,k:
   # update u
   if label(i-1,j,k)==FLUID or label(i,j,k)==FLUID:
      if label(i-1,j,k)==SOLID or label(i,j,k)==SOLID:
         u(i,j,k) = usolid(i,j,k);
      else
         u(i,j,k) -= scale * (p(i,j,k) - p(i-1,j,k));
   else
      mark u(i,j,k) as unknown;
   # update v
   if label(i,j-1,k)==FLUID or label(i,j,k)==FLUID:
      if label(i,j-1,k)==SOLID or label(i,j,k)==SOLID:
         v(i,j,k) = vsolid(i,j,k);
      else
         v(i,j,k) -= scale * (p(i,j,k) - p(i,j-1,k));
   else
      mark v(i,j,k) as unknown;
   # update w
   if label(i,j,k-1)==FLUID or label(i,j,k)==FLUID:
      if label(i,j,k-1)==SOLID or label(i,j,k)==SOLID:
         w(i,j,k) = wsolid(i,j,k);
      else
         w(i,j,k) -= scale * (p(i,j,k) - p(i,j,k-1));
   else
      mark w(i,j,k) as unknown;
```

Figure 5.2. Pseudocode for the pressure gradient update. Fluid velocities are set, and the remainder are marked as unknown.

may well be replaced with simple expressions rather than actually stored in an array. We also highlight where fluid velocities are left unknown: we'll deal with those a little bit later in the chapter.

Boundary conditions can be complicated and are the usual culprit when bugs show up. It could be worth your time going over this section slowly, with a drawing of the MAC grid (like Figure 2.1) in front of you, looking at different configurations of solid, fluid, and air cells until you feel confident about all this.

```
scale = 1 / dx;
loop over i,j,k where label(i,j,k)==FLUID:
    rhs(i,j,k) = -scale * (u(i+1,j,k)-u(i,j,k)
                          +v(i,j+1,k)-v(i,j,k)
                          +w(i,j,k+1)-w(i,j,k));
```

Figure 5.3. Calculating the negative divergence, which will become the right-hand side of the linear system for pressure.

5.2   The Discrete Divergence

Now for the easy part of the chapter! In the continuum case, we want our fluid to be incompressible: $\nabla \cdot \vec{u} = 0$. On the grid, we will approximate this condition with finite differences and require that the divergence estimated at each fluid grid cell be zero for $\vec{u}^{n+1}$.

Remember the divergence in two dimensions is

$$\nabla \cdot \vec{u} = \frac{\partial u}{\partial x} + \frac{\partial v}{\partial y}$$

and in three dimensions is

$$\nabla \cdot \vec{u} = \frac{\partial u}{\partial x} + \frac{\partial v}{\partial y} + \frac{\partial w}{\partial z}.$$

Using the obvious central differences (take a look at the MAC grid again), we approximate the two-dimensional divergence in fluid grid cell (i,j) as

$$(\nabla \cdot \vec{u})_{i,j} \approx \frac{u_{i+1/2,j} - u_{i-1/2,j}}{\Delta x} + \frac{v_{i,j+1/2} - v_{i,j-1/2}}{\Delta x} \tag{5.4}$$

and in three dimensions, for fluid grid cell (i,j,k) as

$$(\nabla \cdot \vec{u})_{i,j,k} \approx \frac{u_{i+1/2,j,k} - u_{i-1/2,j,k}}{\Delta x} + \frac{v_{i,j+1/2,k} - v_{i,j-1/2,k}}{\Delta x}$$
$$+ \frac{w_{i,j,k+1/2} - w_{i,j,k-1/2}}{\Delta x}. \tag{5.5}$$

In terms of the storage convention used earlier, with divergence stored in the same way as pressure, this can be implemented as in the pseudocode of Figure 5.3. It turns out (see below) that we actually are more interested in the negative of divergence, so we store that in a vector we will call **rhs** (standing for the right-hand side of a linear system).

Note that we are only ever going to evaluate divergence for a grid cell that is marked as fluid. For example, our fluid simulation is not concerned with whether solids are changing volume or not.

Another way of interpreting the discrete divergence we have defined here is through a direct estimate of the total rate of fluid entering or exiting the grid cell. Remember that this (in the exact continuum setting) is just the integral of the normal component of velocity around the faces of the grid cell:

$$\iint_{\partial\text{cell}} \vec{u} \cdot \hat{n}.$$

This is the sum of the integrals over each grid cell face. We have the normal component of velocity stored at the center of each face, and can treat that as a good (technically second order accurate) estimate of the average normal velocity over the face. Therefore we can estimate the integral easily by just multiplying the normal component of velocity by the area of the face. Be careful with signs here—in the above integral the normal is always outwards-pointing, whereas the velocity components stored on the grid always are for the same directions, as shown in Figure 2.1, for example). After rescaling, this leads to exactly the same central difference formulas—I'll let you work this out for yourself if you're interested. This numerical technique, where we directly estimate the integral of a quantity around the faces of a grid cell instead of looking at the differential equation formulation, is called the **finite volume** method—more on this later in the chapter when we deal with irregular solid boundaries.

Finally we can explain why the MAC grid is so useful. If we used a regular **collocated** grid, where all components of velocity were stored together at the grid points, we would have a difficult time with the divergence. If we used the central difference formula, for example,

$$(\nabla \cdot \vec{u})_{i,j} \approx \frac{u_{i+1,j} - u_{i-1,j}}{2\Delta x} + \frac{v_{i,j+1} - v_{i,j-1}}{2\Delta x},$$

then we have exactly the null-space issues we mentioned back in Chapter 2. Some highly divergent velocity fields such as $\vec{u}_{i,j} = ((-1)^i, (-1)^j)$ will evaluate to zero divergence. Therefore, the pressure solve won't do anything about correcting them, and so high-frequency oscillations in the velocity field may persist or even grow unstably during the simulation. There are two possible fixes to get around this while still using a collocated grid. The first is to use a biased, one-sided difference approximation—and while this works, it does introduce a peculiar bias to the simulation that can be disturbingly obvious. The second is to filter out the high-frequency divergent modes (i.e., smooth the velocity field, or at least the divergent components) before doing the pressure solve, to explicitly get rid of them—but this can easily introduce more unwanted numerical smoothing. Even with filtering in place, there are some even thornier issues with the linear solve (below) when it comes to collocated velocities, thus we stick to the MAC grid.

5.3   The Pressure Equations

We now have the two ingredients we will need to figure out incompressibility: how to update velocities with the pressure gradient and how to
estimate the divergence.

Recall that we want the final velocity, $\vec{u}^{n+1}$ to be divergence-free inside
the fluid. To find the pressure that achieves this, we simply substitute
the pressure-update formulas for $\vec{u}^{n+1}$, Equations (5.1) in 2D and (5.2) in
3D, into the divergence formula, Equation (5.4) in 2D and (5.5) in 3D.
This gives us a linear equation for each *fluid* grid cell (remember we only
evaluate divergence for a grid cell containing fluid), with the pressures as
unknowns. There are no equations for solid or air cells, even though we
may refer to pressures in them (but we know *a priori* what those pressures
are in terms of the fluid cell pressures).

Let's write this out explicitly in 2D for fluid grid cell (i, j):

$$\frac{u^{n+1}_{i+1/2,j} - u^{n+1}_{i-1/2,j}}{\Delta x} + \frac{v^{n+1}_{i,j+1/2} - v^{n+1}_{i,j-1/2}}{\Delta x} = 0,$$

$$\frac{1}{\Delta x}\left[\left(u_{i+1/2,j} - \Delta t \frac{1}{\rho}\frac{p_{i+1,j} - p_{i,j}}{\Delta x}\right)\right.$$

$$- \left(u_{i-1/2,j} - \Delta t \frac{1}{\rho}\frac{p_{i,j} - p_{i-1,j}}{\Delta x}\right)$$

$$+ \left(v_{i,j+1/2} - \Delta t \frac{1}{\rho}\frac{p_{i,j+1} - p_{i,j}}{\Delta x}\right)$$

$$\left.- \left(v_{i,j-1/2} - \Delta t \frac{1}{\rho}\frac{p_{i,j} - p_{i,j-1}}{\Delta x}\right)\right] = 0,$$

$$\frac{\Delta t}{\rho}\left(\frac{4p_{i,j} - p_{i+1,j} - p_{i,j+1} - p_{i-1,j} - p_{i,j-1}}{\Delta x^2}\right) =$$

$$- \left(\frac{u_{i+1/2,j} - u_{i-1/2,j}}{\Delta x} + \frac{v_{i,j+1/2} - v_{i,j-1/2}}{\Delta x}\right). \quad (5.6)$$

And now in 3D for fluid grid cell (i, j, k):

$$\frac{u_{i+1/2,j,k}^{n+1} - u_{i-1/2,j,k}^{n+1}}{\Delta x} + \frac{v_{i,j+1/2,k}^{n+1} - v_{i,j-1/2,k}^{n+1}}{\Delta x} + \frac{w_{i,j,k+1/2}^{n+1} - w_{i,j,k-1/2}^{n+1}}{\Delta x} = 0,$$
(5.7)

$$\frac{1}{\Delta x} \left[\left(u_{i+1/2,j,k} - \Delta t \frac{1}{\rho} \frac{p_{i+1,j,k} - p_{i,j,k}}{\Delta x} \right) \right.$$

$$- \left(u_{i-1/2,j,k} - \Delta t \frac{1}{\rho} \frac{p_{i,j,k} - p_{i-1,j,k}}{\Delta x} \right)$$

$$+ \left(v_{i,j+1/2,k} - \Delta t \frac{1}{\rho} \frac{p_{i,j+1,k} - p_{i,j,k}}{\Delta x} \right)$$

$$- \left(v_{i,j-1/2,k} - \Delta t \frac{1}{\rho} \frac{p_{i,j,k} - p_{i,j-1,k}}{\Delta x} \right)$$

$$+ \left(w_{i,j,k+1/2} - \Delta t \frac{1}{\rho} \frac{p_{i,j,k+1} - p_{i,j,k}}{\Delta x} \right)$$

$$\left. - \left(w_{i,j,k-1/2} - \Delta t \frac{1}{\rho} \frac{p_{i,j,k} - p_{i,j,k-1}}{\Delta x} \right) \right] = 0,$$

$$\frac{\Delta t}{\rho} \left(\frac{\begin{array}{c} 6p_{i,j,k} - p_{i+1,j,k} - p_{i,j+1,k} - p_{i,j,k+1} \\ - p_{i-1,j,k} - p_{i,j-1,k} - p_{i,j,k-1} \end{array}}{\Delta x^2} \right) =$$

$$- \left(\frac{u_{i+1/2,j,k} - u_{i-1/2,j,k}}{\Delta x} + \frac{v_{i,j+1/2,k} - v_{i,j-1/2,k}}{\Delta x} + \frac{w_{i,j,k+1/2} - w_{i,j,k-1/2}}{\Delta x} \right).$$
(5.8)

Observe that Equations (5.6) and (5.8) are numerical approximations to the **Poisson** problem $-\Delta t / \rho \nabla \cdot \nabla p = -\nabla \cdot \vec{u}$.

If a fluid grid cell is at the boundary, recall that the new velocities on the boundary faces involve pressures outside the fluid that we have to define through boundary conditions: we need to use that here. For example, if grid cell $(i, j + 1)$ is an air cell, then we replace $p_{i,j+1}$ in Equation (5.6) with zero. If grid cell $(i+1, j)$ is a solid cell, then we replace $p_{i+1,j}$ with the value we compute from the boundary condition there, as in formula (5.3).

Assuming $(i-1,j)$ and $(i,j-1)$ are fluid cells, this would reduce the equation to the following:

$$\frac{\Delta t}{\rho} \left(\frac{4p_{i,j} - \left[p_{i,j} + \frac{\rho \Delta x}{\Delta t} \left(u_{i+1/2,j} - u_{\text{solid}} \right) \right] - 0 - p_{i-1,j} - p_{i,j-1}}{\Delta x^2} \right)$$

$$= - \left(\frac{u_{i+1/2,j} - u_{i-1/2,j}}{\Delta x} + \frac{v_{i,j+1/2} - v_{i,j-1/2}}{\Delta x} \right),$$

$$\frac{\Delta t}{\rho} \left(\frac{3p_{i,j} - p_{i-1,j} - p_{i,j-1}}{\Delta x^2} \right) =$$

$$- \left(\frac{u_{i+1/2,j} - u_{i-1/2,j}}{\Delta x} + \frac{v_{i,j+1/2} - v_{i,j-1/2}}{\Delta x} \right) + \left(\frac{u_{i+1/2,j} - u_{\text{solid}}}{\Delta x} \right).$$

We can observe a few things about this example that hold in general and how this will let us implement it in code. First, for the air cell boundary condition, we simply just delete mention of that p from the equation. Second, for the solid cell boundary condition, we delete mention of that p but also reduce the coefficient in front of $p_{i,j}$ by one—in other words, the coefficient in front of $p_{i,j}$ is equal to the number of non-solid grid cell neighbors (this is the same in three dimensions). Third, we increment the

```
scale = 1 / dx;
loop over i,j,k where label(i,j,k)==FLUID:
    if label(i-1,j,k)==SOLID:
        rhs(i,j,k) -= scale * (u(i,j,k) - usolid(i,j,k));
    if label(i+1,j,k)==SOLID:
        rhs(i,j,k) += scale * (u(i+1,j,k) - usolid(i+1,j,k));

    if label(i,j-1,k)==SOLID:
        rhs(i,j,k) -= scale * (v(i,j,k) - vsolid(i,j,k));
    if label(i,j+1,k)==SOLID:
        rhs(i,j,k) += scale * (v(i,j+1,k) - vsolid(i,j+1,k));

    if label(i,j,k-1)==SOLID:
        rhs(i,j,k) -= scale * (w(i,j,k) - wsolid(i,j,k));
    if label(i,j,k+1)==SOLID:
        rhs(i,j,k) += scale * (w(i,j,k+1) - wsolid(i,j,k+1));
```

Figure 5.4. Modifying the right-hand side to account for solid velocities.

negative divergence measured on the right-hand side with a term involving the difference between fluid and solid velocity. This can be implemented in code as an additional loop to modify `rhs`, as shown in Figure 5.4.

5.3.1 Putting It In Matrix-Vector Form

We have now defined a large system of linear equations for the unknown pressure values. We can conceptually think of it as a large coefficient matrix, A, times a vector consisting of all pressure unknowns, p, equal to a vector consisting of the *negative* divergences in each fluid grid cell, b (with appropriate modifications at solid wall boundaries):

$$Ap = b. \qquad (5.9)$$

In the implementation we have discussed so far, of course, p and b are logically stored in a two or three-dimensional grid structure, since each entry corresponds to a grid cell.

We needn't store A directly as a matrix. Notice that each row of A corresponds to one equation, i.e., one fluid cell. For example, if grid cell (i, j, k) is fluid, then there will be a row of the matrix that we can label with the indices (i, j, k). The entries in that row are the coefficients of all the pressure unknowns in that equation: almost all of these are zero except possibly for the seven entries corresponding to $p_{i,j,k}$ and its six neighbors, $p_{i\pm1,j,k}$, $p_{i,j\pm1,k}$, and $p_{i,j,k\pm1}$. (In two dimensions there are at most four neighbors of course.) We only have non-zeros (i, j, k) and its fluid cell neighbors. It is of course pointless to store all the zeros: this is a **sparse** matrix.

Let's take a closer look at A. In the equation for (i, j, k), the coefficients for neighboring fluid cells are all equal to $-\Delta t/(\rho\Delta x^2)$, and if there are $n_{i,j,k}$ fluid- or air-cell neighbors the coefficient for $p_{i,j,k}$ is $n_{i,j,k}\Delta t/(\rho\Delta x^2)$.

One of the nice properties of the matrix A is that it is symmetric. For example, $A_{(i,j,k),(i+1,j,k)}$, the coefficient of $p_{i+1,j,k}$ in the equation for grid cell (i, j, k), has to be equal to $A_{(i+1,j,k),(i,j,k)}$. Either it's zero if one of those two cells is not fluid, or it's the same non-zero value. This symmetry property will hold even with the more advanced discretization at the end of the chapter. Thus we only have to store half of the non-zero entries in A, since the other half are just copies!

This leads us to the following structure for storing A. In two dimensions, we will store three numbers at every grid cell: the diagonal entry $A_{(i,j),(i,j)}$ and the entries for the neighboring cells in the positive directions, $A_{(i,j),(i+1,j)}$ and $A_{(i,j),(i,j+1)}$. We could call these entries `Adiag(i,j)`, `Ax(i,j)`, and `Ay(i,j)` in our code. In three dimensions, we would similarly have `Adiag(i,j,k)`, `Ax(i,j,k)`, `Ay(i,j,k)`, and `Az(i,j,k)`. When we need to refer to an entry like $A_{(i,j),(i-1,j)}$ we use symmetry and instead

```
scale = dt / (density*dx*dx);
loop over i,j,k:
   if label(i,j,k)==FLUID:
      # handle negative x neighbor
      if label(i-1,j,k)==FLUID:
         Adiag(i,j,k) += scale;
      # handle positive x neighbor
      if label(i+1,j,k)==FLUID:
         Adiag(i,j,k) += scale;
         Ax(i,j,k) = -scale;
      else if label(i+1,j,k)==EMPTY:
         Adiag(i,j,k) += scale;
      # handle negative y neighbor
      if label(i,j-1,k)==FLUID:
         Adiag(i,j,k) += scale;
      # handle positive y neighbor
      if label(i,j+1,k)==FLUID:
         Adiag(i,j,k) += scale;
         Ay(i,j,k) = -scale;
      else if label(i,j+1,k)==EMPTY:
         Adiag(i,j,k) += scale;
      # handle negative z neighbor
      if label(i,j,k-1)==FLUID:
         Adiag(i,j,k) += scale;
      # handle positive z neighbor
      if label(i,j,k+1)==FLUID:
         Adiag(i,j,k) += scale;
         Az(i,j,k) = -scale;
      else if label(i,j,k+1)==EMPTY:
         Adiag(i,j,k) += scale;
```

Figure 5.5. Setting up the matrix entries for the pressure equations.

refer to $A_{(i-1,j),(i,j)}$ =Ax(i-1,j). See Figure 5.5 for pseudocode to set up
the matrix in this structure.

5.3.2 The Conjugate Gradient Algorithm

The matrix A is a very well-known type of matrix, sometimes referred to
as the five- or seven-point Laplacian matrix, in two or three dimensions
respectively. It has been exhaustively studied, serves as the subject of
countless numerical linear algebra papers, and is the prototypical first ex-

ample of a sparse matrix in just about any setting. More effort has been put into solving linear systems with this type of matrix than probably all other sparse matrices put together! We won't look very far into this vast body of work, as that could fill a book on its own, but we will look at some effective and easy to implement methods. The first method is called **MICCG(0)**, or more fully **Modified Incomplete Cholesky Conjugate Gradient, Level Zero**. Quite a mouthful! Let's go through it slowly.

One of the many properties that A has is that it is **symmetric positive definite** (SPD). Technically this means that A is symmetric and $q^T A q > 0$ for any non-zero vector q, or equivalently that its eigenvalues are all positive.

Actually, before going on I should be a little more careful. A might just be symmetric positive semi-definite, meaning that $q^T A q \geq 0$ (with zero achieved for some non-zero vector q). If there is some fluid region entirely surrounded by solid walls, with no empty air cells, then A will not be strictly positive definite. In that case, A is singular in fact—it doesn't have an inverse. That doesn't necessarily mean there isn't a solution, however. If the divergences (the right-hand side) satisfy a **compatibility condition** then life is good and there is a solution. The compatibility condition is simply that the velocities of the solid walls are compatible with the fluid contained within being incompressible—i.e., the fluid-solid boundary faces have wall velocities that add up to zero, so that the flow in is balanced by the flow out. (We will discuss how to ensure that this is the case at the end of the chapter.) In fact, not only will there be a solution, but there are infinitely many solutions! You can take any solution for pressure and add an arbitrary constant to it and get another solution, it turns out. However, when we take the pressure gradient for the velocity update, the constant term is annihilated so we don't actually care which solution we get. They're all good.

One of the most useful algorithm for solving symmetric positive semi-definite linear systems in general is called the **conjugate gradient** algorithm, usually abbreviated as CG. It's an iterative method, meaning that we start with a guess at the solution and in each iteration improve on it, stopping when we think we are accurate enough. CG chooses the iterative updates to the guess to minimize a particular measure of the error and can be guaranteed to converge to the solution eventually. Another very nice aspect of CG, as compared to Gaussian elimination for example, is that each iteration only involves multiplying A by a vector, adding vectors, multiplying vectors by scalar numbers, and computing a few dot-products—all of which are very easy to code, even in parallel, and can achieve very high efficiency on modern hardware.

The problem with CG for us, however, is that the larger the grid, the longer it takes to converge. It can be shown that the number of iterations it takes to converge to some desired accuracy is roughly proportional to the width of the grid: the maximum number of grid cells in any one direction. Moreover, the hidden constant isn't particularly good. In practice, when limited to a small maximum number of iterations there are simpler algorithms such as **Gauss-Seidel** and **Successive Over-Relaxation** (SOR) that tend to be much more effective than plain CG, even if they are slower at achieving full accuracy. However, there is a trick up our sleeve that can speed CG up immensely, called **preconditioning**. **Preconditioned conjugate gradient** (PCG) is what we will be using.

Roughly speaking, CG takes more iterations the farther A is from being the identity matrix, I. It should be immediately obvious that solving a system with the identity matrix is pretty easy—the solution of $Ip = b$ is just $p = b$! How exactly we measure how far A is from the identity is beyond the scope of this book—a precise characterization for CG involves the nature of the distribution of eigenvalues of A—but we needn't get too detailed. The idea behind preconditioning is that the solution of $Ap = b$ is the same as the solution of $MAp = Mb$ for any invertible matrix M. If M is *approximately* the inverse of A, so that MA is really close to being the identity matrix, then CG should be able to solve the preconditioned equations $MAp = Mb$ really fast. PCG is just a clever way of applying CG to these preconditioned equations without actually having to explicitly form them.

Before we get to the details of PCG, we need to talk about convergence. When do we know to stop? How do we check to see that our current guess is close enough to the solution? Ideally we would just measure the norm of the difference between our current guess and the exact solution—but of course that requires knowing the exact solution! So we will instead look at a vector called the **residual**:

$$r_i = b - Ap_i.$$

That is, if p_i is the ith guess at the true solution, the ith residual r_i is just how far away it is from satisfying the equation $Ap = b$. When we hit the exact solution, the residual is exactly zero.[1] Therefore, we stop our iteration when the norm of the residual is small enough, below some tolerance.

That brings us to the next question: how small is small enough? And what norm do you use to measure r_i? Think back to what r_i means physically. These equations resulted from deriving that $b - Ap$ is the negative of the finite difference estimate of the divergence of $\vec{u}^{n+1}$, which we want to be zero. Thus the residual measures exactly how much divergence there

---

[1] In fact, it's not hard to see that the residual is just A times the error: $r_i = A(p_{\text{exact}} - p_i)$.

will be in the velocity field after we've updated it with our current estimate of the pressure. It seems sensible, then, to take the infinity norm of the residual (the maximum absolute value of any entry) and compare that to some small number `tol`, so that we know the worst case of how compressible our new velocity field could possibly be. The dimensions of `tol` are one over time: $O(1/\texttt{tol})$ is a lower bound on how long it will take our inexact velocity field to compress the fluid by some fraction. Thus `tol` probably should be inversely proportional to the time length of our simulation. In practice, this either doesn't vary a lot (a few seconds for most shots) or we are doing interactive animation with a potentially infinite time length— so in the end we just pick an arbitrary small fixed number for `tol`, like 10^{-6} s^{-1}. (The s^{-1} is one over seconds: remember again that this quantity has dimensions one over time.) Smaller tolerances will result in less erroneous divergence but will take more iterations (and time) to compute, so there's a clear trade-off in adjusting this number up or down.[2] This is particularly important since typically most of the time in a fluid simulation is spent in the pressure solver: this is the code that usually demands the most optimizing and tuning.

That said, the fact that our absolute tolerance on stopping PCG has physical units (of one over time) can also be worrisome. While most visual effects simulations run in seconds, occasionally we see a need for super slow-motion, or accelerated time, where the time scale is quite different. Later in the book we'll also look at including additional dynamics in the linear system, such as viscosity, where it's peculiar to translate the accompanying residual terms to one-over-time units; it may also be desired to have a generic linear solver available in the code, which doesn't make assumptions about the units of the system. Therefore we often use a *relative* residual measure for convergence: stop when the ratio between the current residual norm and the initial right-hand-side norm is smaller than a given dimensionless tolerance (with no physica units needed). That is, stop when

$$\|r\| = \|b - Ap\| \leq \texttt{tol}\|b\|,$$

where `tol` is typically also on the order of 10^{-6}. Alternatively put, you can scale the relative tolerance set by the user with the maximum absolute value of the input vector b to get the absolute tolerance for convergence. Also note that we use less than or equal to, to handle the case (which happens from time to time) where $b = 0$ and an initial guess of $p = 0$ is the exact solution.

Typically we will also want to guard against inexact floating-point arithmetic causing the algorithm not to converge fully, so we stop at a certain

---

[2]However, one of the great features of PCG is that the rate of convergence tends to accelerate the farther along you go: reducing the tolerance may not slow things down as much as you think.

maximum number of iterations. Or, we may have a computation time constraint that limits the number of iterations we can use—a good default to begin with is 200. The solver shouldn't ordinarily hit the maximum number of iterations (because the solution you get may be of dubious quality), and whenever it does it should be reported as a potential error—maybe there's a bug in the discretization, or the tolerance is nonsensical, and at the very least the user should know that if they get strange results it's probably due to the linear solver failing.

A final issue is what the initial guess for pressure should be. One nice thing about PCG is that if we start with a good guess, we can get to an acceptable solution much faster. In some circumstances, say when the fluid has settled down and isn't changing much, the pressure from the last time step is a very good guess for the next pressure: it won't change much either. However, these situations usually can easily be solved from an initial guess of all zeros also. In the more interesting cases (and really, why would you be simulating fluids that are just sitting still?), the pressure can change significantly from one time step to the next, or in fact may be defined on different grid cells anyhow (e.g., as liquid moves from one grid cell to another) and can't be used. Therefore we usually use the vector of all zeros as the initial guess.

Pseudocode for the PCG algorithm is shown in Figure 5.6. Be aware that this statement of PCG uses different symbols than most text books: I've tried to avoid the use of letters like x and ρ that have other meanings in the context of fluids.

Note that PCG needs storage for an "auxiliary" vector z and a "search" vector s (the same size as p, b, and r), and calls subroutine applyA to multiply the coefficient matrix A times a vector and subroutine applyPreconditioner to multiply M by a vector (which we will talk about next). Also note that the new residual in each iteration is incrementally updated from the previous residual—not only is this more efficient than calculating it from scratch each time, but it in fact tends to reduce the number of iterations required due to some interesting round-off error interactions. Since PCG tends to be the most time-consuming part of the simulation, it pays to use optimized **BLAS**[3] routines for the vector operations here. Finally, it's worth noting that although most of the rest of the fluid simulator may be effectively implemented using 32-bit single precision floating-point numbers, 64-bit double precision is *strongly* recommended for

---

[3]The BLAS, or basic linear algebra subroutines, provide a standardized API for simple operations like dot-products, scaling and adding vectors, multiplying dense matrices, etc. Every significant platform has at least one implementation, which generally is intensely optimized, making full use of vector units, cache prefetching, multiple cores, and the like. It can be very difficult (if not impossible without using assembly language) to match the efficiency attained by the BLAS for vectors of any appreciable size, so it generally pays to exploit it.

- Set initial guess $p = 0$ and residual vector $r = b$ (If $r = 0$ then return p)
- Set auxiliary vector $z = \mathtt{applyPreconditioner}(r)$, and search vector $s = z$
- $\sigma = \mathtt{dotproduct}(z, r)$
- Loop until done (or maximum iterations exceeded):
  - Set auxiliary vector $z = \mathtt{applyA}(s)$
  - $\alpha = \sigma / \mathtt{dotproduct}(z, s)$
  - Update $p \leftarrow p + \alpha s$ and $r \leftarrow r - \alpha z$
  - If $\max |r| \leq \mathtt{tol}$ then return p
  - Set auxiliary vector $z = \mathtt{applyPreconditioner}(r)$
  - $\sigma_{\mathrm{new}} = \mathtt{dotproduct}(z, r)$
  - $\beta = \sigma_{\mathrm{new}} / \sigma$
  - Set search vector $s = z + \beta s$
  - $\sigma = \sigma_{\mathrm{new}}$
- Return p (and report iteration limit exceeded)

Figure 5.6. The preconditioned conjugate gradient (PCG) algorithm for solving $Ap = d$.

PCG—at the very least, for the scalars (in particular when accumulating the dot-products[4]). Single precision rounding errors can cause a significant slow-down in convergence.

5.3.3 Incomplete Cholesky

We still have the question of defining the preconditioner. From the stand-point of convergence the perfect preconditioner would be A^{-1}, except that's obviously far too expensive to compute. The true ideal is something that is both fast to compute and apply, and is effective in speeding up convergence, so as to minimize the total solution time.

There are many, many choices of preconditioner, with more being invented each year. Our default choice, though, is quite an old preconditioner from the **Incomplete Cholesky** (IC) family. It's both simple to implement and fairly efficient, and moreover is highly robust in handling irregular domains (like the shape of a liquid splash). Its chief problems

---

[4]If you do use single precision floating-point values for your vectors (pressure, etc.), you should investigate the BLAS routine dsdot to compute the dot-product in double precision.

are that it's hard to parallelize effectively and that it's not optimally scalable (the number of iterations required for PCG slowly increases with grid size). Algorithms in the **domain decomposition** and **multigrid** family of methods can provide both excellent parallelization and optimal scalability (the time it takes to solve a problem is linearly proportional to the number of grid cells) but are not trivial to implement in a way that is robust to irregular domains. However, we'll discuss below a simple form of domain decomposition that can provide good parallelization for Incomplete Cholesky.

Recall how you might directly solve a system of linear equations with Gaussian elimination. That is, you perform row reductions on the system until the matrix is upper-triangular, and then use back substitution to get the solution one entry at a time. Mathematically, it turns out that this is equivalent to factoring the matrix A as the product of a lower- and an upper-triangular matrix and then solving the triangular systems one after the other. In the case of a symmetric positive definite A, we can actually do it so that the two triangular matrices are transposes of each other:

$$A = LL^T.$$

This is called the **Cholesky** factorization. The original system $Ap = b$ is the same as $L(L^T p) = b$, which we can solve as

$$
\begin{aligned}
\text{solve} \quad & Lq = b \quad && \text{with forward substitution,} \\
\text{solve} \quad & L^T p = q \quad && \text{with backward substitution.}
\end{aligned}
\tag{5.10}
$$

The main reason that we don't typically use this method for fluids is that although A has very few non-zeros, L can have a lot. In three dimensions the amount of **fill-in** (extra non-zeros in L) is particularly bad; **direct solvers** that take this approach can easily fail on 3D problems due to lack of memory.

Basic Incomplete Cholesky tackles this problem with a very simple idea: whenever the Cholesky algorithm tries to create a new non-zero in a location that is zero in A, cancel it—keep it as zero. On the one hand, the resulting L is just as sparse as A, and memory is no longer an issue. On the other hand, we deliberately made errors: $A \neq LL^T$ now. *However,* hopefully the "incomplete" factorization is close enough to A that doing the solves in Equation (5.10) is close enough to applying A^{-1} so that we have a useful preconditioner for PCG!

Technically, performing Incomplete Cholesky only allowing non-zeros in L where there are non-zeros in A is called level zero: IC(0). There are variations that allow a limited number of non-zeros in other locations, but we will not broach that topic here. For the relatively simple Laplacian matrix we are dealing with, they generally are not worth the computational effort.

To make this more precise, IC(0) constructs a lower-triangular matrix L with the same non-zero pattern as the lower triangle of A, such that $LL^T = A$ in the locations where A is non-zero. The only error is that LL^T is non-zero in some other locations where A is zero.

Assume we order our grid cells (and the corresponding rows and columns of A) lexicographically, say along the i-dimension first, then the j-dimension, and finally the k-dimension.[5] Suppose we split A up into its strict lower triangle F and diagonal D:

$$A = F + D + F^T.$$

Then, it can be shown for the particular A we're solving—though we won't show it here—that the IC(0) factor L is of the form

$$L = FE^{-1} + E,$$

where E is a diagonal matrix. That is, all we need to compute and store are the diagonal entries of L, and we can infer the others just from A!

Crunching through the algebra gives the following formulas for computing the entries along the diagonal of E. In two dimensions,

$$E_{(i,j)} = \sqrt{A_{(i,j),(i,j)} - (A_{(i-1,j),(i,j)}/E_{(i-1,j)})^2 - (A_{(i,j-1),(i,j)}/E_{(i,j-1)})^2}.$$

In three dimensions,

$$E_{(i,j,k)} =$$

$$\sqrt{\begin{aligned} &A_{(i,j,k),(i,j,k)} - (A_{(i-1,j,k),(i,j,k)}/E_{(i-1,j,k)})^2 \\ &- (A_{(i,j-1,k),(i,j,k)}/E_{(i,j-1,k)})^2 - (A_{(i,j,k-1),(i,j,k)}/E_{(i,j,k-1)})^2. \end{aligned}}$$

In these equations, we replace terms referring to a non-fluid cell (or cell that lies off the grid) with zero. Also note that the superscript two is an exponent, nothing to do with time steps: those entries of E are squared.

5.3.4 Modified Incomplete Cholesky

Incomplete Cholesky is a good preconditioner that can effectively reduce our iteration count when solving the pressure equations, and is often the

---

[5]It turns out that the order in which we take the dimensions doesn't actually change anything for IC(0) applied to our particular matrix, but that we take some lexicographic order turns out to be critical for ensuring the power of the approximation.

default choice when preconditioning any general matrix. But, for almost no extra cost, we can do better for our particular A! A slight tweak to IC, *Modified* Incomplete Cholesky (MIC), scales significantly better: if our grid is n grid cells wide, regular IC(0) will require $O(n)$ iterations but MIC(0) will converge in only $O(n^{1/2})$ iterations, with a fairly low hidden constant. Modified Incomplete Cholesky works exactly like Incomplete Cholesky, except instead of just discarding those unwanted non-zeros, we account for them by adding them to the diagonal of L.

To make this more precise, MIC(0) constructs a lower-triangular matrix L with the same non-zero pattern as the lower triangle of A, such that

- The off-diagonal non-zero entries of A are equal to the corresponding ones of (LL^T).

- The sum of each row of A is equal to the sum of each row of (LL^T).

This boils down to a slightly different calculation for the diagonal entries: the modified L is also equal to $FE^{-1} + E$, just for a different E. In two dimensions,

$$E_{(i,j)} = \sqrt{\begin{aligned} &A_{(i,j),(i,j)} - \left(A_{(i-1,j),(i,j)}/E_{(i-1,j)}\right)^2 - \left(A_{(i,j-1),(i,j)}/E_{(i,j-1)}\right)^2 \\ &\qquad - A_{(i-1,j),(i,j)}A_{(i-1,j),(i-1,j+1)}/E_{(i-1,j)}^2 \\ &\qquad - A_{(i,j-1),(i,j)}A_{(i,j-1),(i+1,j-1)}/E_{(i,j-1)}^2 \end{aligned}}$$

In three dimensions,

$$E_{(i,j,k)} = \sqrt{\begin{aligned} &A_{(i,j,k),(i,j,k)} - \left(A_{(i-1,j,k),(i,j,k)}/E_{(i-1,j,k)}\right)^2 \\ &- \left(A_{(i,j-1,k),(i,j,k)}/E_{(i,j-1,k)}\right)^2 - \left(A_{(i,j,k-1),(i,j,k)}/E_{(i,j,k-1)}\right)^2 \\ &- A_{(i-1,j,k),(i,j,k)} \\ &\quad \times \left(A_{(i-1,j,k),(i-1,j+1,k)} + A_{(i-1,j,k),(i-1,j,k+1)}\right)/E_{(i-1,j,k)}^2 \\ &- A_{(i,j-1,k),(i,j,k)} \\ &\quad \times \left(A_{(i,j-1,k),(i+1,j-1,k)} + A_{(i,j-1,k),(i,j-1,k+1)}\right)/E_{(i,j-1,k)}^2 \\ &- A_{(i,j,k-1),(i,j,k)} \\ &\quad \times \left(A_{(i,j,k-1),(i+1,j,k-1)} + A_{(i,j,k-1),(i,j+1,k-1)}\right)/E_{(i,j,k-1)}^2 \end{aligned}}$$

If you're curious, the intuition behind MIC (and why it outperforms IC) lies in a Fourier analysis of the problem. If you decompose the error as a superposition of Fourier modes, some low frequency (smooth) and some high frequency (sharp), it turns out IC is only effective at removing the high-frequency components of error. On the other hand, MIC is forced to match the action of A on the lowest frequency mode of all, the constant, and thus is more effective at all frequencies.[6]

In practice, you can squeeze out even better performance by taking a weighted average between the regular Incomplete Cholesky formula and the modified one, typically weighting with 0.97 or more (getting closer to 1 for larger grids). See Figure 5.7 for pseudocode to implement this in three dimensions. We actually compute and store the *reciprocals* of the diagonal entries of E in a grid variable called `precon`, to avoid divides when applying the preconditioner.

The pseudocode in Figure 5.7 additionally has a built-in safety tolerance. In some situations, such as a single-cell–wide line of fluid cells surrounded by solids, IC(0) and MIC(0) become exact—except that A is

---

[6] Continuing this train of thought, looking for methods that work well on all frequency components of the error can lead to multigrid that explicitly solves the equations at multiple resolutions.

- Set tuning constant $\tau = 0.97$ and safety constant $\sigma = 0.25$
- For i=1 to nx, j=1 to ny, k=1 to nz:
  - If cell (i, j, k) is fluid:
    - Set $e = \text{Adiag}_{i,j,k} - (\text{Aplusi}_{i-1,j,k} * \text{precon}_{i-1,j,k})^2$
$$- (\text{Aplusj}_{i,j-1,k} * \text{precon}_{i,j-1,k})^2$$
$$- (\text{Aplusk}_{i,j,k-1} * \text{precon}_{i,j,k-1})^2$$
$$-\tau \left[\text{Aplusi}_{i-1,j,k} * (\text{Aplusj}_{i-1,j,k} \right.$$
$$+ \text{Aplusk}_{i-1,j,k})$$
$$* \text{precon}^2_{i-1,j,k}$$
$$+ \text{Aplusj}_{i,j-1,k}$$
$$* (\text{Aplusi}_{i,j-1,k} + \text{Aplusk}_{i,j-1,k})$$
$$* \text{precon}^2_{i,j-1,k}$$
$$+ \text{Aplusk}_{i,j,k-1}$$
$$* (\text{Aplusi}_{i,j,k-1} + \text{Aplusj}_{i,j,k-1})$$
$$\left. * \text{precon}^2_{i,j,k-1} \right]$$
    - If $e < \sigma \text{Adiag}_{i,j,k}$, set $e = \text{Adiag}_{i,j,k}$
    - $\text{precon}_{i,j,k} = 1/\sqrt{e}$

Figure 5.7. The calculation of the MIC(0) preconditioner in three dimensions.

singular in this case: the exact Cholesky factorization doesn't exist. This is manifested by hitting a zero or—when rounding error is factored in— very small value for e, and it can safely be cured by replacing that small value with, for example, the diagonal entry from A. This safety check also comes in handy if you want to solve more general linear systems, where the Incomplete Cholesky factorization (and even more so the Modified Incomplete Cholesky factorization) may fail to exist without this check.

- (First solve $Lq = r$)
- For i=1 to nx, j=1 to ny, k=1 to nz:
  - If cell (i, j, k) is fluid:
    - Set
      $$t = r_{i,j,k} - \texttt{Aplusi}_{i-1,j,k} * \texttt{precon}_{i-1,j,k} * q_{i-1,j,k}$$
      $$- \texttt{Aplusj}_{i,j-1,k} * \texttt{precon}_{i,j-1,k} * q_{i,j-1,k}$$
      $$- \texttt{Aplusk}_{i,j,k-1} * \texttt{precon}_{i,j,k-1} * q_{i,j,k-1}$$
    - $q_{i,j,k} = t * \texttt{precon}_{i,j,k}$
- (Next solve $L^T z = q$)
- For i=nx down to 1, j=ny down to 1, k=nz down to 1:
  - If cell (i, j, k) is fluid:
    - Set
      $$t = q_{i,j,k} - \texttt{Aplusi}_{i,j,k} * \texttt{precon}_{i,j,k} * z_{i+1,j,k}$$
      $$- \texttt{Aplusj}_{i,j,k} * \texttt{precon}_{i,j,k} * z_{i,j+1,k}$$
      $$- \texttt{Aplusk}_{i,j,k} * \texttt{precon}_{i,j,k} * z_{i,j,k+1}$$
    - $z_{i,j,k} = t * \texttt{precon}_{i,j,k}$

Figure 5.8. Applying the MIC(0) preconditioner in three dimensions ($z = Mr$).

All that's left is how to apply the preconditioner, that is, perform the triangular solves. This is outlined in Figure 5.8 for three dimensions.

Finally, before going on, I should note that the nesting of loops is an important issue for performance. Due to cache effects, it's far faster if you can arrange your loops to walk through memory sequentially. For example, if $p_{i,j,k}$ and $p_{i+1,j,k}$ are stored next to each other in memory, then the i loop should be innermost.

5.3.5 Domain Decomposition

Solving the linear system for pressure is one of the more expensive steps in a typical fluid solve, so parallelization is crucial. Unfortunately, the computation of Incomplete Cholesky described above, running through the system in lexicographic order, is inherently sequential: the forward and backward triangular solves needed at every step of PCG have data dependency that eliminates the possibility for parallelization. It is possible to reorder the matrix and the grid cells in a way that allows a parallel factorization, but interestingly and frustratingly enough, such an ordering seriously harms the power of the preconditioner, rendering it not much better than doing nothing at all [DM89, Doi91, Eij91, BT00]. Research has continued in this vein using graph multicolorings for parallelism, but generally a more complex version of Incomplete Cholesky with more nonzeros in the sparsity pattern is required at a minimum.

Luckily, we can take a different approach to parallelization, domain decomposition. Domain decomposition is essentially the divide-and-conquer principle applied to solving sparse linear systems: we partition our "domain" (the grid of unknowns) into "subdomains" (subsets of the unknowns), solve the smaller linear system restricted to each subdomain independently, and patch the results together into an approximate solution for the original domain. Ideally almost all of the work takes place in solving the subdomains, which can all be done in parallel, leading to excellent parallel efficiency.

Domain decomposition itself could be a topic for an entire book [SBG04], as there are many possibilities for how the subdomains are constructed, how the problem is restricted to them, and how the subdomain solutions are combined at the end. We will go with a particularly simple variant of what is termed "Additive Overlapping Schwarz."

First we need to partition our grid into subdomains. For simplicity, we may as well take them to be subgrids. The critical requirements are:

- We need at least as many subgrids as parallel threads we want to use (fewer is better for convergence, but having more than one subgrid per thread can make dynamic load balancing work better).

- The subgrids, taken all together, have to cover the entire original grid: we can't leave any gaps.

- The subgrids should overlap a bit, i.e. have some grid cells in common with their neighbors. The bigger the overlap, the fewer the number of iterations we will need but the slower to compute each iteration will be (and the more memory required).

For example, if we had a $100 \times 100 \times 100$ original grid, we could split it into eight $52 \times 52 \times 52$ subgrids, with an overlap band of four grid cells—the grid cells in the very center of the domain would be a part of all the subgrids.

For the $z = \texttt{applyPreconditioner}(r)$ call in PCG, we have to first solve or approximately solve each subdomain's part of the equation $Az = r$, independently. For each subdomain, this entails taking just the entries of A and r in the grid cells of that subdomain, and ignoring the offdiagonal entries of A that reference grid cells outside the subdomain. The solve could be a full linear solve to maximum precision using some other technique, but it is likely to be more efficient to just use one call to MIC(0) instead (giving a very approximate solution). Because this is going to part of an outer PCG loop, not every method is allowed here—approximations that are unsymmetric, or nonlinear (such as taking a few "inner" iterations of PCG without converging fully) can cause convergence troubles. Because the solves are completely independent, this step is trivial to parallelize without synchronization or communication required: just some shared reads to A and r (but *not* shared writes). Once each subdomain has its own local estimate of the solution z restricted to its subdomain, we simply add up all the subdomain solves into one global estimate z, which is returned to the outer PCG loop. This addition, in the overlap regions where multiple subdomains contribute, does require some form of synchronization or locking—or the calculation of the overlap entries can be left to a single thread at the end.

When the number of subdomains becomes large, the convergence rate of plain domain decomposition diminishes. To get an optimal high-performance preconditioner, it is necessary to include a **coarse grid correction**. This is basically a step (similar to multigrid) inside the preconditioner where we solve a very coarse version of the problem, with one or just a few variables per subdomain, representing the smoothest components of the error. We won't pursue this in the book, but I will recommend the Discretely-Discontinuous Galerkin (DDG) method of Edwards and Bridson [EB15] as possibly the best option in terms of a very simple implementation that can be applied to just about any sort of PDE problem, while providing extremely good speed-up.

5.4   Projection

The `project`$(\Delta t, \vec{u})$ routine does the following:

- Calculate the negative divergence b (the right-hand side) with modifications at solid wall boundaries.

- Set the entries of A (stored in `Adiag`, etc.).

- Construct the preconditioner (either MIC(0) for single threaded solves, or a more complicated domain decomposition set up for parallel solves).

- Solve $Ap = b$ with PCG.

- Compute the new velocities $\vec{u}^{n+1}$ according to the pressure-gradient update to $\vec{u}$.

We still haven't explained *why* this routine is called `project`. You can skip over this section if you're not interested.

If you recall from your linear algebra, a projection is a special type of linear operator such that if you apply it twice, you get the same result as applying it once. For example, a matrix P is a projection if $P^2 = P$. It turns out that our transformation from $\vec{u}$ to $\vec{u}^{n+1}$ is indeed a linear projection.[7]

If you want, you can trace through the steps to establish the linearity: the entries of b are linear combinations of the entries of $\vec{u}$, the pressures $p = A^{-1}b$ are linear combinations of the entries of d, and the new velocities $\vec{u}^{n+1}$ are linear combinations of $\vec{u}$ and p.

Physically, it's clear that this transformation has to be a projection. The resulting velocity field, $\vec{u}^{n+1}$, has discrete divergence equal to zero. So if we repeated the pressure step with this as input, we'd first evaluate $b = 0$, which would give constant pressures and no change to the velocity.

5.5 More Accurate Curved Boundaries

Reducing the geometry of the problem to just labeling grid cells as solid, fluid, or empty can introduce major artifacts when the boundaries are actually at an angle or curved. For example, in the eyes of the simulator a solid slope becomes a sequence of flat stair steps: obviously water flows down stairs very differently than down an inclined slope. If you render an inclined slope but your water pools at regular intervals along it instead of flowing down, it looks terrible—and isn't easy to fix up later. As a general rule of thumb, you can only expect physically plausible motion for things the simulator can "see" (i.e., those that are taken into account in the numerical discretization of the physics), not details to which only the renderer has access.

To close out this chapter, we will focus on the issue of accurately accounting for solid boundaries that don't line up with the grid. Later, in Chapter 8 on water, we will also look at a more accurate treatment of the free surface. Dealing with solids turns out to be all down to the divergence condition; the pressure gradient we will leave alone (while for the free surface, it turns out to be all about the pressure gradient, irrespective of the divergence condition).

From a finite-difference perspective, the tricky part of handling solids that don't line up with the MAC grid is that the normal component of velocity is no longer conveniently stored on the grid: attempts to interpolate

---

[7]Technically speaking, if we have non-zero solid wall velocities then this is an affine transformation rather than a linear one, but it still is a projection. For the purpose of simplicity, we'll ignore this case here.

that component from the staggered u-, v-, and w-values and then constrain the interpolant to match the solid velocity have met with limited success.

One interesting alternative is to replace the grid with an unstructured tetrahedral mesh, with a boundary that matches up with the solid surfaces. However, this can impose a serious performance overhead in constructing and working with an unstructured mesh which we'd prefer not to be forced into taking if we can avoid it. Luckily we can get around these problems, for most scenarios, with just a regular Cartesian grid if we rethink our discretization.

5.5.1   The Finite Volume Method

The leading solution on grids is to be found in the **finite volume** method, mentioned earlier. Ng et al. have worked this out in detail for our particular case [NMG09]. We begin with the integral form of the incompressibility condition:

$$\iint_{\partial C} \vec{u} \cdot \hat{n} = 0,$$

where ∂C is the boundary of a **control volume** C. In particular, in the interior of the flow, we take each grid cell as a control volume and approximate the boundary integral over each face of the cell as the area Δx^2 of the face times the normal component of velocity stored at the face center. At the boundary, it gets more interesting. If a solid cuts through a face of a grid cell / control volume, the integral of $\vec{u} \cdot \hat{n}$ has two contributions from both the fluid velocity (over the fluid part of the cell faces) and the solid velocity (over the solid part of the cell faces). Our approximation is then likewise the sum of the fluid velocity times the area of the fluid part of the face with the solid velocity times the remaining solid area of the face. Dividing through by Δx^2, the equation for such a **cut cell** is then

$$
\begin{aligned}
&-F_{i-1/2,j,k}u_{i-1/2,j,k} + F_{i+1/2,j,k}u_{i+1/2,j,k} \\
&-F_{i,j-1/2,k}v_{i,j-1/2,k} + F_{i,j+1/2,k}v_{i,j+1/2,k} \\
&-F_{i,j,k-1/2}w_{i,j,k-1/2} + F_{i,j,k+1/2}w_{i,j,k+1/2} \\
&-(1 - F_{i-1/2,j,k})u_{i-1/2,j,k}^{\text{solid}} + (1 - F_{i+1/2,j,k})u_{i+1/2,j,k}^{\text{solid}} \\
&-(1 - F_{i,j-1/2,k})v_{i,j-1/2,k}^{\text{solid}} + (1 - F_{i,j+1/2,k})v_{i,j+1/2,k}^{\text{solid}} \\
&-(1 - F_{i,j,k-1/2})w_{i,j,k-1/2}^{\text{solid}} + (1 - F_{i,j,k+1/2})w_{i,j,k+1/2}^{\text{solid}} \\
&\qquad\qquad\qquad\qquad\qquad\qquad\qquad\qquad\qquad\qquad = 0,
\end{aligned}
\tag{5.11}
$$

where the F terms are the fluid face area fractions, in the range $[0,1]$ (1 meaning fully fluid, 0 meaning fully solid). Plugging our usual pressure gradient into the new finite volume divergence condition results in a symmetric positive semi-definite linear system of exactly the same structure as before (and solvable with exactly the same code) but with modified non-zero entries near boundaries and modified right-hand side. Writing in two dimensions for brevity, this is:

$$-\frac{F_{i-1/2,j}}{\Delta x}p_{i-1,j}$$

$$-\frac{F_{i,j-1/2}}{\Delta x}p_{i,j-1}$$

$$+\frac{F_{i-1/2,j}+F_{i,j-1/2}+F_{i+1/2,j}+F_{i,j+1/2}}{\Delta x}p_{i,j}$$

$$-\frac{F_{i+1/2,j}}{\Delta x}p_{i+1,j}$$

$$-\frac{F_{i,j+1/2}}{\Delta x}p_{i,j+1}$$

$$=F_{i-1/2,j}u_{i-1/2,j}$$

$$+(1-F_{i-1/2,j})u_{i-1/2,j}^{\text{solid}}$$

$$+F_{i,j-1/2}v_{i,j-1/2}$$

$$+(1-F_{i,j-1/2})v_{i,j-1/2}^{\text{solid}}$$

$$-F_{i+1/2,j}u_{i+1/2,j}$$

$$-(1-F_{i+1/2,j})u_{i+1/2,j}^{\text{solid}}$$

$$-F_{i,j+1/2}v_{i,j+1/2}$$

$$-(1-F_{i,j+1/2})v_{i,j+1/2}^{\text{solid}}.$$

$$(5.12)$$

Technically, this discretization so far also assumes that the solid velocity is divergence-free, i.e. that even if a solid is deforming, it won't change its volume. This is almost always true—or close enough to true that we can get by under the assumption for the fluid simulation. In the rare case it isn't, you can change the right-hand-side of this equation to an estimate of the integral of the divergence of solid velocity in the cell, but I have never found this necessary.

It's worth pointing out that in this discretization, unlike the voxelized version from earlier on, pressures associated with cell centers which happen to be inside the solid walls—precisely those that are involved in velocity updates near the wall—can appear as actual unknowns in the equations and cannot be simply eliminated as ghost values as before. Indeed, it's these extra unknowns that ultimately allow a more accurate solution.

However, it's also important to note that this use of pressures inside the walls means that this approach can't perfectly handle thin solids, solids that are thinner than a grid cell—including most models of cloth, for example.

Ideally there should be no direct coupling of pressures or velocities on either side of a fixed, thin solid. To accurately handle such solids, a more complicated data structure than just a simple grid is needed—a voxel containing a thin solid will need more than just one pressure, to handle each separate region the solid cuts the cell into.[8]

5.5.2   Area Fractions

Returning to Equation (5.11), we have a new quantity to estimate: the fluid face fractions, $F_{i-1/2,j,k}$ and friends. If the solid geometry is given in terms of polygonal meshes, this can in principle be computed exactly by intersecting the mesh faces against the grid cell faces, but arriving at a robust and efficient implementation is not for the faint-hearted! It's much simpler if the geometry is given as a level set instead, sampled at the corners of the voxels.

First consider a triangle with corners labeled 0, 1, and 2, and function values ϕ_0, ϕ_1, ϕ_2 sampled there, where $\phi(x)$ is the level set function that implicitly defines the solid geometry. Say that the solid is the region where $\phi(x) < 0$, the fluid is where $\phi(x) > 0$, and the solid surface is the isocontour defined by $\phi(x) = 0$ as usual. Further assume, without loss of generality, that we (re-)labeled the corners of the triangle in order so that $\phi_0 \leq \phi_1 \leq \phi_2$.

If we linearly interpolate ϕ across the triangle from those samples, it should be clear that ϕ_0 is the minimum value over the entire triangle, and ϕ_2 is the maximum value. Then if $\phi_0 > 0$, obviously the zero isocontour doesn't touch the triangle: the triangle is completely solid (so the fluid fraction would be 0). If $\phi_2 < 0$, the zero isocontour also doesn't touch the triangle but the triangle is instead completely fluid (so the fluid fraction would be 1).

In the case $\phi_0 \leq \phi_1 < 0 < \phi_2$, only the "2" corner is in the fluid. Under the linear interpolation model of $\phi(x)$, we must have a tinier subtriangle of fluid, with the remaining quadrilateral in the solid. You can work out that $\phi(x)$ linear interpolates to zero along the $0 - 2$ edge at fraction

$$\theta_{02} = \frac{\phi_2}{\phi_2 - \phi_0} \tag{5.13}$$

going from corner "2" toward corner "0". That is, this is where we estimate the zero isocontour cuts the $0 - 2$ edge. Fraction θ_{02} is one side length of the fluid subtriangle, expressed as a fraction of the side of the full triangle.

---

[8]Of course, one can return to just the inaccurate voxelized approach, with eliminated ghost pressures, which makes the data structure considerably simpler: see Guendelman et al. [GSLF05].

Likewise,

$$\theta_{12} = \frac{\phi_2}{\phi_2 - \phi_1} \tag{5.14}$$

is the fraction of the $1 - 2$ edge in the fluid. A bit of geometry readily shows that the fraction of the area of the triangle in the fluid is just the product:

$$F_{\text{triangle}} = \theta_{02}\theta_{12}. \tag{5.15}$$

In the case $\phi_0 < 0 < \phi_1 \leq \phi_2$, only the "0" corner is in the solid, and the remaining quadrilateral is in the fluid. We can then reverse the above calculation, working out the solid fraction and subtracting it from 1 to get the fluid fraction:

$$F_{\text{triangle}} = 1 - \left(\frac{\phi_0}{\phi_0 - \phi_1}\right)\left(\frac{\phi_0}{\phi_0 - \phi_2}\right). \tag{5.16}$$

Now that we have worked out what to do for triangles, we can estimate a square face fraction by splitting it into subtriangles. To avoid any direction bias, we cut the square along both diagonals into four triangles, with the center of the square as their common vertex. If we only have ϕ given at the corners of the square, we can take the average to estimate the value at the center. The fluid face fraction of the square is just the average of the fluid face fractions of the four subtriangles.

5.5.3 Tiny Fractions Considered Harmful

One fly in the ointment with this "cut-cell finite volume method" is that it can be very sensitive to tiny fluid fractions. If a grid cell has all of its surrounding face fractions close to zero, then a large perturbation in pressure gets scaled down to just a tiny perturbation in the right-hand side. More pessimistically put, a tiny error in the right-hand side (from our approximations to the solid velocity, or the solid geometry, or anything else) can lead to a huge error in the pressure for that cell. This means the pressure associated with a cell with only tiny face fractions is untrustworthy, no matter how accurately the linear solve has converged: using it in the pressure gradient update for velocity can easily cause an unstable spike in velocity, with the fluid suddenly blowing up from that point of the boundary.

The easiest fix for this is to check, when computing a fluid fraction, if it is below some threshold like 0.1: if so, round it all the way down to zero. That way, every nonzero row in the matrix has to have a diagonal entry greater than $0.1/\Delta x$, which roughly means that a small error in the right-hand side can be blown up by at most a factor of ten in the pressure, which is generally just fine.[9]

---

[9]Batty et al. [BBB07] first modified the pressure system in graphics to more accu-

5.5.4   Velocity Extrapolation

To finish off the section, here is a reminder that only the velocity samples with non-zero fluid fractions will be updated. The other velocities are untouched by the pressure and thus may be completely unreliable. As mentioned in Chapter 3, advection may rely on interpolating velocity from these untouched values: clearly we need to do something about them. Also, as mentioned earlier, for inviscid flow it's wrong to simply use the solid velocity there: only the normal component of solid velocity has any bearing on the fluid. Therefore it is usual to extrapolate velocity values from the well-defined fluid samples to the rest of the grid. Typically the breath-first search approach given at the end of Chapter 4 is adequate for this.

5.6   The Compatibility Condition

Naturally a fluid in a solid container cannot simultaneously be incompressible and satisfy solid velocity conditions that are acting to change the volume, a simple result of the divergence theorem:

$$\iiint_\Omega \nabla \cdot \vec{u} = \iint_{\partial\Omega} \vec{u} \cdot \hat{n}.$$

This is the compatibility condition, without which the PDE for pressure has no solution. (Note of course that if there is a free surface as well, no condition is needed.)

More precisely, we want the discrete linear system to have a solution. Even if the solid wall velocity does exactly integrate to zero, once discretized on a grid there may be numerical errors that cause the linear solve to fail. Thus we need a routine which can "correct" the right-hand side of the linear system to make it consistent.

We can view this as a pure linear algebra problem, as outlined by Guendelman et al. [GSLF05]. That is, given a singular A and a vector b, we want to remove from b any components which lie outside the range of A: the modified linear system $Ax = \bar{b}$ then has a solution. If A is symmetric, which it is in our case, this is equivalent to removing components from b that lie in the null-space of A. Luckily, for the pressure problem on a MAC grid, this null-space is very simple: for every set of connected grid

---

rately account for solids, but did it with a quite different approach based on interpreting pressure projection as kinetic energy minimization. This leads to volume fractions instead of face fractions in the linear system, and while these don't give quite as accurate results, they tend to far more robust in the sense of avoiding cells with all surrounding fluid fractions being close to zero. This can be considered another approach to avoiding the instability.

cells with no free surface conditions, there is a null-space basis vector consisting of unit pressures in those voxels. By "connected," we mean with respect to the graph of the matrix A: two grid cells are connected if there is a non-zero entry in A corresponding to the pair; finding these connected sets is a simple graph traversal problem. Note that the sets are necessarily disjoint, so each of the null-space vectors we find is orthogonal to the rest. Therefore we can efficiently remove the incompatibilities in b by orthogonal projection. Boiled down to basics, this simply means adding up the entries of b in the set, dividing by the number of entries, and subtracting this mean off of each entry. It is imperative here to use double precision floating-point in calculating the sum, as otherwise the accumulated rounding errors can seriously undermine the method (necessitating repeating the process and/or subtracting the sum off a single randomly chosen entry). Also note that this process works for both the classic voxelized solve and the more accurate finite volume method from the previous section. From a physical standpoint, this causes us to find a solution that strikes a balance between respecting the boundary conditions and staying divergence-free.

6

Smoke

6.1 Temperature and Smoke Concentration

The first visual fluid phenomena we will consider is smoke, loosely following the standard reference papers by Foster and Metaxas [FM97] and by Fedkiw et al. [FSJ01], with some additional capabilities added. Our fluid in this case is the air in which the smoke particles are suspended. To model the most important effects of smoke, we need two extra fluid variables: the temperature T of the air and the concentration s of smoke particles—what we actually can see. Similar phenomena, such as vapor, can be modeled in much the same way. Generally we'll try to keep to SI units of Kelvin for temperature and keep s as a volume concentration, perhaps expressed in parts-per-million (ppm): depending on how much physics the smoke rendering is simulating, you even might need to track the concentration of different ranges of soot particle sizes separately, but we will not go that far.

Also keep in mind that it's crucial to simulate *all* the air in the simulation, not just the regions with $s > 0$: a lot of the characteristic swirly behavior you see in smoke depends on enforcing the divergence-free constraint in nearby clear regions of air.

Before getting to how these variables will influence the velocity of the air in the next few sections, let's work out how T and s should evolve. It should be immediately apparent that temperature and soot particles are both advected with the fluid, i.e., we'll be using the material derivatives DT/Dt and Ds/Dt to describe them.[1] This gives us the simplest possible equations,

$$\frac{DT}{Dt} = 0,$$
$$\frac{Ds}{Dt} = 0$$

---

[1] The story for temperature, at least, can be rather more complicated when full thermodynamics are considered. However, the assumption of incompressible fluid flow abstracts away most of the interaction between heat, pressure, density, etc. For large-scale atmospheric disturbances, like clouds and volcanic plumes, it may be necessary to dive deeper into thermodynamics than this book allows.

and will be the first step of a numerical method: when we advect $\vec{u}$, we also advect T and s. Typically we would discretize both variables at cell centers, where the pressure values lie.

The boundary conditions for advection can vary. As we saw earlier, these arise in the semi-Lagrangian method in terms of which values should be used when interpolating from non-fluid grid cells or when tracing outside the bounds of the grid. For insulated solids it makes sense to extrapolate T-values from the nearest point in the fluid; for solids that should conduct their heat to the flow, the solid's own temperature can be used. Unless a solid is a source of smoke, like a fire, and can supply a sensible s-value, it should be extrapolated from the fluid. At open boundaries, both T and s should be taken to be "ambient" values—typically T on the order of 273 K and $s = 0$.

To make things interesting, we generally add volume sources to the domain: regions where, at each time step, we add heat and smoke. In the PDE form this could be represented as

$$\frac{DT}{Dt} = r_T(\vec{x})(T_{\text{target}}(\vec{x}) - T),$$
$$\frac{Ds}{Dt} = r_s(\vec{x}),$$

where r_T and r_s are functions that control the rate at which we add heat and smoke—which should be zero outside of sources—and T_{target} gives the target temperature at a source. This can be implemented at each grid point inside a source as an update after advection:

$$T_{ijk}^{\text{new}} = T_{ijk} + (1 - e^{-r_T \Delta t})(T_{\text{target}} - T_{ijk}),$$
$$s_{ijk}^{\text{new}} = s_{ijk} + r_s \Delta t.$$

For additional detail, all of these source values might be modulated by an animated volume texture. To help avoid excesses due to poor choices of parameters, the smoke concentration might also be capped at a maximum concentration of 1.

Another useful animation control is to allow for decay of one or both fields: multiplying all values in a field by $e^{-d\Delta t}$ for a decay rate d. This isn't particularly grounded in real physics, but it is a simple way to mimic effects such as heat loss due to radiation.

Heat and smoke concentration both can diffuse as well, where very small-scale phenomena such as conduction or Brownian motion, together with slightly larger-scale processes such as turbulent mixing, serve to smooth out steep gradients. This can be modeled with a Laplacian term in the PDE, much like viscosity:

$$\frac{DT}{Dt} = k_T \nabla \cdot \nabla T,$$

$$\frac{Ds}{Dt} = k_s \nabla \cdot \nabla s.$$

Here k_T and k_s are non-negative diffusion constants. These could be discretized with finite differences in the obvious way, for example for temperature:

$$T_{i,j,k}^{\text{new}} = T_{i,j,k} + \Delta t k_T$$
$$\times \frac{T_{i+1,j,k} + T_{i,j+1,k} + T_{i,j,k+1} - 6T_{i,j,k} + T_{i-1,j,k} + T_{i,j-1,k} + T_{i,j,k-1}}{\Delta x^2}.$$

The same boundary conditions used in advection provide values of T (or s) at non-fluid points. However, this update is only stable and free of spurious oscillations if

$$\Delta t \lesssim \frac{\Delta x^2}{6k_T}.$$

If this condition cannot be met (or is so far from being met that breaking up the time step into several smaller substeps that do satisfy the condition is too slow), another simple option is to run a Gaussian blur on the variable. In fact, apart from boundary conditions, the *exact* solution to the so-called **heat equation**

$$\frac{\partial T}{\partial t} = k_T \nabla \cdot \nabla T \tag{6.1}$$

over a time Δt is a convolution with the following Gaussian filter, which in this context is called the **heat kernel**:

$$G(\vec{x}) = \frac{1}{(4\pi k_T \Delta t)^{3/2}} e^{-\frac{\|\vec{x}\|^2}{4k_T \Delta t}}.$$

The convolution can be evaluated efficiently dimension by dimension exploiting the separability of the Gaussian filter; see any reference on image processing for details.

If the Gaussian filter radius turns out to be excessively large, this approach too can have flaws: making the filter run fast is nontrivial, and artifacts near boundaries can start to become noticeable. In this case, it can be worth it instead to use implicit integration. One step of Backwards Euler integration looks almost identical to the formula above, but uses the new temperature to evaluate the diffusion term:

$$T_{i,j,k}^{\text{new}} = T_{i,j,k} + \Delta t k_T$$
$$\cdot \frac{T_{i+1,j,k}^{\text{new}} + T_{i,j+1,k}^{\text{new}} + T_{i,j,k+1}^{\text{new}} - 6T_{i,j,k}^{\text{new}} + T_{i-1,j,k}^{\text{new}} + T_{i,j-1,k}^{\text{new}} + T_{i,j,k-1}^{\text{new}}}{\Delta x^2}.$$

At a conducting solid boundary, if a neighboring grid cell is inside the solid (has $\phi_{i+1,j,k}^{\text{solid}} < 0$ for example) then the solid's temperature should be used instead. At an insulating solid boundary or a free surface, that term (say $T_{i+1,j,k}$) should be removed from the equation along with the matching contribution of the central grid point (so instead of $-6T_{i,j,k}$ we would see $-5T_{i,j,k}$, for example). This is actually just a linear system of almost exactly the same form as the one we solve for pressure to make the fluid incompressible, just with slightly different coefficients, and can be solved with exactly the same methods for the new temperature.

Finally, before moving on, it should be noted that although this approach can work well for fairly diffuse situations, the grid resolution limits its ability to handle sharply defined smoke contours. In this case the particle methods discussed later, in Chapter 7, are preferable. Even if smoke concentration is tracked on a grid for the simulation, it still may be preferable to use particles for rendering—running millions of particles through the grid velocity field can provide finer details than really are resolved in the simulation itself!

6.2 Buoyancy

We now turn to the effect that T and s have on velocity. In this section we introduce a simplified buoyancy model commonly used in graphics.

We all know that hot air rises and cool air sinks; similarly it seems plausible that air laden with heavier soot particles will be pulled downwards by gravity. We can model this by replacing the acceleration $\vec{g}$ due to gravity in the momentum equation with a buoyant acceleration

$$\vec{b} = [\alpha s - \beta(T - T_{\text{amb}})]\,\vec{g},$$

where α and β are non-negative coefficients, and T_{amb} is the ambient temperature (say 273 K). Note that we take this proportional to the downward gravity vector—indeed, buoyancy doesn't exist in a zero-G environment. Also note that the formula reduces to zero wherever $s = 0$ and $T = T_{\text{amb}}$, as might be expected.

Since T and s are generally stored at grid cell centers, we need to do some averaging to add the acceleration to the MAC grid velocities, e.g., $T_{i,j+1/2,k} = \frac{1}{2}(T_{i,j,k} + T_{i,j+1,k})$. Alternatively put, when we add buoyancy to the velocity field prior to projection, the contribution of acceleration evaluated at the grid cell center (i, j, k) is equally split between $v_{i,j-1/2,k}$ and $v_{i,j+1/2,k}$.

6.3   Variable Density Solves

Underlying the buoyancy model is the fact that fluid density is a function of temperature and—if we treat the soot as actually dissolved in the air—smoke concentration. Let's begin with just the effect of temperature, for now taking $s = 0$. From the ideal gas law, thermodynamics derives that the density of the air should be

$$\rho_{\text{air}} = \frac{P}{RT},\tag{6.2}$$

where P is the absolute pressure (say $1.01 \times 10^5 Pa$ in SI units), R is the specific gas constant for air (approximately 287 J/kg K in SI units), and T is the temperature. It should be underscored here that the absolute pressure P we propose using here is approximated as a constant—not coupled with the pressure solve for incompressibility—as otherwise we end up in a significantly more complicated compressible flow model; this has been worked out by Bonner [Bon07] in a generalization of the MAC grid incompressible simulation developed in this book, if you are interested.

Adding in some soot of density ρ_{soot} and treating the concentration s as a volume fraction, we can extend this to

$$\rho = \rho_{\text{air}} \left(1 + s \frac{\rho_{\text{soot}} - \rho_{\text{air}}}{\rho_{\text{air}}} \right)$$
$$= \rho_{\text{air}}(1 + \alpha s),\tag{6.3}$$

where we treat the relative density difference $\alpha = (\rho_{\text{soot}} - \rho_{\text{air}})/\rho_{\text{air}}$ as a constant—i.e., the soot has the same thermal expansion as the air. This is of course false, but we consider this error negligible relative to other modeling errors.

At this stage, the buoyancy model from the previous section can be recovered by linearizing Equation (6.3) around standard conditions

$$\rho \approx \rho_0 \left(1 + \alpha s - \frac{1}{T_{\text{amb}}}(T - T_{\text{amb}}) \right)$$
$$= \rho_0 \left[1 + \alpha s - \beta(T - T_{\text{amb}}) \right],$$

where ρ_0 is the smoke-free air density at ambient temperature and $\beta = 1/T_{\text{amb}}$. Plugging it into the momentum equation (where we have multiplied both sides by ρ) gives

$$\rho_0(1 + \alpha s - \beta \Delta T)\frac{D\vec{u}}{Dt} + \nabla p = \rho_0(1 + \alpha s - \beta \Delta T)\vec{g}.$$

The hydrostatic pressure for constant density fluid at rest is $p = \rho_0 \vec{g} \cdot \vec{x}$; write the actual pressure as the sum of this hydrostatic pressure plus a pressure variation p' so that $\nabla p = \rho_0 \vec{g} + \nabla p'$. This simplifies the momentum equation to

$$\rho_0(1 + \alpha s - \beta \Delta T)\frac{D\vec{u}}{Dt} + \nabla p' = \rho_0(\alpha s - \beta \Delta T)\vec{g}.$$

We now make the **Boussinesq** approximation that, assuming $|\alpha s - \beta \Delta T| \ll 1$, we can drop the density variation in the first term, leading to

$$\rho_0 \frac{D\vec{u}}{Dt} + \nabla p' = \rho_0(\alpha s - \beta \Delta T)\vec{g}.$$

Dividing through by ρ_0 gives the buoyancy form of the momentum equation from the previous section. It then becomes clear what α and β "should" be chosen as, though of course these can be left as tunable parameters. (It also makes it clear that the pressure we solve for in the buoyancy model is not the full pressure but actually just the variation above the hydrostatic pressure.)

This is a fine approximation for small density variations. However, for more extreme scenarios that are common in graphics, extra fidelity can be obtained by *not* taking the Boussinesq approximation, i.e., by treating the density as a variable in the pressure solve. Whereas the buoyancy model only generates forces in the vertical direction, the full model can give interesting plumes along any strong pressure gradient, such as radially inward in rotating regions of the flow.

As a first step before the variable-density solve, Equation (6.3) should be used to determine the fluid density at each velocity sample in the MAC grid. This entails averaging the temperatures and smoke concentrations from the grid cell centers to the grid cell faces, in the usual manner. These u-, v- and w-densities modify the pressure projection in two ways. The pressure update is now

$$u_{i+1/2,j,k}^{n+1} = u_{i+1/2,j,k} + \Delta t \frac{p_{i+1,j,k} - p_{i,j,k}}{\rho_{i+1/2,j,k}\Delta x},$$

$$v_{i,j+1/2,k}^{n+1} = v_{i,j+1/2,k} + \Delta t \frac{p_{i,j+1,k} - p_{i,j,k}}{\rho_{i,j+1/2,k}\Delta x},$$

$$w_{i,j,k+1/2}^{n+1} = w_{i,j,k+1/2} + \Delta t \frac{p_{i,j,k+1} - p_{i,j,k}}{\rho_{i,j,k+1/2}\Delta x},$$

and the coefficients of the matrix A similarly incorporate the densities, as illustrated at the end of Chapter 5.

One possible problem that arises when using the variable-density solve is that the matrix may be **ill-conditioned** when large density variations are present. This means PCG will run for more iterations to return an accurate answer. For reasons of practicality it may therefore be worthwhile to clamp density to a lower bound of, say, 0.05 times the background density ρ_0.

6.4 Divergence Control

If you read the last section critically, you might have noticed we violated conservation of mass. The incompressibility constraint implies that fluid volumes remain constant, but if simultaneously the density is changed, it must mean mass is also changed. Perhaps unsurprisingly, however, most audiences aren't troubled by the violation: fluid motion is adequately complex and hard to predict so that this "problem" isn't usually an issue. That said, the solution to the problem can be generalized to one of the most useful simulation controls in smoke: **divergence control**.

In the thermal expansion problem, fundamentally we do want the fluid to expand as it heats up and contract as it cools off. In other words, where the change in temperature DT/Dt is non-zero, we don't want a divergence-free velocity field. Let's derive exactly what we want.

Consider a region of fluid Ω, currently with volume $V = \iiint_\Omega 1$. After a time step of Δt with velocities $\vec{u}$, suppose it changes volume to $V + \Delta V$. Meanwhile, suppose the average density in the region changes from ρ to $\rho + \Delta\rho$. Conservation of mass requires $\rho V = (\rho + \Delta\rho)(V + \Delta V)$ which, after neglecting the quadratic term, gives

$$\Delta V = -\frac{\Delta\rho}{\rho}V. \tag{6.4}$$

Using the divergence theorem, the change in volume is approximately

$$\Delta V = \iint_{\partial\Omega} \Delta t\vec{u} \cdot \hat{n}$$
$$= \iiint_\Omega \Delta t\nabla \cdot \vec{u}.$$

Considering an infinitesimally small region, and dividing both sides of (6.4) by $V\Delta t$, we get

$$\nabla \cdot \vec{u} = -\frac{1}{\Delta t}\frac{\Delta\rho}{\rho}.$$

This is the divergence we want to enforce in the pressure projection step, where we evaluate the change in density at grid cell centers due to changes in temperature and smoke concentration. For example, if the temperature increases, leading to a decrease in density, we need positive divergence to enact that thermal expansion.

This is still a little sloppy—in addition to the approximations made for the change in mass, there is a lag between the change in density in one time step and the resulting motion of fluid in the divergent velocity field in the next time step—and we certainly can't hope to exactly conserve mass. However, it does expose a more general divergence control in the simulation. Define a control field $d(\vec{x})$ at the grid cell centers equal to the desired rate of fractional volume change $\Delta V/V \Delta t$ throughout the volume of the fluid: we then solve for pressure to enforce that divergence. For the classic voxelized pressure solve, this is as simple as adding d to the fluid cells in the right-hand side of the linear system.

Note that adding an arbitrary divergence control inside a closed domain—one without free surfaces—may lead to an incompatible linear system: if we constrain the fluid to maintain its total volume (the container's volume) but require it to expand or contract in the interior, we end up with no solution. Therefore it is imperative to enforce the compatibility condition, as discussed at the end of Chapter 5 for the right-hand side.

Divergence control can be used much more liberally than just to account for mass balance in thermal expansion. For example, Feldman et al. [FOA03] introduced the technique for modeling a large class of explosions: look for more on this, and other techniques that control divergence, in Chapter 9. A constant, or time-varying, positive divergence can be added to the source volume of smoke to make it billow out more; negative divergence inside a target region of space can cause the smoke to be sucked up into the target.

Before leaving the subject of controlling smoke, it should be pointed out that there are, of course, other methods than modifying the divergence. Users may define force fields as additional body forces to coax the air to blow a particular way; these are simply added to the momentum equation much like the buoyancy terms we began with. Fattal and Lischinski [FL04] provide an interesting class of force fields that automatically move smoke to a desired target shape—a particularly useful idea for dealing with characters made out of smoke.

7

Particle Methods

Up until this point, we have discussed continuous fluid fields like velocity represented and solved on Cartesian grids. Now we turn to a very different representation, **particles**: a collection of points with stored positions and attached values for fluid quantities of interest. Particles have long proven their worth in computer graphics as a flexible way to represent phenomena, including fluid-like effects. While numerically it is usually most favorable to solve the fluid equations on grids, in particular the pressure and incompressibility parts, including particles in a grid-centric fluid solver can still be extremely useful. (Later we will look at some schemes which solve everything with particles, which makes some different trade-offs worth considering.) Many secondary fields that we want to be carried around by the fluid, or that weakly effect the flow, can be very profitably represented with particles: smoke (soot concentration), foam, mist, bubbles, temperature, etc. We will begin by examining the big advantage particles have over grids for advection.

7.1   Advection Troubles on Grids

Advection is one of the central themes of fluid simulation in this book. We've already struggled with the excessive numerical dissipation produced by semi-Lagrangian advection with linear interpolation, and improved it significantly with a cubic polynomial interpolant. Even sharper grid-based methods have been developed—however, all Eulerian schemes have a fundamental limit.

One way of looking at a time step of any Eulerian advection schemes is as follows:

- Begin with the field sampled on a grid.

- Reconstruct the field as a continuous function from the grid samples.

- Advect the reconstructed field.

- Resample the advected field on the grid.

Technically speaking, some Eulerian schemes might use more than just the values sampled on the grid—e.g., multistep time integration will also use several past values of the field on the grid—but these details don't change the gist: the key is the resampling at the end.

The problem is that a general incompressible velocity field, though it preserves volumes, may introduce significant distortions: at any point in space, the advected field may be stretched out along some axes and squished together along others. From a rendering perspective, you might think of this as a local magnification (stretching out) along some axes and a local minification (squishing together) along the others. Just as in rendering, while resampling a stretched out or magnified field doesn't lose any information, resampling a shrunken or minified field *can* lead to information loss. If the advected field has details varying at the grid scale Δx, as soon as those get shrunk in advection, resampling will at best destroy them—or worse, if care is not taken in the numerical method, cause them to alias as spurious lower-frequency artifacts—again, just as in rendering.

It's actually a little worse: the Nyquist limit essentially means that even in a pure translation velocity field with no distortion, the maximum spatial frequency that can be reliably advected has period $4\Delta x$. Higher-frequency signals, even though you might resolve them on the grid at a particular instant in time, cannot be handled in general: e.g., just in one dimension the highest-frequency component you can see on the grid, $\cos(\pi x/\Delta x)$, exactly disappears from the grid once you advect it by a distance of $\frac{1}{2}\Delta x$.

A "perfect" Eulerian scheme would filter out the high-frequency components that can't be reliably resampled at each time step, even as a bad one will allow them to alias as artifacts. The distortions inherent in non-rigid velocity fields mean that as time progresses, some of the lower-frequency components get transferred to higher frequencies—and thus must be destroyed by a good scheme. But note that the fluid flow, after squeezing the field along some axes at some point, may later stretch it back out—transferring higher frequencies down to lower frequencies. However, it's too late if the Eulerian scheme has already filtered them out.

At small enough length scales, viscosity and other molecular diffusion processes end up dominating advection: if Δx is small enough, Eulerian schemes can behave perfectly well since the physics itself is effectively band-limiting everything, dissipating information at higher frequencies. This brute-force approach leads to the area called direct numerical simulation (DNS), which comes in handy in the scientific study of turbulence, for example. However, since many scenarios of practical interest would require Δx less than a millimeter, DNS is usually far too expensive for graphics work.

A more efficient approach is to use adaptive grids, where the grid resolution is increased wherever higher resampling density is required to avoid information loss, and decreased where the field is smooth enough that low resolution suffices. This can be done using octrees (see for example Losasso et al. [LGF04]) or unstructured tetrahedral meshes (covered later). However, these approaches can suffer from considerable implementation complexity, increased overhead in execution, and typically lower accuracy compared to regular grids of similar resolution—and still must enforce a maximum resolution that, for practical purposes, tends to be much coarser than the DNS ideal. Adaptive methods have some excellent properties, but they are not really a solution to unwanted grid-caused diffusion.

However, if we store a field on particles that move with the flow, it doesn't matter how the flow distorts the distribution of particles: the advection equation $Dq/Dt = 0$ says the values stored on the particles shouldn't change, rather the particles just should move with fixed values. Therefore there is no filtering and no information loss. In some sense particles are perfect for advection.

It should also be pointed out, before we get into details, that these particle methods apply best to fields with essentially zero diffusion (or viscosity, or conduction, or whatever other name is appropriate for the quantity in question). If there is significant physical diffusion, strong enough to show up on the grid length scale, then using an Eulerian advection scheme should work perfectly well without the need for particles. We will take a look at incorporating small amounts of diffusion into particle methods, but the emphasis is on small: for large diffusion Eulerian methods may be equally as good or better.

7.2   Particle Advection

The core operation for particles in a fluid solver is advection, where we update particle positions based on the MAC grid velocity field. As we discussed back in Chapter 3, the simplest time integration scheme, forward Euler, really is insufficient. In fact, the requirements for particle advection are probably a bit stricter than for tracing trajectories in semi-Lagrangian advection, since errors in particle advection are accumulated over many time steps instead of being reset each time step as in the semi-Lagrangian method.

The simplest and cheapest method that makes sense to use is a second-order Runge-Kutta integrator, an example of which we introduced before. However, it's actually slightly unstable in regions of rigid rotation: particles will steadily migrate away from the center of rotation, perturbing the distribution. A much better choice, albeit sometimes a little more expensive choice, is to use a "three-stage third-order Runge-Kutta scheme:" these *are* stable for rigid rotations as long as Δt isn't too large. There are infinitely many such schemes, but Ralston [Ral62] showed the following scheme is probably the best when it comes to minimizing error:

$$\vec{k}_1 = \vec{u}(\vec{x}_n),$$
$$\vec{k}_2 = \vec{u}(\vec{x}_n + \tfrac{1}{2}\Delta t \vec{k}_1),$$
$$\vec{k}_3 = \vec{u}(\vec{x}_n + \tfrac{3}{4}\Delta t \vec{k}_2),$$
$$\vec{x}_{n+1} = \vec{x}_n + \tfrac{2}{9}\Delta t \vec{k}_1 + \tfrac{3}{9}\Delta t \vec{k}_2 + \tfrac{4}{9}\Delta t \vec{k}_3.$$

Here I've ignored the time dependence of the velocity field, which technically reduces the accuracy back to first order in time, just like our overall time-splitting algorithm; the error we care more about here has to do with the variation of velocity in space.

Chapter 3 also mentions the possibility of using substeps in time integration to better control error, say constraining each particle to at most move Δx or some small multiple each substep. This can easily be incorporated into Runge-Kutta schemes by first evaluating $\vec{u}(\vec{x}_n)$, which will be used regardless of the time-step size and then setting the substep size $\Delta \tau$ to keep $\|\Delta \tau \vec{u}(\vec{x}_n)\|$ below a threshold.[1] Of course, substep sizes must be adjusted so that when you add them up they exactly equal the global time step Δt. A fairly effective solution is given in Figure 7.1.

There's finally also the question of boundaries: what should happen to a particle when it leaves the fluid? For the usual solid wall boundaries, this is presumably just due to small numerical errors, which in the limit should go to zero. The obvious fix if a particle does end up on the other side of a solid wall is to project it out to the closest point on the boundary, perhaps plus a small fraction of Δx back into the fluid—or just delete the particle if it has traveled too far into a solid and projecting it back out is geometrically troublesome. Luckily, with level set representations of solid geometry, finding out if a particle is inside a solid, how deep inside it is, and projecting it back to the closest point on the surface are all easy operations.

For open edges on the grid with a $p = 0$ "free surface" condition, or inflow/outflow boundaries where we specify $\vec{u} \cdot \hat{n}$ to be something different than the solid's normal velocity, it makes sense instead to simply delete particles that stray outside the fluid. In these cases, however, it might also be critical to add new particles at those boundaries when the velocity field is pulling new fluid into the problem. We'll address the seeding problem below.

---

[1] For aggressively large time steps, it may even be necessary to check each velocity sample in the course of RK3 and re-do the advection based on the largest velocity magnitude seen, if it's much too large.

- Set substep time $\tau = 0$.
- Set flag `finished` to false.
- While `finished` is false:
  - Evaluate $\vec{u}(\vec{x})$.
  - Find the maximum substep size $\Delta\tau = C\Delta x/(\|\vec{u}(\vec{x})\| + \epsilon)$.
    (ϵ is a small number like 10^{-37} used to guard against divide-by-zero.)
  - If $\tau + \Delta\tau \geq \Delta t$:
    - Set $\Delta\tau = \Delta t - \tau$ and `finished` to true.
  - Else if $\tau + 2\Delta\tau \geq \Delta t$:
    - Set $\Delta\tau = \frac{1}{2}(\Delta t - \tau)$
  - Update $\vec{x}$ with RK3 for substep size $\Delta\tau$, reusing the evaluated $\vec{u}(\vec{x})$.
  - Update $\tau \leftarrow \tau + \Delta\tau$.

Figure 7.1. Pseudocode for substepping particle advection, loosely restricting a particle $\vec{x}$ to travel no more than $C\Delta x$ per substep. For very large time steps, it may be necessary to check how far the particle actually did travel with RK3, and re-do the step with a smaller Δt if this is too large.

7.3 Transferring Particles to the Grid

The most common use of particles is to track secondary fields, such as smoke concentration, foam, bubbles, or other things that would show up in rendering, but aren't primary fluid variables like velocity. Let us use soot or smoke concentration as a concrete example for this section. It is quite possible to directly render smoke as particles, but some global illumination effects are simpler if the soot concentration is sampled instead on a grid, and likewise some dynamic effects (if it ties into a buoyancy acceleration) require it on a grid: in this section we look at the general problem of going from particle samples to a grid-based field.

Assume each particle, in addition to its position $\vec{x}_p$, has a smoke concentration s_p. This value should represent the concentration of smoke in the "volume" we will associate with the particle. At it simplest, s_p could be a constant for all particles, but if we have additional rules for reducing it over time as an artistic control it might make more sense to track this per particle. At the moment a particle is created, it will take a default initial value S; if s_p is reduced below some threshold, the particle could be deleted. For extra variability, the initial S itself could be modulated by an animated volume texture in the emission region.

We now need a way to determine the smoke concentration on the simulation grid from the particle data. The simplest thing is to sum, at each grid point, the particle values modulated by a kernel function k that only gives weight to nearby particles, normalized by a weight value W which we'll discuss in a moment:

$$s_{i,j,k} = \sum_p s_p \frac{k(\vec{x}_p - \vec{x}_{i,j,k})}{W}. \tag{7.1}$$

Note the convention in this chapter is to always use p for particle indices and reserve i, j, and k for grid indices: thus $s_{i,j,k}$ is unambiguously the smoke concentration at grid point (i, j, k) which is at position $\vec{x}_{i,j,k}$. Also note that in practice it can make sense to order the computation as a loop over particles, each contributing to the nearby grid points:[2]

- Reset all grid $s_{i,j,k}$ values to zero.
- Loop over particle index p:
  - Loop over grid indices i, j, k where $k(\vec{x}_p - \vec{x}_{i,j,k})$ might be non-zero:
    - Add $s_p k(\vec{x}_p - \vec{x}_{i,j,k})/W$ to $s_{i,j,k}$

The kernel function k should be adapted to the grid spacing, just as in rendering—if its support is less than Δx then some particles between grid points may momentarily vanish from the grid (i.e. not contribute to any grid points), but if the support is too much larger than Δx, the method becomes inefficient and we'll have blurred away a lot of the desirable sharpness of particle methods. The simplest choice that makes sense is to use the trilinear hat function:

$$k(x, y, z) = h\left(\frac{x}{\Delta x}\right) h\left(\frac{y}{\Delta x}\right) h\left(\frac{z}{\Delta x}\right)$$

$$\text{with} \quad h(r) = \begin{cases} 1 - r & : \ 0 \leq r \leq 1, \\ 1 + r & : -1 \leq r \leq 0, \\ 0 & : \text{otherwise.} \end{cases}$$

This may not be smooth enough for quality rendering, however. Something

---

[2]When implementing this in a multithreaded environment the actual code pattern will probably be more complex: it is best to make sure only one thread is allowed to write to a particular region in the grid, to avoid excessive overhead due to locking or atomic operations.

like a quadratic B-spline may be more useful in that case:

$$k_2(x, y, z) = h_2\left(\frac{x}{\Delta x}\right) h_2\left(\frac{y}{\Delta x}\right) h_2\left(\frac{z}{\Delta x}\right)$$

$$\text{with} \quad h_2(r) = \begin{cases} \frac{1}{2}(r + \frac{3}{2})^2 & : -\frac{3}{2} \le r < -\frac{1}{2}, \\ \frac{3}{4} - r^2 & : -\frac{1}{2} \le r < \frac{1}{2}, \\ \frac{1}{2}(\frac{3}{2} - r)^2 & : \frac{1}{2} \le r < \frac{3}{2}, \\ 0 & : \text{otherwise.} \end{cases}$$

So what about the normalization weight W? This is intimately tied up with the sampling density of the particles. Let V be the volume associated with each particle: you can think of it as the limit of a volume of space divided by the number of particles contained within, for uniform sampling. For example, if you initialize with eight particles per grid cell in a smoky region, then $V = \Delta x^3 / 8$. We can estimate the total amount of smoke in the simulation, i.e., the integral of smoke concentration over the simulation volume, either from the particles as

$$S_{\text{total}} \approx \sum_p s_p V$$

or from the grid as

$$S_{\text{total}} \approx \sum_{i,j,k} s_{i,j,k} \Delta x^3.$$

We now choose W so these two estimates are equal. For the trilinear hat kernel function k (or indeed, any other B-spline, like k_2 above), the sum of $k(\vec{x}_p - \vec{x}_{i,j,k})$ over all grid points is exactly one, which nicely simplifies the calculation:

$$\sum_{i,j,k} s_{i,j,k} \Delta x^3 = \sum_{i,j,k} \sum_p s_p \frac{k(\vec{x}_p - \vec{x}_{i,j,k})}{W} \Delta x^3$$

$$= \sum_p s_p \left(\sum_{i,j,k} k(\vec{x}_p - \vec{x}_{i,j,k})\right) \frac{\Delta x^3}{W}$$

$$= \sum_p s_p \frac{\Delta x^3}{W}.$$

Therefore, we take $W = \Delta x^3 / V$, or more simply, the average number of particles per grid cell.

We can of course get a little fancier and introduce a normalization weight W_p per particle, tying into a non-uniform particle seeding. This brings up the question of how to seed particles in the first place. There are a lot of possibilities, and not necessarily any single best choice, but we will outline one strategy.

7.4   Particle Seeding

There are many possible schemes for seeding or emitting particles. Whatever you choose, the most important guiding principle with this as just about everything else in simulation is: make sure it's *consistent* across different time steps and grid sizes. That is, make sure the main parameters that a user will control are "physical," in the sense of not referring to time steps or grid cells, and that in turn your algorithm will give consistent behavior as time steps and grid sizes are refined.

As an example of what not to do, imagine a rule which says to emit 8 particles in each grid cell of an emission region every time step, with fixed value s. If the same simulation is run with a time step half the size, instead of just giving more accurate behavior, the emitter will emit twice as much smoke into the simulation! Things get even worse if the time step varies adaptively during the simulation for a CFL condition, say—at certain times the emitter will be emitting more smoke than at others, just because somewhere else in the domain the fluid is moving faster. This can be a disaster.

So what can we do? Let's break the problem down into two common cases: spatially smooth emission vs. sharply defined emission areas.

7.4.1   Smoothly Varying Emission

If we start the simulation with a region where the emission smoke density smoothly varies, reducing to zero at the edges, it makes sense to begin by seeding W particles at jittered random locations in any grid cell with nonzero emission density, and in each particle set its value s_p to the interpolated (or otherwise evaluated) emission density. This should be very close to an Eulerian scheme just starting with that continuous value of s.

If we have continuous emission from a region somewhere in the simulation, we need the emitter to specify an emission rate, the value of ds/dt. In an Eulerian scheme we would increment the smoke value at a grid cell by $\Delta t \, ds/dt$; we need to approximate the same with particles instead. For this we need a target rate of particle creation dW/dt, expressed in particles per voxel per second. Then in one time step, in one grid cell with nonzero smoke emission rate ds/dt, we should emit $n = \Delta t \, dW/dt$ particles. If n is an integer, this is clear enough; if not, we should emit $\lfloor n \rfloor$ particles and with probability $n - \lfloor n \rfloor$ emit an extra one (check if a uniform random number from the range $[0, 1]$ is below this fraction). Each particle should again be at a random jittered location in the grid cell, and take a value $s_p = \Delta t \, ds/dt$ interpolated from the emitter.

We take one further step with this scheme for continuous emission, taking into account the velocity field in which the smoke particles are supposed to be moving. If we emit a puff of particles in the emission region at the start of each frame, and then advect them through the velocity field for the time step, if the velocity is fast we will see those discrete puffs moving through space. To avoid this, each particle should also get a random creation time uniformly distributed through the time step, and be advected for the remainder of the time step through the velocity field to get its actual location. This is especially important for "in-flow" boundaries, where we typically have a narrow region or even just a surface patch where we emit particles, but they are coming in with a strong velocity.

7.4.2 Sharp Regional Emission

Another common scenario is where the emission density is even just constant within some sharply defined region (given by a level set, most likely) and drops sharply to zero outside the region. In this case we should test if a particle's random location (before advecting through part of the step) is inside the level set of the emission region: if not, it shouldn't be emitted.

In some cases, especially if we have relatively few particles per grid cell and we want a really smoothly defined emission volume that matches the emission geometry without any raggedness, we might play some additional tricks to get a sampling which places more particles on the emission boundary surface. When we propose a candidate random particle location $\vec{x}_p$, we check the signed distance function of the emission region $\phi(\vec{x}_p)$. If $\phi(\vec{x}_p) > \frac{1}{4}\Delta x$, i.e. the point is outside the emission region by a quarter of a grid cell, we don't emit. If $\phi(\vec{x}_p) < -\frac{1}{4}\Delta x$, so the point is well inside the emission region, we emit as usual. But in the remaining band near to the surface, if $\phi(\vec{x}_p) > 0$, we move $\vec{x}_p$ to the closest point on the surface, and cut the emission value in half; if $\phi(\vec{x}_p) \leq 0$, we leave $\vec{x}_p$ where it is but also cut the emission value in half. In this way we emit roughly the same "amount" of smoke into a grid cell, even when its a fractional grid cell, but we end up with more points than usual precisely on the surface of the emitter, giving better definition to the output.

7.5 Diffusion

There is one further small tweak we can add to simulate the effect of a small amount of diffusion. Some non-trivial stochastic calculus shows that diffusing a quantity, i.e., including a Laplacian term $Dq/Dt = k\nabla \cdot \nabla q$, is equivalent in the limit to adding a component of random Brownian motion to particle trajectories (i.e., solving $Dq/Dt = 0$ with a randomly perturbed velocity field). That is, we can add an independent random-walk contribution to each particle's position each time step, such as a random vector chosen uniformly from the sphere of radius $\sqrt{2k\Delta t}$. Obviously this is only an effective technique if the perturbations are reasonably small compared to a grid cell. For stronger diffusion, we can use the techniques in the next section (transferring values back and forth between particles and the grid), or simply keep the field stored on a grid and use the semi-Lagrangian approach to advection, possibly with additional grid-based diffusion.

Finally, there are several other quantities for which we can use this machinery. Temperature of course can go hand-in-hand with smoke concentration, storing both quantities with each particle. Feldman et al. [FOA03] also include unburnt fuel as a particle variable for their volumetric combustion model (see Chapter 9), albeit with a slightly more advanced particle system that gives particles mass and inertia (see Chapter 15).

7.6   Particle-in-Cell Methods

A major part of the numerical viscosity we have battled is due to the Eulerian advection. We already considered using a sharper cubic interpolation scheme to significantly reduce diffusion, but as it turns out, we can do even better. In this section, we will replace the velocity advection step $D\vec{u}/Dt = 0$ itself with particle advection.

Simply storing velocity vectors on particles and advecting them around isn't enough, of course: pressure projection to keep the velocity field divergence-free globally couples all the velocities together. Somehow we need to account for particle-particle interactions on top of advection. We'll now take a look at a general class of methods that can efficiently treat particle-particle interaction by way of a grid.

The particle-in-cell (PIC) approach was pioneered at Los Alamos National Laboratory in the early 1950s, though Harlow's 1963 paper [Har63] is perhaps the first journal article describing it.[3] The basic PIC method begins with all quantities—velocities included—stored on particles that sample the entire fluid region. For graphics work, eight particles per grid cell, initialized as usual from a jittered grid, is a good place to start. For

---

[3] Harlow and other team members in the T-3 Division at Los Alamos also created the MAC grid and marker particle method, and pioneered the use of the vorticity-streamfunction formulation used in the previous section, to name just a few of their many contributions to computational fluid dynamics; see the review article by Harlow [Har04] for more on the history of this group.

efficiency, where the flow is not as important to resolve, reducing this to as low as one particle per grid cell makes a lot of sense (e.g. in the clear air away from the smoky regions).

In each time step, we first transfer the quantities such as velocity from the particles to the grid—perhaps just as we did with smoke concentration earlier in this chapter. All the non-advection terms, such as acceleration due to gravity, pressure projection and resolution of boundary conditions, viscosity, etc., are integrated on the grid, just as in a fully Eulerian solver. Finally we interpolate back from the grid to the particles, and then advect the particles in the grid velocity field.

To more accurately do the particle-to-grid transfer, and be more robust in the face of non-uniform particle distributions, it's recommended that at least for velocity the normalization weight W actually be calculated per grid point, making the value at each grid point a weighted average of nearby particle values. For example, the u-component of velocity on the grid ends up as

$$u_{i+1/2,j,k} = \frac{\sum_p u_p k(\vec{x}_p - \vec{x}_{i+1/2,j,k})}{\sum_p k(\vec{x}_p - \vec{x}_{i+1/2,j,k})}, \tag{7.2}$$

though of course to actually calculate it we instead loop over the particles accumulating both $u_p k(\vec{x}_p - \vec{x}_{i+1/2,j,k})$ and the weight $k(\vec{x}_p - \vec{x}_{i+1/2,j,k})$ on the grid, and then do the divide in a second pass over the grid.

Also note that the particle-to-grid transfer only provides grid values near particles; it may be imperative to extrapolate those grid values out to the rest of the grid as discussed before. If an aggressively low particle sampling (like one per grid cell), errors in advection, or a positive divergence control result in "gaps" between particles opening up on the grid, it may also be a good idea to include a reseeding stage where new particles are added to grid cells with too few particles, taking particle values interpolated from the grid. Similarly particles can be dynamically deleted from grid cells with an excess of particles (say, more than twelve).

While plain PIC worked admirably—albeit only with first-order accuracy—for the compressible flow problems to which it was originally applied, it also suffered from severe numerical dissipation. The problem is that fluid quantities are averaged from particles to the grid, introducing some smoothing, and then the smoothed grid values are interpolated back to the particles, compounding the smoothing. Even if nothing is happening—particles aren't moving at all—a significant amount of smoothing takes place at every time step.

To counteract this, Brackbill and Ruppel [BR86] developed the fluid implicit particle (FLIP) method, a beautifully simple variation on PIC. In FLIP, instead of interpolating a quantity back to the particles, the *change* in the quantity (as computed on the grid) is interpolated and used to *incre-*

ment the particle value, not replace it. Each increment to a particle's value undergoes one smoothing (from interpolation) but that's all: smoothing is not accumulated, and thus FLIP is virtually free of numerical diffusion. In pseudocode, the method can be interpreted as

- Transfer particle values q_p to the grid $q_{i,j,k}$, through equations like (7.1) or (7.2), and extrapolate on the grid as necessary.
- Save the grid values $q_{i,j,k}$.
- Compute all other terms on the grid, such as pressure projection, to get an updated $q_{i,j,k}^{\text{new}}$.
- For each particle, interpolate the change $\Delta q_{i,j,k} = q_{i,j,k}^{\text{new}} - q_{i,j,k}$ from the grid to add it to the particle's value.
- Advect the particles in the grid velocity field.

Zhu and Bridson [ZB05] introduced FLIP to incompressible flow and demonstrated how effective it can be at producing highly detailed motion on fairly coarse grids. It essentially eliminates all numerical diffusion from advection, though of course the loss of vorticity from our first-order time-splitting remains. At the same time, it is almost trivial to implement, and especially if you are using particles for other tasks (e.g., marker particles for liquid tracking, as we will in Chapter 8) it is highly recommended.

One issue with FLIP is that it may develop noise. Typically we use eight particles per grid cell, meaning there are more degrees of freedom in the particles than in the grid: velocity fluctuations on the particles may, on some time steps, average down to zero and vanish from the grid, and on other time steps show up as unexpected perturbations. Of course basic PIC doesn't have this problem, since the particle velocities are simply interpolated from the grid there. Therefore it may be useful to actually blend in a small amount of the PIC update with the FLIP update, causing any noise to decay to zero while hopefully not introducing significant dissipation. That is, for some small **regularization** parameter α in the range $[0, 1]$, set the new particle velocities to

$$\vec{u}_p^{\text{new}} = \alpha \operatorname{interp}(\vec{u}_{\text{grid}}^{\text{new}}, \vec{x}_p) + (1 - \alpha) \left[\vec{u}_p^{\text{old}} + \operatorname{interp}(\Delta \vec{u}_{\text{grid}}, \vec{x}_p) \right].$$

When $\alpha = 0$ this is the pure FLIP update; when $\alpha = 1$ it is the basic PIC update.

A little analysis of the numerical dissipation implied by PIC, similar to our analysis of the first-order semi-Lagrangian method back in Chapter 3, shows that we can actually relate α to the kinematic viscosity of the fluid ν:

$$\alpha = \frac{6\Delta t \nu}{\Delta x^2}.$$

Of course, if this formula gives an $\alpha > 1$, you should clamp it to one, use the PIC update (or just a regular Eulerian advection scheme) and probably even add in a viscous step as in Chapter 10.

Part II

More Types of Fluids

8

Water

We now have most of the machinery in place to simulate water as well. Our starting point is treating water as a fluid with a free surface boundary condition where it's in contact with air. The main new ingredient is geometric: the free surface condition allows the water to change shape, and thus we need to track or capture[1] that shape somehow.

Before jumping in, a note on terminology: the air-water surface or boundary is also often called an **interface**. Most of this chapter is about how to work with this interface.

8.1 Marker Particles and Voxels

We'll begin with the simplest possible water simulator. Here we'll use the voxelized pressure solve covered first in Chapter 5, which only required us to classify each grid cell as being fluid (i.e., water), empty (i.e., air), or solid. While the solid cells should be straightforward to identify, determining when to switch a cell to fluid or empty as water moves in or out of it due to advection under the velocity field is the tricky part.

One possibility is to define an initial level set of the water, and advect it using the sharp cubic interpolant. Even with the cubic, however, this tends to have a lot of problems. Water splashing very naturally creates thin structures, and as we noted before, fundamentally a level set on the grid can't reliable handle structures thinner than about two grid cells. Wherever the water thins out, it will tend to soon simply vanish from the grid, as if the water is rapidly evaporating. Droplets rarely can travel more than a few grid cells before disappearing.

This is where we turn instead to **marker particles**, used all the way back in Harlow and Welch's seminal marker-and-cell paper, which also introduced the MAC grid [HW65]. We begin the simulation by emitting

---

[1]In some numerical contexts, tracking and capturing are technical terms referring to different approaches to solving this problem: tracking loosely corresponds to methods using explicit descriptions of surfaces, such as meshes, whereas capturing refers to methods built on implicit descriptions of surfaces.

water particles to fill the volume of water (presumably defined by a level set) and viewing them as a sampling of the water geometry. If there are sources adding water during the course of the simulation, we emit particles from them as well. Within each advection step we move the particles according to the grid velocity field, so that they naturally follow where the water should be going—using RK2 or better, just like we did for semi-Lagrangian trajectory tracing.[2] Finally, we in turn use the marker particles to mark which grid cells are fluid for the pressure solve: any non-solid cell containing a marker particle is water, and the rest of the non-solid cells are left empty by default.

This algorithm can be justified conceptually by imagining taking it to the limit, where each individual molecule of water is identified with a marker particle: then the set of grid cells containing marker particles is exactly the set of grid cells containing water.

This raises the question of how densely to sample with marker particles —clearly one per molecule isn't practical! Obviously there should be at least one particle per water grid cell, and to avoid gaps in the fluid randomly opening up during advection we probably want at least double that resolution: four particles per cell in 2D and eight per cell in 3D. However, going above double won't necessarily give much improvement: ultimately these particles will be moved by velocities sampled at the grid resolution, which places a limit on how much detail we can expect in the water geometry. If higher-resolution geometry is required, the simulation grid must be refined too.

As we discussed in Chapter 7, it's a good idea to emit particles in a random jittered pattern, not just a regular lattice. This is super important for water marker particles: a shearing flow that compresses along one axis and stretches along another can turn a regular lattice into weird anisotropic stripe-like patterns, far from a good uniform sampling. Thus we require at least jittering the initial grid, as one might do for sampling patterns in rendering.

The first problem apparent with the marker particle approach is in rendering: ultimately we want a smooth surface, describing the boundary between water and air, but right now we only have a mass of points filling the water volume. Clearly we don't want to simply render the water-filled voxels as blocks.

One option is to construct a smooth implicit surface wrapped around the particles. For example, Blinn [Bli82] introduced **blobbies**: given the

---

[2]Just to remind you, for RK2 and many other integrators, we'll need to look up fluid velocity at locations that might not be inside the current water region, necessitating extrapolation. We'll get to that soon.

positions of the particles $\{\vec{x}_i\}$ define

$$F(\vec{x}) = \sum_i k\left(\frac{\|\vec{x} - \vec{x}_i\|}{h}\right),$$

where k is a suitable smooth kernel function and h is a user parameter intended to be the extent of each particle. A Gaussian might be a reasonable choice for k; a cheaper and simpler alternative would be a spline, such as

$$k(s) = \begin{cases} (1 - s^2)^3 : s < 1, \\ 0 : s \geq 1. \end{cases}$$

This spline has the advantage that it depends only on s^2, not s, allowing one to avoid taking a square root when evaluating at $s = \|\vec{x} - \vec{x}_i\|/h$. The extent h should generally be several times the average inter-particle spacing r, for example $h = 3r$, but it can be tweaked as needed. (For our recommended sampling, r is half the grid spacing Δx.) The blobby surface is implicitly defined as the points $\vec{x}$ where $F(\vec{x}) = \tau$ for some threshold τ, or in other words the τ-isocontour of F. A reasonable default for τ is $k(r/h)$, which produces a sphere of radius r for an isolated particle, but this too can be a tweakable parameter.

Unfortunately, the blobby surface can have noticeable artifacts, chief among them that it can look, well, blobby. Many water scenarios include expanses of smooth water; after sampling with particles and then wrapping the blobby surface around the particles, generally bumps for each particle become apparent. This is especially noticeable from specular reflections on the water surface, though it can be masked by foam or spray. The bumps can be smoothed out to some extent by increasing the h-parameter—however, this also smooths out or even eliminates small-scale features we *want* to see in the render. Typically there is a hard trade-off involved.

An improvement on blobbies is given by Zhu and Bridson [ZB05], where instead the implicit surface function is given by

$$\phi(\vec{x}) = \|\vec{x} - \bar{X}\| - \bar{r},$$

where $\bar{X}$ is a weighted average of nearby particle locations:

$$\bar{X} = \frac{\sum_i k\left(\frac{\|\vec{x} - \vec{x}_i\|}{h}\right) \vec{x}_i}{\sum_i k\left(\frac{\|\vec{x} - \vec{x}_i\|}{h}\right)}$$

and $\bar{r}$ is a similar weighted average of nearby particle radii:

$$\bar{r} = \frac{\sum_i k\left(\frac{\|\vec{x} - \vec{x}_i\|}{h}\right) r_i}{\sum_i k\left(\frac{\|\vec{x} - \vec{x}_i\|}{h}\right)}.$$

For now we'll take all the particle radii to be the same r, though better results can be obtained if a particle's radius is actually its distance to the closest point on the desired water surface—see the paper by Adams et al. [APKG07] for an example of how to compute this practically, using a point-based fast marching algorithm similar to Corbett's [Cor05]. Finally, the surface is defined as the points $\vec{x}$ where $\phi(\vec{x}) = 0$, the zero isocontour or level set of ϕ. Once again, for an isolated particle this gives a perfect sphere of radius r. The advantage of this formula over regular blobbies is that it gives somewhat flatter, smoother results where the particles should be sampling smooth geometry, and it is less sensitive to non-uniformities in sampling; however, it does have the disadvantage of potentially introducing small-scale "chaff" in concavities (gaps) in the particle distribution. Sampling this on a grid and doing a small amount of smoothing can be helpful.

A faster and generally quite good option is to simply take a union-of-balls, but sampled on a grid and turned into a level set. This can be done efficiently by computing the distance to the particles on a grid, as in chapter 4, then subtracting the particle radius r (typically just a little less than the grid cell size Δx) from the distance to dilate those points by radius r. The interior is typically far from signed distance at this point, even though the exterior is fine: redistancing is needed where $\phi < 0$. The resulting level set can then be further processed, for example with a smoothing kernel, or a hole-filling step where $\phi_{i,j,k}$ is replaced with the average of its neighbors if and only if the average is less:

$$\phi_{i,j,k}^{\text{avg}} = \frac{\phi_{i-1,j,k}^{\text{old}} + \phi_{i+1,j,k}^{\text{old}} + \phi_{i,j-1,k}^{\text{old}} + \phi_{i,j-1,k}^{\text{old}} + \phi_{i,j,k-1}^{\text{old}} + \phi_{i,j,k+1}^{\text{old}}}{6}$$

$$\phi_{i,j,k}^{\text{new}} = \begin{cases} \phi_{i,j,k}^{\text{avg}} & : \quad \phi_{i,j,k}^{\text{avg}} < \phi_{i,j,k}^{\text{old}} \\ \phi_{i,j,k}^{\text{old}} & : \quad \text{otherwise.} \end{cases}$$

This causes small holes to be filled as if shrink-wrapped, but never erodes away the surface: its limit behaviour if you iterate for a long time is to reconstruct the convex hull of the original level set, so one or two iterations could be considered a "local" convex hull operation.

While a level set of the water—created either by sampling a blobby function or using the union-of-balls construction—can be directly raytraced, it is very common to then construct a mesh approximating the surface as we discussed in Chapter 4, and potentially run further mesh fairing algorithms to improve the quality of the result, or "shrink" it with averaging to get closer to the underlying water particles. These meshes can then be rendered very effectively.

One exciting direction taken in recent years is to skip the level set construction and directly use a triangle mesh to track the surface of the water. While advecting a mesh through a velocity field is at first glance no harder than advecting particles—just move the vertices like particles— there are several problems that arise. First, the flow can deform the mesh significantly, stretching some triangles to be too big or compressing others to be too small, so remeshing operations are necessary, subdividing or collapsing edges if they are too big or small respectively. Second, when the water pinches off to separate a drop, or two parts of water are supposed to merge, those topology change operations have to be carried out in the mesh connectivity. Finally, numerical errors can cause the mesh to collide with itself, self-intersecting when it is not supposed to. Resolving all these issues robustly and efficiently is hard! There are several approaches to try [BB06,BB09,MÖ9,BBB10,WTGT10,WMFB11,DBG14]. Their promise is providing much higher quality tracking of small features, like thin sheets and delicate ripples, but they haven't yet been as "battle tested" as marker particle methods, so I won't go further here.

Getting back to marker particles: if we are using particles to track where the water is, we may as well get the full benefit from them and use FLIP instead of semi-Lagrangian methods for velocity advection. This leads to a simulation step something like this:

1. From the particles, construct the level set for the liquid.

2. Transfer velocity (and any other additional state) from particles to the grid, and extrapolate from known grid values to at least one grid cell around the fluid, giving a preliminary velocity field $\vec{u}^*$.

3. Add body forces such as gravity or artistic controls to the velocity field.

4. Construct solid level sets and solid velocity fields.

5. Solve for and apply pressure to get a divergence-free velocity $\vec{u}^{n+1}$ that respects the solid boundaries.

6. Update particle velocities by interpolating the grid update $\vec{u}^{n+1} - \vec{u}^*$ to add to the existing particle velocities (FLIP), or simply interpolating the grid velocity (PIC), or a mix thereof.

7. Advect the particles through the divergence-free velocity field $\vec{u}^{n+1}$.

8.2   More Accurate Pressure Solves

The methods we have developed so far still fall short when it comes to visual plausibility. The culprit is the voxelized treatment of the free surface boundary condition $p = 0$. Even if we can track and render an accurate water surface, so far the core of the simulation—the pressure solve—only sees a block voxelized surface, with some cells marked as water and some as air. Thus the velocity field, and from there the motion and shape of the surface itself, cannot avoid significant voxel artifacts. For example, small "ripples" less than a grid cell high do not show up at all in the pressure solve, and thus they aren't evolved correctly but rather persist statically in the form of a strange displacement texture. Somehow we need to inform the pressure solve about the location of the water-air interface within each grid cell. More precisely, we are going to modify how we compute the gradient of pressure near the water-air interface for updating velocities, which naturally will also change the matrix in the pressure equations.[3]

The standard solution is to use the ghost fluid method, as laid out by Gibou et al. [GFCK02]. We'll illustrate this by looking at the update to $u_{i+1/2,j,k}$, which in the interior of the water would be

$$u_{i+1/2,j,k}^{n+1} = u_{i+1/2,j,k} - \frac{\Delta t}{\rho_{i+1/2,j,k}} \frac{p_{i+1,j,k} - p_{i,j,k}}{\Delta x}.$$

Suppose further that (i, j, k) is in the water, i.e., $\phi_{i,j,k} \leq 0$, and that $(i + 1, j, k)$ is in the air, i.e., $\phi_{i+1,j,k} > 0$ (treating the case where it's the other way around will be obvious). The simple solver before then set $p_{i+1,j,k} = 0$. However, it would be more accurate to say that $p = 0$ at the water-air interface, which is somewhere between (i, j, k) and $(i + 1, j, k)$. Linearly interpolating between $\phi_{i,j,k}$ and $\phi_{i+1,j,k}$ gives the location of the interface at $(i + \theta \Delta x, j, k)$ where

$$\theta = \frac{\phi_{i,j,k}}{\phi_{i,j,k} - \phi_{i+1,j,k}}.$$

Linearly interpolating between the real pressure $p_{i,j,k}$ and a fictional "ghost" pressure $p_{i+1,j,k}^G$, then setting it equal to zero at the interface, gives

$$(1 - \theta)p_{i,j,k} + \theta p_{i+1,j,k}^G = 0$$

$$\Rightarrow \quad p_{i+1,j,k}^G = -\frac{1 - \theta}{\theta} p_{i,j,k}$$

$$= \frac{\phi_{i+1,j,k}}{\phi_{i,j,k}} p_{i,j,k}.$$

Now plug this into the velocity update:

$$u_{i+1/2,j,k}^{n+1} = u_{i+1/2,j,k} - \frac{\Delta t}{\rho} \frac{\frac{\phi_{i+1,j,k}}{\phi_{i,j,k}} p_{i,j,k} - p_{i,j,k}}{\Delta x}$$

$$= u_{i+1/2,j,k} - \frac{\Delta t}{\rho} \frac{\phi_{i+1,j,k} - \phi_{i,j,k}}{\phi_{i,j,k}} \frac{p_{i,j,k}}{\Delta x}.$$

---

[3]Note that this is quite orthogonal to our previously covered accurate finite volume approach to solid wall boundaries, where we use face area fractions to get better estimates of fluid flow in and out of cells, independent of how the pressure updates velocity.

The end effect in the matrix is to increase the diagonal. At this point you should probably get worried about the case where $\phi_{i,j,k} = 0$ or is very close to zero—we are dividing by this quantity! This is a "safe" case, however, in that boosting the diagonal of the matrix makes it simpler to solve and (after Incomplete Cholesky preconditioning) better conditioned. Still, to limit the possibility of numerical strangeness it is still wise to limit the coefficient in the pressure update $(\phi_{i+1,j,k} - \phi_{i,j,k})/\phi_{i,j,k}$ and matrix to some maximum value, say 10^3.

A closely related solution, more in line with the volume fraction approach we've already used extensively, is to instead modify the fluid density $\rho_{i+1/2,j,k}$ to account for the fractions of the u-cell occupied by water versus air. Compute $\rho_{i+1/2,j,k}$ as the average fluid density in the u-cell, ignoring solids. The ghost fluid method above is in fact equivalent to using $\rho_{\text{air}} = 0$ and estimating the volume fraction from just $\phi_{i,j,k}$ and $\phi_{i+1,j,k}$. We can in fact track the velocity field in the air, or use a smooth extrapolation of the water velocity at each step, and solve for pressure in both water and air using the true non-zero density of air. This leads to a full two-phase flow simulator, though getting all the details right w.r.t. advection, level set estimation, etc. requires a lot more work: see Boyd and Bridson's article [BB12], for example, for an approach to extending FLIP to water and air mixes. Solving for pressure throughout water and air gives a much harder linear system, but it does mean that the implied velocity field in the air will be divergence-free so, in particular, air bubbles will be incompressible, conserving their volume instead of collapsing as they do with the usual $p = 0$ free surface condition. In fact, one can go even further and model the thermodynamics governing air compressibility in bubbles, as Patkar et al. showed [PAKF13].

8.3 Topology Change and Wall Separation

One of the trickiest parts of free surface flow, at least from a theoretical perspective, is how separation occurs. Assuming the water starts off as a path-connected component (meaning any two points in the water can be connected by a continuous path going only in the water region), and is advected only in a continuous velocity field, then it must remain path-connected. In particular, a drop cannot separate from the rest of the water: it will always remain connected by an ever-thinner tendril.

With level set and marker particle methods, it turns out this is not a problem in practice: droplets separate quite naturally. However, the theory indicates to us this is merely numerical error in fact, due to us only sampling the liquid's presence at a finite set of grid points and/or particles. Unfortunately, there is no simple resolution to this problem, as the actual physics of topology change (separation, merging) is not yet properly modeled at the continuum level. We will leave this, therefore, as a problem to worry about in the middle of a sleepless night.

It is also worth pointing out, on the subject of topology change, that water merging can cause some trouble too. At low speeds, more specifically low velocities relative to the grid size divided by time step, two water components merge the instant they come within one grid cell of each other, due to our level set approach to describing the geometry to the pressure solve. In splashing scenarios, this may even cause appreciable volume gain. However, at high speeds (high velocities relative to grid cell divided by time step) we can have the opposite problem: a water drop can penetrate quite deeply into a solid wall or into another water region during advection, effectively losing volume in the process.

Another related issue is how liquid can separate from solid walls. In fact, exactly what happens at the **moving contact line** where air, water, and solid meet is again not fully understood. Complicated physical chemistry, including the influence of past wetting (leaving a nearly invisible film of water on a solid), is at play. What is clear is that our "no-stick" boundary condition $\vec{u} \cdot \hat{n} = \vec{u}_{\text{solid}} \cdot \hat{n}$ both prevents water from penetrating into a solid as well as *separating* from the surface of a solid. However, there is no denying we can observe water separating from surfaces, albeit usually leaving droplets or a wet film behind. Again, in practice using marker particles we find that numerical errors allow water to separate fairly naturally, while also modeling cohesion of water to solids that looks quite reasonable at small scales. However, the time of separation does depend critically and unphysically on grid size and time step size, and at large scales the degree of cohesion can look unnatural. Foster and Fedkiw [FF01] proposed a simple unsticking trick that only enforces $\vec{u} \cdot \hat{n} \geq \vec{u}_{\text{solid}} \cdot \hat{n}$, which unfortunately fails in several common scenarios; Batty et al. [BBB07] later demonstrated a more robust, physically consistent, though expensive treatment inspired by contact problems, extending the inequality constraint into a complementary condition with pressure (so pressure cannot exert more than a critical suction at solid walls). Chentanez and Müller illustrate how this condition can be efficiently solved with multigrid [CMF12].

8.4   Volume Control

Between iterative solves for pressure, truncation error in level set representations and errors in advection, as well as the topology change issues noted above, it is not surprising that a typical water simulation doesn't exactly conserve the volume of water it begins with. Typically the errors are biased to steadily lose volume, but noticeable volume gain can occur too. Kim et al. [KLL$^+$07] demonstrate a simple correction to this drift by enforcing a non-zero divergence control in the pressure projection step, similar to how we can enforce expansion when heating up smoke.

8.5 Surface Tension

Another subject we'll only briefly touch on is adding surface-tension forces for small-scale water phenomena. This is, it should be warned, a subject of ongoing research both within graphics and scientific computing. For example, the test case of running a sphere of water at rest in zero-G with surface tension (which should result in surface-tension forces exactly canceling pressure forces, so velocity remains zero) is surprisingly hard to get right.

The physical chemistry of surface tension is conceptually simple. Water molecules are more attracted to other water molecules than to air molecules, and vice versa. Thus, water molecules near the surface tend to be pulled in towards the rest of the water molecules and vice versa. In a way they are seeking to minimize the area exposed to the other fluid, bunching up around their own type. The simplest linear model of surface tension can in fact be phrased in terms of a potential energy equal to a surface-tension coefficient γ times the surface area between the two fluids (γ for water and air at normal conditions is approximately $0.073 J/m^2$). The force seeks to minimize the surface area.

The surface area of the fluid is simply the integral of 1 on the boundary:

$$A = \iint_{\partial\Omega} 1.$$

Remembering our signed distance properties, this is the same as

$$A = \iint_{\partial\Omega} \nabla\phi \cdot \hat{n}.$$

Now we use the divergence theorem in reverse to turn this into a volume integral:

$$A = \iiint_{\Omega} \nabla \cdot \nabla\phi$$

Consider a virtual infinitesimal displacement of the surface, δx. This changes the volume integral by adding or subtracting infinitesimal amounts of the integrand along the boundary. The resulting infinitesimal change in surface area is

$$\delta A = \iint_{\partial\Omega} (\nabla \cdot \nabla\phi)\delta x \cdot \hat{n}.$$

Thus, the variational derivative of surface area is $(\nabla \cdot \nabla \phi)\hat{n}$. Our surface-tension force is proportional to this, and since it is in the normal direction we can think of it in terms of a pressure jump at the air-water interface (as pressure only applies in the normal direction). Since air pressure is zero in our free surface model, we have that the pressure at the surface of the water is

$$p = \gamma \nabla \cdot \nabla \phi.$$

It turns out that $\kappa = \nabla \cdot \nabla \phi$ is termed the **mean curvature** of the surface, a well-studied geometric quantity that measures how curved a surface is.

This property has been incorporated into the ghost fluid pressure discretization by Kang et al. [KFL00]. Here, we take the ghost pressures in the air so that we linearly interpolate to $\gamma\kappa$ at the point where $\phi = 0$, rather than interpolating to zero. The mean curvature κ can easily be estimated at that point by using the standard central difference for the Laplacian, on trilinearly interpolated values of ϕ. Though not immediately apparent, there is also a fairly severe stability restriction on the time step, $\Delta t \leq O(\Delta x^{3/2}\sqrt{\rho/\gamma})$, since this is essentially an explicit treatment of the surface-tension forces. Things are also rather more complicated at triple junctions between water, solid, and air; we refer to Wang et al. [WMT05] for more on this.

To ease the severe time step restriction, two interesting possibilities are out there. One is to make the surface tension treatment more implicit in time, solving for fluid motion which simultaneously will be incompressible and act to minimize surface area (in balance with inertia). With a tetrahedral mesh discretizing the fluid, Misztal et al. have shown the power of this approach [MEB+12], but it remains open how best to incorporate this idea into a more conventional water solver. Alternatively, Sussman and Ohta [SO09] have demonstrated a more stable evaluation of the surface tension force compared to using a finite difference estimate of curvature: essentially they run a smoothing PDE on the level set for a certain amount of time, and measure the difference in level set values to arrive at a more stable estimate of curvature.

9

Fire

This is a short chapter: while the physics and chemistry of combustion can be extraordinarily complicated, and to this day aren't fully understood, we will boil it down to a very simplified model. Our two main sources in graphics are the papers by Nguyen et al. [NFJ02] for thin flames, and those by Melek and Keyser [MK02] and Feldman et al. [FOA03] for volumetric combustion. There are of course many other approaches that avoid fluid simulation and directly model flames procedurally, but we will not cover them in this book.

Combustion is simply a chemical reaction[1] triggered by heat where an oxidizer (like oxygen gas) and a fuel (like propane) combine to form a variety of products, giving out more heat in the process. Thus, at a minimum, our fluid solver will need to be able to track fuel/oxidizer versus burnt products along with temperature—and if it's not a clean flame, we also need smoke concentration to track the resulting soot. In the following sections we'll take a look at two strategies for tracking the fuel/oxidizer appropriate for different classes of combustion.

Just to clarify before proceeding: throughout this chapter we are assuming that both fuel and oxidizer are either themselves gases, or suspended in the air. If you analyze even a wood fire or a candle, you'll find that the flames are the result of gaseous fuel—pyrolyzed from the wood as it heats up, or evaporated wax—not the solid itself directly. Thus when we model a solid (or even liquid) object that is on fire, we treat it as a source emitting gaseous fuel, which then burns. Part of the emission is enforcing a velocity boundary condition $\vec{u} \cdot \hat{n} = \vec{u}_{\text{solid}} \cdot \hat{n} + u_{\text{emission}}$ similar to the usual moving solid wall boundary condition: gaseous fuel is injected into the grid at this relative velocity u_{emission}. In addition, fields describing the presence of fuel (see the following sections) should have the appropriate boundary condition for advection. Various authors have looked at further

---

[1]One of the complexities hidden here is that in most situations in reality, there are actually hundreds of different chemical reactions in play, with a multitude of different chemical species. For example, we all know that the gasoline burned in a car engine doesn't simply combine with the oxygen in the air to produce water and carbon dioxide: a vast range of other chemicals from carbon monoxide to nitrous oxide to all sorts of carbon structures in soot particles end up in the exhaust.

eroding away the solid or liquid source as it emits gaseous fuel, which is particularly important for thin objects like sheets of paper—see for example the articles by Melek and Keyser [MK03] and Losasso et al. [LIGF06]. Whether or not (and where) a solid is emitting gaseous fuel is usually directly specified by the animator, often modulated by an animated texture to produce more interesting effects, though procedural models simulating the spread of fire according to burn rates or temperature thresholds can also easily be concocted.

9.1   Thin Flames

Nguyen et al. [NFJ02] detail an approach to fire, in which the region where combustion takes place is modeled as an infinitely thin flame front, i.e., a surface, not a volume. In addition, it's assumed that fuel and oxidizer are **premixed** before ignition, as in blow torches—while not really true for other phenomena where the mixing of fuel and oxidizer is an integral part of the fire (technically known as **diffuse flames**), the simplifying premixed assumption can still serve just fine for a visually plausible result.

The flame front divides the fluid region into two parts: premixed fuel/oxidizer on one side and burnt products (and/or background air) on the other side. To track the flame surface we model it with a level set ϕ sampled on the grid, as we did for water in Chapter 8.

The first problem to address is how to evolve the flame front: at what speed does it move? If no combustion were taking place, the flame front would be nothing more than the material interface between the two fluids—just like the free surface in water simulation. Thus our first velocity term is simply the fluid velocity: the flame front is advected along with the flow. For definiteness (this will be important in a moment) we'll use the velocity of the unburnt fuel, $\vec{u}_{\text{fuel}}$. However, when combustion is taking place, the flame front also is "moving:" fuel at the flame surface gets combusted into burnt products, effectively shrinking the surface inwards. The simplest model for this is to assume a constant burn speed S, the rate at which the flame surface burns into the fuel region along the normal direction. Nguyen et al. [NFJ02] suggest a default value of $S = 0.5 m/s$. Assuming that ϕ is negative in the fuel region by convention, this gives our level set equation

$$\frac{\partial \phi}{\partial t} + \vec{u}_{\text{fuel}} \cdot \nabla \phi = S. \qquad (9.1)$$

With $S \neq 0$, note that the volume of the fuel region is *not* conserved, and thus a lot of the worries for tracking level sets for water don't bother us here—just the usual advection approaches can be used as if ϕ were any other scalar, along with an addition of $S\Delta t$ each time step, and perhaps periodic reinitialization to signed distance. Note also that if an object is supposed to be on fire, a boundary condition forcing $\phi \leq 0$ on the burning sections of its surface should be included; otherwise ϕ should be extrapolated into solids to avoid artifacts near the surface, as with liquids.

As an aside, Hong et al. [HSF07] have more recently added additional detail to this technique by using higher-order non-linear equations for the speed and acceleration of the flame front (rather than keeping it as a constant burn speed S). These promote the formation of "cellular patterns" characteristic of some fires.

The next problem to address is how the fire affects the velocity field. If the density of the burnt products is less than the density of the fuel mix (as is often the case, either due to differences in a specific gas constant or temperature), then conservation of mass demands that the fluid should instantaneously expand when going through the flame front from the fuel region to the burnt-products region. The rate of mass leaving the fuel region per unit area is $\rho_{\text{fuel}}S$, which must match the rate of mass entering the burnt region per unit area, $\rho_{\text{burnt}}(S + \Delta V)$, where ΔV is the jump in the normal component of fluid velocity across the interface. Solving gives

$$\Delta V = \left(\frac{\rho_{\text{fuel}}}{\rho_{\text{burnt}}} - 1 \right) S.$$

Since the tangential component of velocity is continuous across the flame, this means the full velocity satisfies the following jump at the flame front:

$$\vec{u}_{\text{burnt}} = \vec{u}_{\text{fuel}} + \Delta V \hat{n}$$

$$= \vec{u}_{\text{fuel}} + \left(\frac{\rho_{\text{fuel}}}{\rho_{\text{burnt}}} - 1 \right) S \hat{n}, \tag{9.2}$$

where $\hat{n}$ is the normal pointing outward from the fuel region into the burnt region. This naturally defines a **ghost velocity** for use in advection: if you trace through the flame front and want to interpolate velocity on the other side, you need to add or subtract this change in normal velocity for the advection to make sense (where normal, in this case, might be evaluated from the normalized gradient of the level set ϕ wherever you happen to be interpolating). This is one example of the **ghost fluid method** developed by Fedkiw and coauthors.

This expansion also has to be modeled in the pressure projection step, enforcing a non-zero divergence at the flame front—indeed, this is one of the critical visual qualities of fire. The simplest discrete approach is to build Equation (9.2) into the evaluation of divergence that defines the right-hand side of the pressure equation. For example, when evaluating the divergence at a cell where $\phi \leq 0$ (i.e., in the fuel region) then any of the surrounding u-, v-, or w-velocity samples, where the averaged $\phi > 0$ (i.e., in the burnt region) should be corrected by the x-, y- or z-component of $-\Delta V \hat{n}$, respectively. Similarly if $\phi > 0$ at the cell center, then, at surrounding velocity samples where the averaged $\phi \leq 0$, ϕ should be corrected by the appropriate components of $+\Delta V \hat{n}$. This can be interpreted as yet another use for divergence controls. When setting up the matrix in the pressure solve, greater fidelity can be obtained by accounting for the different densities of fuel and burnt products: this shows up as variable densities just as in water or the advanced smoke model discussed earlier in the book. We can estimate the density in, say, a u-cell $(i+1/2, j, k)$ as a weighted average of ρ_{fuel} and ρ_{burnt}:

$$\rho_{i+1/2,j,k} = \alpha \rho_{\text{fuel}} + (1-\alpha)\rho_{\text{burnt}},$$

where the weight α could be determined from the level set values $\phi_{i,j,k}$ and $\phi_{i+1,j,k}$:

$$\alpha = \begin{cases} 1: & \phi_{i,j,k} \leq 0 \text{ and } \phi_{i+1,j,k} \leq 0, \\[2mm] \dfrac{\phi_{i,j,k}}{\phi_{i,j,k} - \phi_{i+1,j,k}}: & \phi_{i,j,k} \leq 0 \text{ and } \phi i+1, j, k > 0, \\[2mm] 1 - \dfrac{\phi_{i,j,k}}{\phi_{i,j,k} - \phi_{i+1,j,k}}: & \phi_{i,j,k} > 0 \text{ and } \phi i+1, j, k \leq 0, \\[2mm] 0: & \phi_{i,j,k} > 0 \text{ and } \phi_{i+1,j,k} > 0. \end{cases}$$

This of course blends very elegantly with the variable density smoke solve, where density is a function of temperature T and the specific gas constant R; this constant R can be taken as different for the fuel region and the burnt-products region.

Speaking of temperature, we don't yet have a model for it. The simplest approach is to keep a constant $T = T_{\text{ignition}}$, the temperature at which combustion starts, inside the fuel region and establish a discontinuous jump to T_{max} on the burnt products side of the flame front. The temperature on the burnt side is advected and dissipated as before for smoke, but using the trick that—just as was done for velocity above—when crossing over the flame front and referring to a temperature on the fuel side, the "ghost" value of T_{max} is used. Let's make that clear: the actual temperature T in the fuel side is kept constant at T_{ignition}, but when advecting and diffusing T on the burnt side, if reference is made to a T value in the fuel (e.g., when doing interpolation in semi-Lagrangian advection) T_{max} is used instead. For the extreme temperatures apparent in fires, hot enough to make an incandescent glow, a black-body radiation formula for the decay of T might be used instead of the simple exponential decay mentioned earlier, where the rate of cooling is proportional to the fourth power of the temperature difference

$$\frac{DT}{Dt} = -c\left(\frac{T - T_{\text{ambient}}}{T_{\text{max}} - T_{\text{ambient}}}\right)^4$$

for some cooling constant c defined as a user parameter. After advecting temperature around to get an intermediate $\tilde{T}$ for a time step Δt, this cooling equation can be solved analytically to give

$$T^{n+1} = T_{\text{ambient}} + \left[\frac{1}{(\tilde{T} - T_{\text{ambient}})^3} + \frac{3c\Delta t}{(T_{\text{max}} - T_{\text{ambient}})^4}\right]^{-\frac{1}{3}}.$$

Similar to this treatment of temperature, we can also feed a smoke concentration s_{max} into the burnt region from the flame front, allowing it to be advected and dissipated as usual. Temperature and smoke concentration can feed into either a buoyancy force (if we make the Boussinesq approximation) or modify density, as discussed in Chapter 6.

The final issue is rendering, which mostly lies outside the scope of this book. The actual flame front itself is sometimes referred to as the "blue core," referring to the spectral emissions made when burning typical hydrocarbons (other fuels give rise to different spectra, giving different colors): the level set itself is a light emitter. For a dirty flame, where soot is produced, the bulk of the visual effect though is the black-body incandescence of the soot particles. That is, light is emitted from the burnt region as well, proportional to the smoke concentration s and following the black-body spectrum for the temperature T. Simultaneously, the soot is somewhat opaque, so light emitted elsewhere should be absorbed at a rate proportional to s. Further scattering effects can be included of course.

9.2 Volumetric Combustion

We now turn to an alternate model where combustion may take place throughout the volume, loosely following Feldman et al. [FOA03]. This is appropriate particularly for modeling the fireballs due to deflagration of fuel suspended in the air, whether flammable powder or liquid-fuel mist. It's also slightly simpler to implement than the preceding thin-flame model, since level sets are not involved, yet it can still achieve some of the look of regular flames and thus might be preferred in some instances.

To a standard smoke simulation, which includes temperature T, smoke concentration s, and divergence controls, we add another field F, the concentration of unburnt fuel in each grid cell. The fuel gets advected along with the flow as usual, may be additional diffused, and may be seeded at fuel sources or emitted from boundaries. (In Feldman et al.'s work, fuel is instead represented as the unburnt mass of discrete fuel particles; we'll come back to using particle systems in grid-based fluid solvers in Chapter 7.)

To this we add some simple rules. If the temperature T at a grid cell, following advection and dissipation steps, is above some ignition threshold $T_{ignition}$ and the fuel concentration F is above zero, we burn some of the fuel. At the simplest we reduce F by $z\Delta t$, where z is the burn speed (volume fraction combusted per second), clamping it to zero to avoid negative F. Let ΔF be the change in F; we then increase the smoke concentration s by some amount proportional to ΔF, increase the temperature T also proportional to ΔF, and add an amount to the divergence control proportional to $\Delta F/\Delta t$ (recall the divergence is percent expansion per unit of time, thus we need to divide by Δt). Note that this rule burns the fuel at a constant rate z without regard to the availability of oxidizer; Feldman et al. argue that for suspended particle explosions (coal dust, sawdust, flour, etc.) oxygen availability in the air is never the limiting factor, and thus this rule is justified. However, if need be you could limit the rate based on $1 - s - F$, the volume fraction left for plain air.

Rendering is based on black-body radiation as in the previous section, though here we don't have any representation of the "blue core" available so the rendering possibilities are slightly more limited.

10

Viscous Fluids

After briefly discussing viscosity in Chapter 1, we dispensed with it and until now have only looked at inviscid simulations. In fact our major problem has been that our numerical methods have too much numerical dissipation which, in the velocity field, looks like viscosity. We now will turn our attention to simulating highly viscous fluids, like molasses, and even variable viscosity fluids where some parts are more viscous than others perhaps due to heating or cooling, or desired animation effects.

10.1 Stress

To properly understand viscosity and avoid some potential mistakes when handling variable viscosity situations, we need to first understand the concept of stress.

In reality, at least as a first approximation, matter is composed of small particles with mass that interact by applying forces on each other. However, since we're not interested in phenomena at that microscopic scale, in fluid mechanics we make the continuum assumption, that matter is a continuous field with no discrete particles. One way of thinking about this assumption is that we're taking the limit as the particles become infinitesimally small and packed together with infinitesimal space between them. For dynamics this poses the problem that the masses drop to zero, and for accelerations to remain bounded the forces must drop to zero too. To get around this, we measure things in bulk: how much mass there is in a volume of space, or what the net force is on a volume.

While it makes no sense to ask what the mass of a continuum fluid is at a point in space (it has to be zero), we can define the density at any point, which is a useful quantity. By integrating density in a volume we get the total mass of the volume. Similarly it makes no sense to ask what the force on a continuum fluid is at a point in space (it has to be zero), but we can define quantities analogous to density: force densities in a sense, that when integrated over a region give a net force.

We've already seen two examples of force density, body forces (such as gravity) and pressure. These are fundamentally different however: to get the net gravitational force on a region of fluid you integrate the gravitational body force density $\rho\vec{g}$ over the *volume*, but to get the net pressure force on the volume you integrate the pressure times the normal $p\hat{n}$ over the *surface* of the region. The difference is that a body force acts over a distance to influence everything inside the volume, whereas other forces (like pressure) can only act locally on the surface of contact. It is these local contact forces that we need to generalize from pressure to figure out viscosity and more exotic fluid effects.

An accepted assumption (verified to be accurate in many experiments), called Cauchy's Hypothesis, is that we can represent the local contact forces by a function of position and orientation only. That is, there is a vector field called **traction**, $\vec{t}(\vec{x}, \hat{n})$, a function of where in space we are measuring it and what the normal to the contact surface there is. It has units of force per area: to get the net contact force on a volume of fluid Ω, we integrate the traction over its surface:

$$\vec{F} = \iint_{\partial\Omega} \vec{t}(\vec{x}, \hat{n}).$$

I'd like to underscore here that this volume can be an arbitrary region containing fluid (or in fact, any continuum substance); e.g., it could be a tiny subregion in the interior of the fluid, or a grid cell, etc.

Once we accept this assumption, it can be proven that the traction must depend linearly on the normal; that is, the traction must be the result of multiplying some matrix by the normal. Technically speaking this is actually a rank-two tensor, not just a matrix, but we'll gloss over the difference for now and just call it a tensor from now on.[1] The tensor is called the **stress tensor**, or more specifically the **Cauchy stress tensor**,[2] which we label σ. Thus we can write

$$\vec{t}(\vec{x}, \hat{n}) = \sigma(\vec{x})\hat{n}.$$

Note that the stress tensor only depends on position, not on the surface normal. It can also be proven from conservation of angular momentum that the stress tensor must be symmetric: $\sigma = \sigma^T$.

---

[1] Basically a matrix is a specific array of numbers; a rank-two tensor is a more abstract linear operator that can be represented as a matrix when you pick a set of basis vectors with which to measure it. For the purposes of this book, you can think of them interchangeably, as we will always use a fixed Cartesian basis where y is in the vertical direction.

[2] There are other stress tensors, which chiefly differ in the basis in which they are represented. For elastic solids, where it makes sense to talk of a rest configuration to which the object tries to return, it can be convenient to set up a stress tensor in terms of rest-configuration coordinates, rather than the world-space coordinates in which Cauchy stress operates.

Since the unit normal has no units, the stress tensor is also measured as force per area, just like traction. However, it's a little harder to interpret; it's easier instead to think in terms of traction on a specific plane of contact.

As a concrete example using continuum materials that are a little easier to experience, put your hand down on a flat desk. The flesh of your hand and the wood of the desk are essentially each a continuum, and thus there is conceptually a stress tensor in each. The net force you apply on the desk with your hand is the integral of the traction over the area of contact. The normal in this case is the vertical vector $(0, 1, 0)$, so the traction at any point is

$$\vec{t} = \sigma\hat{n} = \begin{bmatrix} \sigma_{11} & \sigma_{12} & \sigma_{13} \\ \sigma_{21} & \sigma_{22} & \sigma_{23} \\ \sigma_{31} & \sigma_{32} & \sigma_{33} \end{bmatrix} \begin{bmatrix} 0 \\ 1 \\ 0 \end{bmatrix} = \begin{bmatrix} \sigma_{12} \\ \sigma_{22} \\ \sigma_{32} \end{bmatrix}.$$

Note that the normal force comes from the vertical component σ_{22} of traction—how hard you are pushing down on the desk. The other components of the traction, σ_{12} and σ_{32}, are tangential—how hard you are pushing the desk forwards, backwards, or to the side.

Those tangential forces are due to friction; without it there could only be a normal force. Viscosity is in many ways similar to friction, in particular that a fluid without viscosity only exerts forces in the normal direction. That is, the traction $\vec{t} = \sigma\hat{n}$ in an inviscid fluid is always in the normal direction: it must be parallel to $\hat{n}$. Since this is true for any normal vector, it can be proven that the stress tensor of an inviscid fluid must be a scalar times the identity. That scalar is, in fact, the negative of pressure. Thus, for the inviscid case we have considered up until now, the stress tensor is just

$$\sigma = -p\delta, \tag{10.1}$$

where we use δ to mean the identity tensor. When we model viscosity, we will end up with a more complicated stress tensor that can give tangential tractions.

10.2   Applying Stress

The net force due to stress on a volume Ω of fluid is the surface integral of traction:

$$\vec{F} = \iint_{\partial\Omega} \sigma\hat{n}.$$

We can use the divergence theorem to transform this into a volume integral:

$$\vec{F} = \iiint_{\Omega} \nabla \cdot \sigma.$$

Note that the notation $\nabla \cdot \sigma$ is the accepted short-hand for the vector whose elements are the divergences of the rows (or columns) of σ:

$$\nabla \cdot \sigma = \begin{bmatrix} \frac{\partial \sigma_{11}}{\partial x} + \frac{\partial \sigma_{12}}{\partial y} + \frac{\partial \sigma_{13}}{\partial z} \\ \frac{\partial \sigma_{21}}{\partial x} + \frac{\partial \sigma_{22}}{\partial y} + \frac{\partial \sigma_{23}}{\partial z} \\ \frac{\partial \sigma_{31}}{\partial x} + \frac{\partial \sigma_{32}}{\partial y} + \frac{\partial \sigma_{33}}{\partial z} \end{bmatrix}.$$

Ignoring body forces for simplicity, we set this net force equal to the mass times center-of-mass acceleration:

$$\vec{F} = M\vec{A} = \iiint_\Omega \rho \frac{D\vec{u}}{Dt},$$

i.e., we have an equality between the two volume integrals:

$$\iiint_\Omega \rho \frac{D\vec{u}}{Dt} = \iiint_\Omega \nabla \cdot \sigma.$$

Since this holds for any arbitrary volume, the integrands must be equal:

$$\rho \frac{D\vec{u}}{Dt} = \nabla \cdot \sigma.$$

Adding back in the body force term, we actually have the general momentum equation for a continuum (elastic solids as well as fluids):

$$\frac{D\vec{u}}{Dt} = \frac{1}{\rho}\vec{g} + \frac{1}{\rho}\nabla \cdot \sigma.$$

In the particular case of an inviscid fluid, as we discussed above, the stress tensor is just the negative of pressure times the identity—see Equation (10.1). In this case, it's not hard to see that $\nabla \cdot \sigma$ simplifies to $-\nabla p$, giving the familiar momentum equation.

For general fluid flow, pressure is still a very important quantity, so we will explicitly separate it out from the rest of the stress tensor:

$$\sigma = -p\delta + \tau,$$

where τ is also a symmetric tensor. We will let the pressure term handle the incompressibility constraint and model other fluid behavior with τ.

10.3   Strain Rate and Newtonian Fluids

Our model of viscosity is physically based on the fact that when molecules traveling at different speeds collide or closely interact, some energy may be transferred to vibrational or rotational modes in the molecule—i.e., heat —and thus the difference in center-of-mass velocity between the two molecules is reduced. At the continuum level, the net effect of this is that as a region of fluid slips past another, momentum is transferred between them to reduce the difference in velocity, and the fluids get hotter. The critical thing to note is that this occurs when fluid moves *past* other fluid: in a rigid body rotation there are differences in velocity, but the fluid moves together and there is no viscous effect. Thus we really only care about how the fluid is deforming, that is how far from rigidly moving it is.

To measure differences in velocity locally, the natural quantity to consider is the gradient of velocity: $\nabla \vec{u}$. However, mixed up in the gradient is also information about the rigid rotation[3] as well as the deformation induced by the flow. We will want to separate out just the deformation part to define viscous stress.

One way to characterize rigid motion is that the dot-product of any two vectors remains constant. (If the two vectors are the same, this is just saying lengths remains constant; for different vectors we're saying the angle between them also stays the same.) How much the dot-product between two vectors changes is thus a measure of how fast the fluid is deforming. Let's look at a point $\vec{x}$: in a small time interval Δt it moves to approximately $\vec{x} + \Delta t \vec{u}(\vec{x})$. Now look at two nearby points, $\vec{x} + \Delta \vec{x}$ and $\vec{x} + \Delta \vec{y}$: linearizing appropriately, they approximately move to

$$\vec{x} + \Delta \vec{x} + \Delta t(\vec{u}(\vec{x}) + \nabla \vec{u} \Delta \vec{x})$$
$$\text{and} \quad \vec{x} + \Delta \vec{y} + \Delta t(\vec{u}(\vec{x}) + \nabla \vec{u} \Delta \vec{y}),$$

respectively. The dot-product of the vectors from $\vec{x}$ to these points begins as

$$[(\vec{x} + \Delta \vec{x}) - \vec{x}] \cdot [(\vec{x} + \Delta \vec{y}) - \vec{x}] = \Delta \vec{x} \cdot \Delta \vec{y}$$

and after the time interval is approximately

$$[(\vec{x} + \Delta \vec{x} + \Delta t(\vec{u}(\vec{x}) + \nabla \vec{u} \Delta \vec{x})) - (\vec{x} + \Delta t \vec{u}(\vec{x}))]$$
$$\cdot [(\vec{x} + \Delta \vec{y} + \Delta t(\vec{u}(\vec{x}) + \nabla \vec{u} \Delta \vec{y})) - (\vec{x} + \Delta t \vec{u}(\vec{x}))]$$
$$= [\Delta \vec{x} + \Delta t \nabla \vec{u} \Delta \vec{x}] \cdot [\Delta \vec{y} + \Delta t \nabla \vec{u} \Delta \vec{y}].$$

Then the change in the dot-product, ignoring $O(\Delta t^2)$ terms, is

$$\Delta t \left(\Delta \vec{x} \cdot \nabla \vec{u} \Delta \vec{y} + \Delta \vec{y} \cdot \nabla \vec{u} \Delta \vec{x} \right) = \Delta t \Delta \vec{x}^T \left(\nabla \vec{u} + \nabla \vec{u}^T \right) \Delta \vec{y}.$$

That is, the rate of change of dot-products of vectors in the flow is determined by the symmetric part of the velocity gradient, the matrix $D =$

---

[3]Later in the book, we will take a look at the curl of velocity which is called vorticity, $\vec{\omega} = \nabla \times \vec{u}$; it measures precisely the rotational part of the velocity field.

$\frac{1}{2}(\nabla\vec{u}+\nabla\vec{u}^T)$. This is called the **strain rate tensor** or rate of strain, since it's measuring how fast **strain**—the total deformation of the continuum—is changing.

Incidentally, the rest of the velocity gradient, the skew-symmetric part $\frac{1}{2}(\nabla\vec{u}-\nabla\vec{u}^T)$ naturally has to represent the other source of velocity differences in the flow: rotation. We'll explore this further later in the book.

We'll also immediately point out that for incompressible fluids, which is all we focus on in this book, the trace of D (the sum of the diagonal entries, denoted $\text{tr}(D)$) is simply $\nabla \cdot \vec{u} = 0$.

We are looking for a symmetric tensor τ to model stress due to viscosity; the rate of strain tensor D is symmetric and measures how fast the fluid is deforming. The obvious thing to do is assume τ is proportional to D. Fluids for which there is a simple linear relationship are called **Newtonian**. Air and water are examples of fluids which are, to a very good approximation, Newtonian. However, there are many liquids (generally with a more complex composition) where a non-linear relationship is essential; they go under the catch-all category of **non-Newtonian** fluids.[4] We won't go into any more detail, except to say that two classes of non-Newtonian fluids, **shear-thickening** and **shear-thinning** fluids, can be easily modeled with a viscosity coefficient μ that is a function of $\|D\|_F$, the Frobenius norm of the strain rate:[5]

$$\|D\|_F = \sqrt{\sum_{i,j=1}^{3} D_{i,j}^2}.$$

Often a power-law is assumed:

$$\mu = K\|D\|_F^{n-1}, \tag{10.2}$$

where $n = 1$ corresponds to a Newtonian fluid, $n > 1$ a shear-thickening fluid where apparent viscosity increases as you try to deform the fluid faster (e.g., cornstarch suspended in water), and $0 < n < 1$ a shear-thinning

---

[4]Also sometimes included in the non-Newtonian class are **viscoelastic** fluids, which blur the line between fluid and solid as they can include elastic forces that seek to return the material to an "undeformed" state—in fact these are sometimes best thought of instead as solids with permanent (**plastic**) deformations. You might refer to the article by Goktekin et al. [GBO04] and Irving's thesis [Irv07] for a fluid-centric treatment in graphics.

[5]Technically this is assuming again that the fluid is incompressible, so the trace of D is zero, which means it represents only **shearing** deformations, not expansions or contractions.

fluid where apparent viscosity increases as the fluid comes to rest (e.g., paint). Granular materials such as sand can even be modeled as the limit $n = 0$ of shear-thinning where the magnitude of "viscous" stress depends instead on pressure, not the magnitude of the strain rate, making it more akin to dry Coulomb friction; see Zhu and Bridson [ZB05] for more on this subject.

Getting back to simple Newtonian fluids, the relationship for incompressible flow is

$$\tau = 2\mu D + \lambda \mathrm{tr}(D)\delta, \tag{10.3}$$

where μ is the **coefficient of dynamic viscosity**. The second term, involving $\mathrm{tr}(D) = \nabla \cdot \vec{u}$, is of course zero for incompressible flow for any λ (which is termed the **second coefficient of viscosity**, and is also associated with the term "bulk viscosity," i.e. viscous resistance to changing bulk a.k.a. volume). For compressible flow λ is often taken to be $-\frac{2}{3}\mu$, though theoretically this is only an idealization of monatomic gases. However, for an incompressible fluid we are free to choose λ as we please,[6] and thus for simplicity's sake we'll set $\lambda = 0$ for now.

Plugging this into the momentum equation, we get

$$\frac{D\vec{u}}{Dt} + \frac{1}{\rho}\nabla p = \frac{1}{\rho}\nabla \cdot \left(\mu(\nabla\vec{u} + \nabla\vec{u}^T)\right). \tag{10.4}$$

You may notice that this isn't quite the same as our first statement of the momentum equation, Equation (1.1). It turns out that for the common case where μ is constant, the correct equation (10.4) does in fact simplify to Equation (1.1): but be aware, for simulations with variable viscosity, only Equation (10.4) is correct. For example, Equation (1.1) doesn't conserve angular momentum in the variable viscosity case. The simplification also is unhelpful in applying the correct free surface boundary condition (see below), which is critical for viscous liquid simulations, and since highly viscous gases are rarely of interest for graphics, I actually recommend **not** bothering with the simplification, since it's hardly ever useful.

However, for completeness' sake, let's work through the simplification so it at least doesn't remain a mystery. If μ is constant, then we can take

---

[6]This isn't quite true: for $\lambda < -\frac{2}{3}\mu$, basic thermodynamics are violated, with viscosity actually accelerating expansion or contraction, increasing the energy of the system. In a numerical method, where divergence probably isn't exactly zero even for incompressible flow, problems are bound to arise.

it out from under the divergence:

$$\frac{D\vec{u}}{Dt} + \frac{1}{\rho}\nabla p = \frac{\mu}{\rho}\nabla \cdot (\nabla\vec{u} + \nabla\vec{u}^T)$$

$$= \frac{\mu}{\rho}\left[\nabla \cdot \nabla\vec{u} + \nabla \cdot (\nabla\vec{u}^T)\right]$$

$$= \frac{\mu}{\rho}\left[\nabla \cdot \nabla\vec{u} + \begin{pmatrix} \frac{\partial}{\partial x}\frac{\partial u}{\partial x} + \frac{\partial}{\partial y}\frac{\partial v}{\partial x} + \frac{\partial}{\partial z}\frac{\partial w}{\partial x} \\ \frac{\partial}{\partial x}\frac{\partial u}{\partial y} + \frac{\partial}{\partial y}\frac{\partial v}{\partial y} + \frac{\partial}{\partial z}\frac{\partial w}{\partial y} \\ \frac{\partial}{\partial x}\frac{\partial u}{\partial z} + \frac{\partial}{\partial y}\frac{\partial v}{\partial z} + \frac{\partial}{\partial z}\frac{\partial w}{\partial z} \end{pmatrix}\right]$$

$$= \frac{\mu}{\rho}\left[\nabla \cdot \nabla\vec{u} + \begin{pmatrix} \frac{\partial}{\partial x}(\frac{\partial u}{\partial x} + \frac{\partial v}{\partial y} + \frac{\partial w}{\partial z}) \\ \frac{\partial}{\partial y}(\frac{\partial u}{\partial x} + \frac{\partial v}{\partial y} + \frac{\partial w}{\partial z}) \\ \frac{\partial}{\partial z}(\frac{\partial u}{\partial x} + \frac{\partial v}{\partial y} + \frac{\partial w}{\partial z}) \end{pmatrix}\right].$$

In the last step we simply changed the order of partial derivatives in the last term and regrouped. But now we see that the last term is simply the gradient of $\nabla \cdot \vec{u}$:

$$\frac{D\vec{u}}{Dt} + \frac{1}{\rho}\nabla p = \frac{\mu}{\rho}\left[\nabla \cdot \nabla\vec{u} + \nabla(\nabla \cdot \vec{u})\right].$$

If the flow is incompressible, i.e., $\nabla \cdot \vec{u} = 0$. Finally, substituting the **kinematic viscosity** $\nu = \mu/\rho$ in, we end up back at Equation (1.1). I emphasize that this only happens when both the viscosity is constant through the flow and the velocity field is incompressible. The second point also becomes important numerically since at intermediate stages in our time integration our velocity field may not be discretely incompressible—and then this last term can't be blithely ignored.

Getting back to variable viscosity, some formula needs to be decided for μ. For a non-Newtonian fluid, it might be a function of the magnitude of the strain rate, as we have seen. For regular Newtonian fluids it might instead be a function of temperature—assuming we're tracking temperature in the simulation as we saw how to do with smoke and fire—which is most important for liquids. Carlson et al. [CMIT02] suggest that modeling melting and solidifying (freezing) can be emulated by making the viscosity a low constant for temperatures above a transition zone (centered on the melting point) and a high constant for temperatures below the transition zone (thus giving near-rigid behavior), and smoothly varying between the two in the narrow transition zone itself.

10.4 Boundary Conditions

The two types of boundaries considered in this book are free surfaces and solid walls, and each has particular conditions associated with viscosity.

In the case of a free surface, things are fairly straightforward. On the other side of the boundary there is a vacuum, or another fluid of much smaller density whose effect we assume is negligible. Thus there is nothing with which to transfer momentum: there can be no traction at the free surface. In other words, the boundary condition for the stress at the free surface is

$$\sigma\hat{n} = -p\hat{n} + \tau\hat{n} = 0.$$

Note that if the viscous stress τ is zero, this reduces to $p = 0$ as before; however, this becomes significantly more complex when τ isn't zero. In terms of the velocity, and assuming no special treatment of bulk viscosity, this condition is:

$$-p\hat{n} + (\nabla\vec{u} + \nabla\vec{u}^T)\hat{n} = 0.$$

In particular, the true free surface condition is quite different from separately specifying $p = 0$ and $\nabla\vec{u} \cdot \hat{n} = 0$, an erroneous and physically meaningless boundary condition which unfortunately crops up regularly in research papers. Batty and Bridson [BB08] worked through the first correct treatment of a viscous free surface in graphics, illustrating how this error destroys many of the critical visual features in highly viscous flow.

At solid walls, things are also a little different. Physically speaking once we model viscosity, it turns out the velocity field must be continuous everywhere: if it weren't, viscous transfer of momentum would in the next instant make it continuous again. This results in the so-called **no-slip** boundary condition:

$$\vec{u} = \vec{u}_{\text{solid}},$$

which of course simplifies to $\vec{u} = 0$ at stationary solids. Recall that in the inviscid case, only the normal component of velocities had to match: here we are forcing the tangential components to match as well.

The no-slip condition has been experimentally verified to be more accurate than the inviscid no-stick condition. However, the caveat is that in many cases something called a **boundary layer** develops. Loosely speaking, a boundary layer is a thin region next to a solid where the tangential velocity rapidly changes from $\vec{u}_{\text{solid}}$ at the solid wall to $\vec{u}^\star$ at the other side of the layer, where $\vec{u}^\star$ is the velocity the inviscid no-stick boundary condition ($\vec{u} \cdot \hat{n} = \vec{u}_{\text{solid}} \cdot \hat{n}$) would have given. That is, the effect of viscous drag at the surface of the solid is restricted to a very small region next to the solid, and can be ignored elsewhere. When we discretize the fluid flow on a relatively coarse grid, that boundary layer may be much thinner than a grid cell, and thus it's no longer a good idea to implement the no-slip condition numerically—we would artificially be expanding the boundary layer to at least a grid cell thick, which would be a much worse approximation than going back to the inviscid no-stick boundary condition. In this case, we have

$$\vec{u} \cdot \hat{n} = \vec{u}_{\text{solid}} \cdot \hat{n},$$
$$(\tau \hat{n}) \times \hat{n} = 0,$$

where the second boundary equation is indicating that the viscous stress causes no tangential traction. There is even an intermediate case, the Navier slip condition, which allows some tangential slip but also some tangential "drag" at the solid surface. However, for simplicity's sake, we will stick with the simpler no-slip condition for the rest of the chapter.

10.5   Implementation

The first simplification we will make is to use time-splitting again, handling viscosity in a separate step from advection and body forces. It can be profitably combined with the pressure solve, enforcing incompressibility while simultaneously integrating viscous effects, which sometimes is called an "unsteady Stokes" solve.[7] Batty and Bridson [BB10] show how, if you solve for p and the components of τ you can still do this with an SPD matrix, and use the same linear solver code as we used for pressure.

However, for this book, we'll take one more common simplification, time splitting viscosity from pressure projection. That is, we'll project out pressure to make the flow incompressible, and then solve for the effect of viscosity on velocity. For one time step Δt, this update is

$$\frac{\partial \vec{u}}{\partial t} = \frac{1}{\rho} \nabla \cdot \left(\mu (\nabla \vec{u} + \nabla \vec{u}^T) \right),$$

with any or all of the boundary conditions given above. Although we will use the full form of viscosity in equation (10.4), which can help damp away any remaining divergence in the field, this step can also trade reduced a shear rate for an increased divergence, so it's generally necessary to perform a second pressure projection afterwards, before continuing with advection in the resulting velocity field.[8]

---

[7]Stokes flow, as opposed to Navier-Stokes, is used to model slow-moving and viscous incompressible flow; it is what you get when you drop the nonlinear $\vec{u} \cdot \nabla \vec{u}$ term from the momentum equation arguing it is a negligible high-order effect, reducing the equations to much simpler linear equations.

[8]Increasing the bulk viscosity coefficient λ to a substantial positive multiple of μ can lessen the need for a second projection, but also causes convergence troubles for the linear solver in an implicit step, so it's probably cheaper nevertheless to stick with a second projection.

Likewise, we will time split the boundary conditions, enforcing $p = 0$ at free surfaces and $\vec{u} \cdot \hat{n} = \vec{u}_{\text{solid}} \cdot \hat{n}$ at solid boundaries in the pressure solve, and then $(\nabla \vec{u} + \nabla \vec{u}^T)\hat{n} = 0$ at free surfaces and $\vec{u} = \vec{u}_{\text{solid}}$ at solid boundaries in the viscous solve.

Staggered grids make life easier for viscosity, as they did for pressure. Let's take a look at the contribution to the horizontal component of velocity, given the viscous stress tensor τ:

$$u^{n+1} = u^P + \frac{\Delta t}{\rho}\left(\frac{\partial \tau^{11}}{\partial x} + \frac{\partial \tau^{12}}{\partial y} + \frac{\partial \tau^{13}}{\partial z} \right).$$

(Here I am using u^P as the velocity field *after* pressure projection, and u^{n+1} is the finalized velocity field after viscosity is included.) Since u is located in the grid at, say, $(i+1/2, j, k)$, it's natural to ask for τ^{11} to be at grid cell centers (i, j, k), for τ^{12} to be at the edge-center $(i+1/2, j+1/2, k)$, and for τ^{13} at $(i+1/2, j, k+1/2)$. This gives an elegant discretization:

$$u^{n+1}_{i+1/2,j,k} = u^P_{i+1/2,j,k} + \frac{\Delta t}{\rho}\left(\frac{\tau^{11}_{i+1,j,k} - \tau^{11}_{i,j,k}}{\Delta x} \right.$$

$$\left. + \frac{\tau^{12}_{i+1/2,j+1/2,k} - \tau^{12}_{i+1/2,j-1/2,k}}{\Delta x} + \frac{\tau^{13}_{i+1/2,j,k+1/2} - \tau^{13}_{i+1/2,j,k-1/2}}{\Delta x} \right).$$

Similarly for the other components of velocity:

$$v^{n+1}_{i,j+1/2,k} = v^P_{i,j+1/2,k} + \frac{\Delta t}{\rho}\left(\frac{\tau^{12}_{i+1/2,j+1/2,k} - \tau^{12}_{i-1/2,j+1/2,k}}{\Delta x} \right.$$

$$\left. + \frac{\tau^{22}_{i,j+1,k} - \tau^{22}_{i,j,k}}{\Delta x} + \frac{\tau^{23}_{i,j+1/2,k+1/2} - \tau^{23}_{i,j+1/2,k-1/2}}{\Delta x} \right),$$

$$w^{n+1}_{i,j,k+1/2} = w^P_{i,j,k+1/2} + \frac{\Delta t}{\rho}\left(\frac{\tau^{13}_{i+1/2,j,k+1/2} - \tau^{13}_{i-1/2,j,k+1/2}}{\Delta x} \right.$$

$$\left. + \frac{\tau^{23}_{i,j+1/2,k+1/2} - \tau^{23}_{i,j-1/2,k+1/2}}{\Delta x} + \frac{\tau^{33}_{i,j,k+1} - \tau^{33}_{i,j,k}}{\Delta x} \right).$$

Note that these formulas make use of the symmetry of τ, e.g., $\tau^{12} = \tau^{21}$. In 2D, they simplify the obvious way. But how do we determine the values of τ on the staggered grid?

10.5.1   Explicit Treatment

The simplest thing of all is to just use central differences on the given velocity field. From the definition $\tau = \mu(\nabla \vec{u} + \nabla \vec{u}^T)$ we get

$$\tau_{i,j,k}^{11} = 2\mu_{i,j,k}\frac{u_{i+1/2,j,k}^P - u_{i-1/2,j,k}^P}{\Delta x}$$

$$\tau_{i+1/2,j+1/2,k}^{12} =$$
$$\mu_{i+1/2,j+1/2,k}\left(\frac{u_{i+1/2,j+1,k}^P - u_{i+1/2,j,k}^P}{\Delta x} + \frac{v_{i+1,j+1/2,k}^P - v_{i,j+1/2,k}^P}{\Delta x}\right)$$

$$\tau_{i+1/2,j,k+1/2}^{13} =$$
$$\mu_{i+1/2,j,k+1/2}\left(\frac{u_{i+1/2,j,k+1}^P - u_{i+1/2,j,k}^P}{\Delta x} + \frac{w_{i+1,j,k+1/2}^P - w_{i,j,k+1/2}^P}{\Delta x}\right)$$

$$\tau_{i,j,k}^{22} = 2\mu_{i,j,k}\frac{v_{i,j+1/2,k}^P - v_{i,j-1/2,k}^P}{\Delta x}$$

$$\tau_{i,j+1/2,k+1/2}^{23} =$$
$$\mu_{i,j+1/2,k+1/2}\left(\frac{v_{i,j+1/2,k+1}^P - v_{i,j+1/2,k}^P}{\Delta x} + \frac{w_{i,j+1,k+1/2}^P - w_{i,j,k+1/2}^P}{\Delta x}\right)$$

$$\tau_{i,j,k}^{33} = 2\mu_{i,j,k}\frac{w_{i,j,k+1/2}^P - w_{i,j,k-1/2}^P}{\Delta x}$$

This can be simplified in the obvious way for 2D.

Beyond boundaries, we need ghost velocity values to plug into these formulas. For viscous solid walls with the no-slip condition, it's natural to simply use the solid velocity itself. For free surfaces we have to be a little more careful. The obvious first approach to try is to just extrapolate the velocity into the air, as we have done before, effectively setting $\vec{u}$ at a point in the air to the velocity at the closest point on the surface.

However, this simple extrapolation induces a non-negligible error. As a thought experiment, imagine a blob of fluid moving rigidly in free flight: it has zero deformation since its internal velocity field is rigid, therefore it should experience no viscous forces—i.e., τ should evaluate to zero, even at the boundary. However, if a rigid rotation is present, τ only evaluates to zero if the ghost velocities keep that same rotation: extrapolating as a constant doesn't, and will induce erroneous viscous resistance at the boundary. Ideally a more sophisticated extrapolation scheme such as linear extrapolation should be used. That said, at present our first-order time-splitting of advection from pressure also will induce a similar erroneous drag on rotational motion, which we'll discuss in Chapter 11. Reducing one error but not the other is probably not worth the bother, and thus we'll leave this question open for further research.

The chief problem with the method as presented is stability. Unfortunately this method is liable to blow up if Δt is too large. Let's examine a simple 1D model diffusion problem to understand why,

$$\frac{\partial q}{\partial t} = k \frac{\partial^2 q}{\partial x^2},$$

where q models a velocity component and k models μ/ρ, the kinematic viscosity. Our explicit discretization would give

$$q_i^{n+1} = q_i^n + \Delta t k \frac{q_{i+1}^n - 2q_i^n + q_{i-1}^n}{\Delta x^2}.$$

Consider the highest spatial-frequency component possible in the numerical solution, say $q_i^n = Q^n(-1)^i$. Here Q^n is the time n scalar coefficient multiplying the ± 1 underlying basis function, with grid index i the exponent of (-1). Plug this in to see what Q^{n+1} is:

$$Q^{n+1}(-1)^i = Q^n(-1)^i + \Delta t k \frac{Q^n(-1)^{i+1} - 2Q^n(-1)^i + Q^n(-1)^{i-1}}{\Delta x^2}$$

$$= Q^n(-1)^i \left(1 + \frac{\Delta t k}{\Delta x^2}(-1 - 2 - 1)\right)$$

$$= Q^n(-1)^i \left(1 - \frac{4\Delta t k}{\Delta x^2}\right),$$

$$Q^{n+1} = \left(1 - \frac{4\Delta t k}{\Delta x^2}\right) Q^n.$$

This can only exponentially and monotonically decay, as we would expect viscosity to do, if

$$\Delta t < \frac{\Delta x^2}{4k}.$$

Otherwise we end up with q oscillating in time—a physically incorrect vibration—and possibly even exponential *increase*, which is thermodynamically impossible and potentially disastrous numerically.

For the full 3D viscous problem, a similar time step restriction applies:

$$\Delta t < \frac{\Delta x^2 \rho}{12 \mu_{\max}}. \tag{10.5}$$

This is pretty severe: while we discussed the merit of restricting Δt to be $O(\Delta x)$ to control errors in advection, this possibly reduces it a whole order of magnitude further. More to the point, there is no accuracy requirement to keep Δt this small: the physics of viscous dissipation essentially boils down to the exponential decay of deformation modes, which can be well approximated even with large time steps. In numerical lingo, this means that the problem is **stiff**: accuracy is saying it should be fine to take large Δt, but stability is requiring punishingly small Δt. The usual numerical solution is to use **implicit** time integration.

10.5.2 Implicit Treatment

The simplest implicit time integration scheme is called **backward Euler**. In this case it means rather than evaluating the stress tensor based on the old velocities $\vec{u}^n$, we'll base it on the new velocities $\vec{u}^{n+1}$, which of course, we don't know yet, until we get the stress tensor—which again depends on knowing the new velocities. This isn't a paradox: it's merely an *implicit* definition of the new velocities, giving us simultaneous equations we must solve to find them.

Let's first do it with the 1D model problem from the last section. The backward Euler discretization is

$$q_i^{n+1} = q_i^n + \Delta t k \frac{q_{i+1}^{n+1} - 2q_i^{n+1} + q_{i-1}^{n+1}}{\Delta x^2}.$$

This is the ith linear equation: we can complete the system by enforcing, say, no-slip boundary conditions $q_0 = q_{m+1} = 0$, leaving m equations in m unknowns $q_1^{n+1}, \ldots q_m^{n+1}$. Rearranging gives

$$-\frac{\Delta t k}{\Delta x^2} q_{i+1}^{n+1} + \left(1 + \frac{2\Delta t k}{\Delta x^2}\right) q_i^{n+1} - \frac{\Delta t k}{\Delta x^2} q_{i-1}^{n+1} = q_i^n.$$

This can now be thought of as a classic matrix-times-unknown-vector-equals-known-vector problem,

$$\left(I + \frac{\Delta t k}{\Delta x^2} A\right) q^{n+1} = q^n,$$

where I is the identity matrix, and A is a tridiagonal matrix with 2 down the main diagonal and -1 along the sub- and super-diagonals:

$$A = \begin{pmatrix} 2 & -1 & & \\ -1 & 2 & -1 & \\ & \ddots & \ddots & \ddots \\ & & -1 & 2 \end{pmatrix}.$$

This is almost the same, up to scaling, as a 1D version of the Poisson problem for pressure, except now we are increasing the positive diagonal entries even further. The matrix is symmetric positive definite—in fact slightly better conditioned than the pressure matrix thanks to the incremented diagonal—and so solving it with PCG works very efficiently.

Does this solve the stability problem? Well, let's rewrite the ith equation again:

$$\left(1 + \frac{2\Delta t k}{\Delta x^2}\right) q_i^{n+1} = \frac{\Delta t k}{\Delta x^2} q_{i+1}^{n+1} + \frac{\Delta t k}{\Delta x^2} q_{i-1}^{n+1} + q_i^n$$

$$\Rightarrow \quad q_i^{n+1} = \left(\frac{\Delta t k/\Delta x^2}{1 + 2\Delta t k/\Delta x^2}\right) q_{i+1}^{n+1} + \left(\frac{\Delta t k/\Delta x^2}{1 + 2\Delta t k/\Delta x^2}\right) q_{i-1}^{n+1}$$

$$+ \left(\frac{1}{1 + 2\Delta t k/\Delta x^2}\right) q_i^n.$$

That is, the new value at a grid point is a weighted average (with guaranteed positive weights, summing to 1) of its neighbors' new values and the old value at that grid point. Here we're including ghost values of q in the boundaries for some of those averages. Therefore, the maximum new value of q has to be less than or equal to the maximum old value of q, and similarly the minimum new value of q has to be greater than or equal to the minimum old value. So unstable growth is impossible. A more detailed analysis further can prove that spurious oscillations (the unphysical vibration we could hit before) are ruled out as well. This is all true no matter how large Δt is taken: it's unconditionally stable and monotone![9]

10.5.3 Variational Form of Implicit Integration

Before we get back to the full 3D problem of viscosity, we will take one more step with this 1D model problem. The issue is that the free surface boundary condition in 3D, $(\nabla \vec{u} + \nabla \vec{u}^T)\hat{n} = 0$, is difficult to directly incorporate into finite differences. To make progress, we need another tool in our belt: the calculus of variations. We hinted at this before in Chapter 8, discussing surface tension. Here we will use it to rephrase an implicit, Backwards Euler step as the search for a velocity field which minimizes a special quantity. Batty and Bridson [BB08] introduced this numerical approach to viscosity specifically because it naturally captures the free surface boundary condition without any extra work.

This might just be the most intimidating bit of math in this book. I'm including it because I think it is one of the most wonderful tools in applied

---

[9]This of course doesn't mean we're necessarily getting the correct answer if Δt is very large—there is still an approximation error. However, a Fourier analysis can show that for large Δt the only "problem" is that the diffusion, the exponential decay of all the deformation modes, is effectively slower than it should be, though it still takes place.

mathematics, and worth seeing, but if you have a tough time following this, don't worry: you can skip on to the next section and just trust that the math there can be justified.

Instead of discretizing first in space and then in time, let's discretize the 1D problem $\partial q/\partial t = k\partial^2 q/\partial x^2$ first in time, with Backwards Euler:

$$q^{n+1} = q^n + \Delta tk\frac{\partial^2 q^{n+1}}{\partial x^2}.$$

We will want the analog of free-surface boundaries, by setting $\partial q/\partial x = 0$ at $x = 0, 1$. We already have an idea that the solution q^{n+1} will be like a smoothed out version of q^n: the smaller Δtk is the closer q^{n+1} will be to q^n, and the bigger Δtk is the more it will be smoothed out to a fully diffused constant average value.

For any 1D function q, take a look at this special combination of integrals on the interval $[0, 1]$:

$$E[q] = \int_0^1 \frac{1}{2}\Big(q(x) - q^n(x)\Big)^2 dx + \int_0^1 \frac{\Delta tk}{2}\left(\frac{\partial q(x)}{\partial x}\right)^2 dx.$$

This "functional" $E[q]$ takes a function q and returns a single real number which is a sum of two terms. The first term measures how far q is from q_n, by integrating the squared difference; the second term measures how big the first spatial derivative of q is, i.e. how far from being constant q is, and is weighted by Δtk. Assuming $k > 0$ and $\Delta t > 0$, also note that $E[q]$ is always non-negative, since it's integrating positive factors times squares.

We can then ask for what function q does $E[q]$ take a minimal value? If E were a regular function that took numbers instead of functions as its argument, we could use the usual calculus trick of looking for where the derivative of E is zero—but it's a bit of a leap to take the derivative of a functional with respect to another function!

There is a clever end-run around this though. Suppose that $q(x)$ actually was the function for which $E[q]$ is minimized.[10] Now say that $r(x)$ is any nonzero smooth function on $[0, 1]$, and define the *regular* function $g(s)$ as follows:

$$g(s) = E[q + sr]$$
$$= \int_0^1 \frac{1}{2}\Big(q(x) + sr(x) - q^n(x)\Big)^2 dx + \int_0^1 \frac{\Delta tk}{2}\left(\frac{\partial q(x)}{\partial x} + s\frac{\partial r(x)}{\partial x}\right)^2 dx.$$

---

[10]We actually are assuming a lot here, both that a minimum is achieved by any function, and that it is unique: some higher-powered math is required to make this all rigorous, but the derivation we're following gives the right impression of what's going on nevertheless.

The important thing to keep in mind is that $g(s)$ just maps a single real number s to another real number: the definition is a bit complicated, but our usual calculus approach can be used on it. In fact, let's rewrite $g(s)$ a bit to show that it's nothing more complicated than a quadratic equation, with some fancy but constant coefficients. We'll multiply out the squared terms in the integrals, and then move the factor s out of the integrals since it is just a real number, not a function of x:

$$g(s) = \int_0^1 \frac{1}{2} \left((q(x) - q^n(x))^2 + 2 \left(q(x) - q^n(x) \right) r(x)s + r(x)^2 s^2 \right) dx$$

$$+ \int_0^1 \frac{\Delta t k}{2} \left(\left(\frac{\partial q(x)}{\partial x} \right)^2 + 2 \frac{\partial q(x)}{\partial x} \frac{\partial r(x)}{\partial x} s + \left(\frac{\partial r(x)}{\partial x} \right)^2 s^2 \right) dx$$

$$= \left[\int_0^1 \frac{1}{2} \left(q(x) - q^n(x) \right)^2 dx + \int_0^1 \frac{\Delta t k}{2} \left(\frac{\partial q(x)}{\partial x} \right)^2 dx \right]$$

$$+ \left[\int_0^1 \left(q(x) - q^n(x) \right) r(x)\, dx + \int_0^1 \Delta t k \left(\frac{\partial q(x)}{\partial x} \frac{\partial r(x)}{\partial x} \right) dx \right] s$$

$$+ \left[\int_0^1 \frac{1}{2} r(x)^2\, dx + \int_0^1 \frac{\Delta t k}{2} \left(\frac{\partial r(x)}{\partial x} \right)^2 dx \right] s^2$$

$$= C + Bs + As^2.$$

Now, under the assumption that $q(x)$ is the true minimum of $E[q]$, it must be the case that $g(s) = E[q + sr]$ is minimized at $s = 0$. Otherwise, the function $q(x) + sr(x)$ would have an E value even lower than the minimum! If $s = 0$ is the minimum of the quadratic function $g(s) = C + Bs + As^2$, then $g'(0) = B$ has to be zero.

That is, we have argued that if $q(x)$ minimizes the functional $E[q]$, then for any smooth function $r(x)$, we must have that

$$\left[\int_0^1 \left(q(x) - q^n(x) \right) r(x)\, dx + \int_0^1 \Delta t k \left(\frac{\partial q(x)}{\partial x} \frac{\partial r(x)}{\partial x} \right) dx \right] = 0.$$

It's nice to have an equation, but it doesn't tell us much about the minimizing function $q(x)$ yet. Let's use another calculus trick, integration-by-parts, on the second integral:

$$\int_0^1 \left(q(x) - q^n(x) \right) r(x)\, dx - \int_0^1 \Delta t k \left(\frac{\partial^2 q(x)}{\partial x^2} r(x) \right) dx + \left[\frac{\partial q(x)}{\partial x} r(x) \right]_0^1 = 0.$$

We can now unite the integrals, identifying a common factor of $r(x)$:

$$\int_0^1 \left(q(x) - q^n(x) - \Delta t k \frac{\partial^2 q(x)}{\partial x^2} \right) r(x)\, dx + \left[\frac{\partial q(x)}{\partial x} r(x) \right]_0^1 = 0.$$

This last equation has to hold no matter what we choose for the nonzero function $r(x)$. With each choice of $r(x)$, of course the quadratic $g(s)$ has different coefficients, but the argument still holds giving us this equation. The only way this integral, plus the boundary terms, can always evaluate to zero regardless of the choice of $r(x)$ is if

$$\left(q(x) - q^n(x) - \Delta t k \frac{\partial^2 q(x)}{\partial x^2} \right) = 0$$

for all $x \in (0, 1)$, and at the boundary if

$$\left. \frac{\partial q(x)}{\partial x} \right|_{x=0} = 0 \quad \left. \frac{\partial q(x)}{\partial x} \right|_{x=1} = 0.$$

That is, the function q which minimizes $E[q]$ has to satisfy this differential equation in $(0, 1)$,

$$q(x) = q^n(x) + \Delta t k \frac{\partial^2 q(x)}{\partial x^2},$$

and also is subject to the "free" boundary condition $\partial q / \partial x = 0$ at the ends of the domain.

This gives us a new way to express Backwards Euler: instead of working straight from the PDE, we can instead say the next time step function q^{n+1} is whatever minimizes $E[q]$. The marvellous bonus is that this automatically implies the free boundary conditions without any extra work.

In fact, we can discretize $E[q]$ in space, approximating the integrals with sums over n discrete intervals:

$$E[q] \approx E_{\Delta x}[q] = \sum_{i=0}^{n} \frac{\omega_i}{2} \left(q_i - q_i^n \right)^2 \Delta x + \sum_{i=0}^{n-1} \frac{\Delta t k}{2} \left(\frac{q_{i+1} - q_i}{\Delta x} \right)^2 \Delta x$$

The special weight ω_i is 1 except at the ends of the interval $i = 0, n$ where $\omega_0 = \omega_n = 1/2$, in order to give a consistent estimate of the integral.

Once we have a discrete $E_{\Delta x}[q]$, our actual Backwards Euler step is defined by minimizing it. With some effort (which we won't go through here), you can show that $E_{\Delta x}[q]$ is just a big quadratic in q, and setting its gradient with respect to q_i to zero gives the i'th linear equation we derived for Backwards Euler already. However, the important point is that the discrete solution will again automatically satisfy free boundary conditions $\partial q / \partial x = 0$ without us having to explicitly handle them.

10.5.4　Implicit Viscosity with Free Surfaces

At last we have the tools we need to do an accurate viscous solve, with free surfaces included. Following Batty and Bridson [BB08], we look for the new velocity field which minimizes the energy

$$E[\vec{u}] = \iiint_\Omega \frac{\rho}{2}\|\vec{u} - \vec{u}^P\|^2 + \iiint_\Omega \Delta t\mu \left\|\frac{\nabla\vec{u} + \nabla\vec{u}^T}{2}\right\|_F^2$$

The new velocity field (which will be $\vec{u}^{n+1}$, the finalized velocity at the end of the time step) is thus a balance between staying close to $\vec{u}^P$ (the velocity after pressure projection) and trying to eliminate all deformation to get just rigid motion, with the exact balance decided by the density, the time step, and the viscosity coefficient. At solid boundaries we enforce $\vec{u} = \vec{u}_{\text{solid}}$, but at free surfaces we don't have to do anything special, thanks to the variational magic. This will give us a stable Backwards Euler step of viscosity.

To discretize in space, we just approximate $E[\vec{u}]$ with sums and finite differences as above. For a basic first order accurate solution, which nevertheless gives all the right visual behavior of viscous flow, it suffices to simply include in the sums those staggered grid points which are inside the fluid, without any special weights. The first integral then breaks up into three sums:

$$\iiint_\Omega \frac{\rho}{2}\|\vec{u} - \vec{u}^P\|^2$$

$$= \iiint_\Omega \frac{\rho}{2}(u - u^P)^2 + \iiint_\Omega \frac{\rho}{2}(v - v^P)^2 + \iiint_\Omega \frac{\rho}{2}(w - w^P)^2$$

$$\approx \sum_{(i+1/2,j,k)\in\Omega} \frac{\rho_{i+1/2,j,k}}{2}(u_{i+1/2,j,k} - u^P_{i+1/2,j,k})^2 \Delta x^3 +$$

$$+ \sum_{(i,j+1/2,k)\in\Omega} \frac{\rho_{i,j+1/2,k}}{2}(v_{i,j+1/2,k} - v^P_{i,j+1/2,k})^2 \Delta x^3 +$$

$$+ \sum_{(i,j,k+1/2)\in\Omega} \frac{\rho_{i,j,k+1/2}}{2}(w_{i,j,k+1/2} - w^P_{i,j,k+1/2})^2 \Delta x^3$$

Here the sums are over staggered grid points where the fluid velocity is going to be defined, say where the liquid-air level set interpolates to negative but the solid level set interpolates to positive. Note that the fluid density ρ can vary across the grid.

The second integral similarly breaks up into six sums, one for each of the distinct components of the Frobenius norm, taking into account symmetry. We switch to short-hand derivative notation again for brevity:

$$\left\|\frac{\nabla\vec{u} + \nabla\vec{u}^T}{2}\right\|_F^2 =$$

$$u_x^2 + \tfrac{1}{4}(u_y + v_x)^2 + \tfrac{1}{4}(u_z + w_x)^2 + v_y^2 + \tfrac{1}{4}(v_z + w_y)^2 + w_z^2$$

Let's look at the first two of these for example, u_x^2 and $\frac{1}{4}(u_y + v_x)^2$, approximating their integrals separately as a sum over the staggered grid points (i, j, k) and $(i+1/2, j+1/2, k)$ respectively, inside the fluid domain. By *inside* we mean that all the nearby velocity values used in the finite difference are either real fluid velocities (appearing in the sums above) or are solid velocities (which we use from the solid, respecting the no-slip boundary condition). The first:

$$\iiint_\Omega \Delta t \mu u_x^2 \approx \sum_{i,j,k} \Delta t \mu_{i,j,k} \left(\frac{u_{i+1/2,j,k} - u_{i-1/2,j,k}}{\Delta x} \right)^2 \Delta x^3.$$

The second:

$$\iiint_\Omega \frac{\Delta t \mu}{4} (u_y + v_x)^2 \approx$$

$$\sum \frac{\Delta t \mu}{4} \left(\frac{u_{i+1/2,j+1,k} - u_{i+1/2,j,k} + v_{i+1,j+1/2,k} - v_{i,j+1/2,k}}{\Delta x} \right)^2 \Delta x^3.$$

I left the indices off the dynamic viscosity coefficient $\mu_{i+1/2,j+1/2,k}$ in the second to save space, but as with ρ it can vary across the domain for variable or non-Newtonian viscosity simulations. If the viscosity coefficient is only specified at grid points, then the appropriate averages can be used to estimate it at staggered locations.

Once we have these discrete sums in hand, we can differentiate with respect to the unknown velocities and set the gradient to zero to find the minimizer. This will be a system of linear equations (SPD as before, so PCG works) to solve for the new velocity field. Here is the equation taken from differentiating $E_{\Delta x}[\vec{u}]$ by $u_{i+1/2,j,k}$, for example, and dropping the Δx^3 common factor:

$$\rho_{i+1/2,j,k}(u_{i+1/2,j,k} - u_{i+1/2,j,k}^P)$$

$$+ 2\Delta t \mu_{i,j,k} \left(\frac{u_{i+1/2,j,k} - u_{i-1/2,j,k}}{\Delta x^2} \right)$$

$$- 2\Delta t \mu_{i+1,j,k} \left(\frac{u_{i+3/2,j,k} - u_{i+1/2,j,k}}{\Delta x^2} \right)$$

$$+ \frac{\Delta t \mu_{i+1/2,j-1/2,k}}{2} \left(\frac{u_{i+1/2,j,k} - u_{i+1/2,j-1,k} + v_{i+1,j-1/2,k} - v_{i,j-1/2,k}}{\Delta x^2} \right)$$

$$- \frac{\Delta t \mu_{i+1/2,j+1/2,k}}{2} \left(\frac{u_{i+1/2,j+1,k} - u_{i+1/2,j,k} + v_{i+1,j+1/2,k} - v_{i,j+1/2,k}}{\Delta x^2} \right)$$

$$+ \frac{\Delta t \mu_{i+1/2,j,k-1/2}}{2} \left(\frac{u_{i+1/2,j,k} - u_{i+1/2,j,k-1} + w_{i+1,j,k-1/2} - w_{i,j,k-1/2}}{\Delta x^2} \right)$$

$$- \frac{\Delta t \mu_{i+1/2,j,k+1/2}}{2} \left(\frac{u_{i+1/2,j,k+1} - u_{i+1/2,j,k} + w_{i+1,j,k+1/2} - w_{i,j,k+1/2}}{\Delta x^2} \right)$$

$$= 0.$$

Here any velocity values that lie inside the solid should be replaced by the known solid velocity. Entire terms that involve one or more velocity samples "in the air", neither in the solid nor the fluid, should be dropped entirely, even if some of the velocities are fluid velocities. This is a consequence of how the energy is defined (summing just over grid points where the deformation rate is well-defined) and is what gives us the correct free-surface boundary condition.

The equations corresponding to $v_{i,j+1/2,k}$ and $w_{i,j,k+1/2}$ can similarly be derived to complete the system of equations:

$$\rho_{i,j+1/2,k}(v_{i,j+1/2,k} - v_{i,j+1/2,k}^P)$$

$$+ 2\Delta t \mu_{i,j,k} \left(\frac{v_{i,j+1/2,k} - v_{i,j-1/2,k}}{\Delta x^2} \right)$$

$$- 2\Delta t \mu_{i,j+1,k} \left(\frac{v_{i,j+3/2,k} - v_{i,j+1/2,k}}{\Delta x^2} \right)$$

$$+ \frac{\Delta t \mu_{i-1/2,j+1/2,k}}{2} \left(\frac{u_{i-1/2,j+1,k} - u_{i-1/2,j,k} + v_{i,j+1/2,k} - v_{i-1,j+1/2,k}}{\Delta x^2} \right)$$

$$- \frac{\Delta t \mu_{i+1/2,j+1/2,k}}{2} \left(\frac{u_{i+1/2,j+1,k} - u_{i+1/2,j,k} + v_{i+1,j+1/2,k} - v_{i,j+1/2,k}}{\Delta x^2} \right)$$

$$+ \frac{\Delta t \mu_{i,j+1/2,k-1/2}}{2} \left(\frac{v_{i,j+1/2,k} - v_{i,j+1/2,k-1} + w_{i,j+1,k-1/2} - w_{i,j,k-1/2}}{\Delta x^2} \right)$$

$$- \frac{\Delta t \mu_{i,j+1/2,k+1/2}}{2} \left(\frac{v_{i,j+1/2,k+1} - v_{i,j+1/2,k} + w_{i,j+1,k+1/2} - w_{i,j,k+1/2}}{\Delta x^2} \right)$$

$$= 0,$$

$$\rho_{i,j,k+1/2}\left(w_{i,j,k+1/2} - w^P_{i,j,k+1/2}\right)$$

$$+ 2\Delta t\mu_{i,j,k}\left(\frac{w_{i,j,k+1/2} - w_{i,j,k-1/2}}{\Delta x^2}\right)$$

$$- 2\Delta t\mu_{i,j,k+1}\left(\frac{w_{i,j,k+3/2} - w_{i,j,k+1/2}}{\Delta x^2}\right)$$

$$+ \frac{\Delta t\mu_{i-1/2,j,k+1/2}}{2}\left(\frac{u_{i-1/2,j,k+1} - u_{i-1/2,j,k} + w_{i,j,k+1/2} - w_{i-1,j,k+1/2}}{\Delta x^2}\right)$$

$$- \frac{\Delta t\mu_{i+1/2,j,k+1/2}}{2}\left(\frac{u_{i+1/2,j,k+1} - u_{i+1/2,j,k} + w_{i+1,j,k+1/2} - w_{i,j,k+1/2}}{\Delta x^2}\right)$$

$$+ \frac{\Delta t\mu_{i,j-1/2,k+1/2}}{2}\left(\frac{v_{i,j-1/2,k+1} - v_{i,j-1/2,k} + w_{i,j,k+1/2} - w_{i,j-1,k+1/2}}{\Delta x^2}\right)$$

$$- \frac{\Delta t\mu_{i,j+1/2,k+1/2}}{2}\left(\frac{v_{i,j+1/2,k+1} - v_{i,j+1/2,k} + w_{i,j+1,k+1/2} - w_{i,j,k+1/2}}{\Delta x^2}\right)$$

$$= 0.$$

Rearranging these into sparse matrix and vector form is left to you.

Part III

More Algorithms

Turbulence

This chapter takes a look at methods aimed to capture more of the fine-scale swirly motion characteristic of turbulence. This is far from a scientific examination of turbulence, and in fact scientific work on the subject tends to concentrate on averaging or smoothing over the details of turbulent velocity fields—whereas we want to get to those details as cheaply as possible, even if they fall short of true accuracy.

11.1 Vorticity

Our first stop is getting at a precise measurement of the "swirliness" characteristic of turbulent flow. That is, at any point in space, we would like to measure how the fluid is rotating. In Chapter 10 on viscosity we saw how the gradient of the velocity field gives a matrix whose symmetric part measures deformation—independent of rigid body motions. It's not surprising then that what's left over, the skew-symmetric part, gives us information about rotation. (And of course, $\vec{u}$ itself without any derivatives tells us the translational component of the motion.)

Let's take a look at a generic rigid motion velocity field in 3D:

$$\vec{u}(\vec{x}) = \vec{U} + \vec{\Omega} \times \vec{x}.$$

Here $\vec{U}$ is the translation, and $\vec{\Omega}$ is the angular velocity measured around the origin. Let's work out the gradient of this velocity field in three dimensions to see how we can extract the angular velocity:

$$\frac{\partial \vec{u}}{\partial \vec{x}} = \frac{\partial}{\partial \vec{x}} \begin{pmatrix} U_1 + \Omega_2 z - \Omega_3 y \\ U_2 + \Omega_3 x - \Omega_1 z \\ U_3 + \Omega_1 y - \Omega_2 x \end{pmatrix}$$

$$= \begin{pmatrix} 0 & -\Omega_3 & \Omega_2 \\ \Omega_3 & 0 & -\Omega_1 \\ -\Omega_2 & \Omega_1 & 0 \end{pmatrix}.$$

Thus for a rigid body rotation, the gradient has no symmetric part—there's no deformation after all—and the skew-symmetric part lets us read out the components of angular velocity directly.

Take a look at the skew-symmetric part of the velocity gradient (in general, not just for rigid body motions):

$$\frac{1}{2}\left(\frac{\partial \vec{u}}{\partial \vec{x}} - \frac{\partial \vec{u}}{\partial \vec{x}}^T\right) = \frac{1}{2}\begin{pmatrix} 0 & \frac{\partial u}{\partial y} - \frac{\partial v}{\partial x} & \frac{\partial u}{\partial z} - \frac{\partial w}{\partial x} \\ \frac{\partial v}{\partial x} - \frac{\partial u}{\partial y} & 0 & \frac{\partial v}{\partial z} - \frac{\partial w}{\partial y} \\ \frac{\partial w}{\partial x} - \frac{\partial u}{\partial z} & \frac{\partial w}{\partial y} - \frac{\partial v}{\partial z} & 0 \end{pmatrix}.$$

Reading off the local measure of angular velocity this represents, just as we saw in the rigid case, we get

$$\vec{\Omega}(\vec{x}) = \frac{1}{2}\left(\frac{\partial w}{\partial y} - \frac{\partial v}{\partial z},\ \frac{\partial u}{\partial z} - \frac{\partial w}{\partial x},\ \frac{\partial v}{\partial x} - \frac{\partial u}{\partial y}\right).$$

This is exactly half the curl of the velocity field.

In fact we define **vorticity** $\vec{\omega}$ to be the curl of the velocity field, which will then be twice the local angular velocity. Again, in three dimensions this is a vector:

$$\vec{\omega} = \nabla \times \vec{u}$$
$$= \left(\frac{\partial w}{\partial y} - \frac{\partial v}{\partial z},\ \frac{\partial u}{\partial z} - \frac{\partial w}{\partial x},\ \frac{\partial v}{\partial x} - \frac{\partial u}{\partial y}\right).$$

In two dimensions it reduces to a scalar:

$$\omega = \nabla \times \vec{u} = \frac{\partial v}{\partial x} - \frac{\partial u}{\partial y}.$$

This turns out to be one of the most useful "derived" quantities for a fluid flow.

Take the curl of the momentum equation (1.1), assuming constant viscosity:

$$\nabla \times \frac{\partial \vec{u}}{\partial t} + \nabla \times (\vec{u} \cdot \nabla \vec{u}) + \nabla \times \left(\frac{1}{\rho}\nabla p\right) = \nabla \times \vec{g} + \nabla \times \nu \nabla \cdot \nabla \vec{u}.$$

Switching the order of some derivatives, and assuming that density ρ is constant so it can be brought outside the curl for the pressure term, gives

$$\frac{\partial \nabla \times \vec{u}}{\partial t} + \nabla \times (\vec{u} \cdot \nabla \vec{u}) + \frac{1}{\rho}\nabla \times \nabla p = \nabla \times \vec{g} + \nu \nabla \cdot \nabla(\nabla \times \vec{u}).$$

Recalling that the curl of a gradient is automatically zero (see Appendix A for identities such as this) and assuming that $\vec{g}$ is constant or the gradient of some potential, and substituting in vorticity, reduces this to

$$\frac{\partial \vec{\omega}}{\partial t} + \nabla \times (\vec{u} \cdot \nabla \vec{u}) = \nu \nabla \cdot \nabla \vec{\omega}.$$

The advection term can be simplified with some work (and exploiting the divergence-free condition $\nabla \cdot \vec{u} = 0$) to eventually get, in three dimensions:

$$\frac{\partial \vec{\omega}}{\partial t} + \vec{u} \cdot \nabla \vec{\omega} = -\omega \cdot \nabla \vec{u} + \nu \nabla \cdot \nabla \vec{\omega}. \tag{11.1}$$

This is known as the **vorticity equation**, which you can see has the material derivative $D\vec{\omega}/Dt$ on the left-hand side, a viscosity term on the right-hand side, and a new term $\vec{\omega} \cdot \nabla \vec{u}$, which we can write in components as

$$\vec{\omega} \cdot \nabla \vec{u} = \begin{pmatrix} \omega_1 \frac{\partial u}{\partial x} + \omega_2 \frac{\partial v}{\partial x} + \omega_3 \frac{\partial w}{\partial x} \\ \omega_1 \frac{\partial u}{\partial y} + \omega_2 \frac{\partial v}{\partial y} + \omega_3 \frac{\partial w}{\partial y} \\ \omega_1 \frac{\partial u}{\partial z} + \omega_2 \frac{\partial v}{\partial z} + \omega_3 \frac{\partial w}{\partial z} \end{pmatrix}.$$

This term is sometimes called the **vortex-stretching** term from a geometric point of view which we won't get into in this book. In two dimensions, the vorticity equation actually simplifies further: the vortex-stretching term is automatically zero. (This is easy to verify if you think of a 2D flow as being a slice through a 3D flow with u and v constant along the z-direction and $w = 0$.) Here it is in 2D, now written with the material derivative to emphasize the simplicity:

$$\frac{D\omega}{Dt} = \nu \nabla \cdot \nabla \omega. \tag{11.2}$$

In fact, if we are talking about inviscid flow where viscosity is negligible (as we have done throughout this book except in Chapter 10 on highly viscous flow), the 2D vorticity equation reduces simply to $D\omega/Dt = 0$. That is, vorticity doesn't change, but is just advected with the flow.

It turns out you can build an attractive fluid solver based on vorticity, particularly in 2D where the equation is even simpler, though there are decidedly non-trivial complications for boundary conditions and reconstructing the velocity field for advection from vorticity (more on this in Chapter 14). For example, Yaeger et al. [YUM86], Gamito et al. [Gam95], Angelidis et al. [AN05, ANSN06], Park and Kim [PK05], and Elcott et al. [ETK+07] have all taken this route. However, our chief concern now is in what happens to vorticity in our regular fluid solver, based on velocity and pressure.

We already know that we run the risk of numerical dissipation in our Eulerian advection schemes: we saw that for first-order linear interpolation, the error behaves like additional viscosity, and so it should be no surprise that the vorticity of the velocity field similarly gets dissipated. So far we've dealt with this by increasing the sharpness of the interpolation—though even this doesn't fully avoid dissipation—or switching to particles with FLIP. However, this is not the only cause of vorticity dissipation.

   The other big source lies in the time-splitting algorithm itself. We mentioned before that our algorithm for separately advecting and then projecting velocity is only first-order accurate in time; it turns out this can be a fairly problematic error when attempting to capture small-scale vortices. As a motivating example, imagine starting with just a 2D rigid rotation of constant-density fluid around the origin, say

$$\vec{u}^0 = (-y, x).$$

Ignoring boundary conditions and body forces, the exact solution of the Navier-Stokes equations, given this initial velocity field, is for $\vec{u}$ to stay constant—the rotation should continue at exactly the same speed. However, if we advance it with our time-splitting algorithm, things go wrong. Even with *perfect* error-free advection, for a time step of $\Delta t = \frac{1}{2}\pi$ which corresponds in this velocity field to a counterclockwise rotation of 90°, we get this intermediate velocity field:

$$\vec{u}^A = (x, y).$$

It no longer has any vorticity (easy to check) and moreover is divergent: our advection step transferred all the energy from rotation to expansion. It's not hard to verify that the pressure solution is

$$p = \frac{x^2 + y^2}{2\pi\rho}.$$

After updating the intermediate velocity field with this pressure, we end up with

$$\vec{u}^{n+1} = 0.$$

Oops! The flow comes to a standstill, never to move again. If we had taken a smaller time step it would have just been slowed down, but only in the limit $\Delta t \to 0$ does it approach the vorticity it should be preserving. (If we had taken a larger time step, the fluid might even have reversed direction and rotated the other way!)

   In fact, at least when density is constant, since the curl of a gradient is automatically zero the pressure projection stage can't affect the fluid's vorticity: the damage is already done when we advect velocities. With a little more effort, it's not hard to verify that starting with a rigid rotation of vorticity ω, one time step of perfect advection will change that to vorticity $\omega \cos(\omega \Delta t/2)$. If Δt is small enough, this is approximately

$$\omega_{n+1} \approx \left(1 - \frac{\omega_n^2 \Delta t^2}{8}\right) \omega_n.$$

Thus our next step is to look at a way of adding back some of the missing vorticity.

11.2 Vorticity Confinement

The **vorticity confinement** technique developed by Steinhoff and Underhill [SU94] is a modification of the Navier-Stokes equations by a term that tries to preserve vorticity. Fedkiw et al. [FSJ01] introduced it to graphics, introducing a Δx factor so that in the limit (as the grid is refined) the term disappears and we get back the true fluid solution. The underlying idea is to detect where vortices are located and add a body force to boost the rotational motion around each vortex.

In this context, a vortex is loosely speaking a peak in the vorticity field, a place that's spinning faster than all the fluid nearby. We can construct unit vectors $\vec{N}$ that point to these maximum points simply by normalizing the gradient of $\|\vec{\omega}\|$:

$$\vec{N} = \frac{\nabla\|\vec{\omega}\|}{\|\nabla\|\vec{\omega}\|\|}.$$

Now $\vec{N}$ points toward the center of rotation of a vortex, and $\vec{\omega}$ itself points along the axis of rotation, so to get a force vector that increases the rotation, we just take a cross-product:

$$f_{\text{conf}} = \epsilon\Delta x(\vec{N} \times \vec{\omega}).$$

The ϵ here is a parameter that can be adjusted to control the effect of vorticity confinement. The Δx factor, as mentioned above, makes this physically consistent: as we refine the grid and Δx tends to zero, the erroneous numerical dissipation of vorticity also tends to zero, so our fix should too.

Let's step through numerically implementing this. We begin by averaging velocities from the MAC grid to the cell centers (as discussed in Chapter 2) and then use central derivatives to approximate the vorticity:[1]

$$\vec{\omega}_{i,j,k} = \left(\frac{w_{i,j+1,k} - w_{i,j-1,k}}{2\Delta x} - \frac{v_{i,j,k+1} - v_{i,j,k-1}}{2\Delta x}, \right.$$

$$\frac{u_{i,j,k+1} - u_{i,j,k-1}}{2\Delta x} - \frac{w_{i+1,j,k} - w_{i-1,j,k}}{2\Delta x},$$

$$\left. \frac{v_{i+1,j,k} - v_{i-1,j,k}}{2\Delta x} - \frac{u_{i,j+1,k} - u_{i,j-1,k}}{2\Delta x} \right).$$

The gradient of $\|\vec{\omega}\|$ is similarly estimated with central differences at the

---

[1]Note that the null-space problem we discussed earlier isn't particularly alarming here: we just will lack the ability to "see" and boost the very smallest vortices. We still get the benefit of boosting slightly larger ones.

grid cell centers, for use in defining $\vec{N}$:

$$\nabla\|\vec{\omega}\|_{i,j,k} = \left(\frac{\|\vec{\omega}\|_{i+1,j,k} - \|\vec{\omega}\|_{i-1,j,k}}{2\Delta x}, \ \frac{\|\vec{\omega}\|_{i,j+1,k} - \|\vec{\omega}\|_{i,j-1,k}}{2\Delta x}, \ \frac{\|\vec{\omega}\|_{i,j,k+1} - \|\vec{\omega}\|_{i,j,k-1}}{2\Delta x} \right).$$

When we normalize this to get $\vec{N}$, we should of course guard against a divide-by-zero by using, for example,

$$\vec{N}_{i,j,k} = \frac{\nabla\|\vec{\omega}\|_{i,j,k}}{\|\nabla\|\vec{\omega}\|_{i,j,k}\| + 10^{-20}M},$$

where M is a characteristic value of units $\text{m}^{-1}\text{s}^{-1}$ for the simulation—nothing to be too concerned about; $M = 1/(\Delta x \Delta t)$ is fine just to make sure this scales properly. Finally, we take the cross-product to get f_{conf} at the grid cell centers; we can take the appropriate averages to apply this to the different components of velocity on the MAC grid.

Ideally we would connect the confinement parameter ϵ with the expected numerical dissipation of vorticity. However, this has yet to be done, but in the meantime serves as another tweakable parameter for the simulation. If set too high, the simulation can go quasi-unstable, reducing the velocity field to essentially just random chaos; more moderate values encourage fine-scale vortices and keep the flow more lively.

Finding a single number which restores some of the lost vorticity where we feel the flow is too boring, but which doesn't break up coherent features like smoke rings which we like, is tricky. Often we want a more localized way of injecting apparent turbulence into only some regions. Selle et al. [SRF05] provide just such a tool. The core of their idea is to seed extra "spin particles"[2] in regions where we want turbulence, which are advected with the flow, and whose strength is added into a local per-grid-cell vorticity confinement parameter.

11.3   Procedural Turbulence

Ultimately, there is a practical limit to the resolution a fluid simulator can run at. For an $n \times n \times n$ grid, we obviously require $O(n^3)$ memory—and the hidden constant is a bit hefty, as you can see when you add up all the additional arrays needed for time integration, pressure solves, etc. Furthermore, if we keep Δt proportional to Δx as recommended, and use the MICCG(0)

---

[2]Selle et al. call these vortex particles, but this is a bit confusing compared to the usual meaning of vortex particles, coming up in Chapter 14, so I prefer to call them spin particles.

linear solver developed in Chapter 5 which requires $O(\sqrt{n})$ iterations to converge, we end up with the total cost of a simulation scaling like $O(n^{4.5})$. That puts a pretty severe bottleneck on going to higher resolution.

However, real turbulence can show features—vortices—on a huge range of length scales. As a point of reference, for example, turbulence in the atmosphere can span from kilometers down to millimeters. There simply is no practical way to directly simulate with a grid capable of capturing that range ($n \sim 10^5$). However, the turbulent features below a certain length scale tend to lose structure and become isotropic and easily described statistically: if you filter out the large-scale motion of the fluid and zoom in on just the small-scale turbulence, any region looks pretty much like any other region. This is our saving grace. Below the scale of the actual simulation, we can add in procedural models of turbulent velocity fields to fake additional detail. For turbulent smoke, instead of tracking the grid-level smoke concentration field, we instead trace and render millions of marker particles running through this enhanced velocity field (see Rasmussen et al. [RNGF03], for example).

We now take a look at two approaches to generating the required procedural velocity fields. The critical requirements are allowing control over the spectrum of the velocity (i.e., looking at the velocity variation over different length-scales) and making sure the velocity is still divergence-free.

11.3.1   Fourier Synthesis

One of the simpler methods for generating plausible turbulent velocity fields is to do it in Fourier space. If we take the Fourier transform of a velocity field $\vec{u}(\vec{x})$, which we'll assume is periodic over a cube of side length L, we can write it as

$$\vec{u}(\vec{x}) = \sum_{i,j,k=-\infty}^{\infty} \hat{u}_{ijk} e^{\sqrt{-1}2\pi(ix+jy+kz)/L}.$$

Here we're using $\sqrt{-1}$ as a symbol to denote an imaginary number, instead of the more common i or j since this book uses i and j as indices. This Fourier series is also obviously using complex exponentials instead of sines and cosines, which implies the Fourier coefficients $\hat{u}_{ijk}$ may be complex even though $\vec{u}$ is real-valued: this helps to simplify some of the other notation, and more to the point, matches the API of most Fast Fourier Transform packages. Note also that the Fourier coefficients $\hat{u}_{ijk}$ are 3D vectors of complex numbers, not just scalars: you can think of this really being the Fourier transform of u, the separate Fourier transform of v, and the further separate Fourier transform of w all wrapped up into one equation.

In practice, of course, we'll use just a discrete Fourier transform, over an $m \times m \times m$ array of Fourier coefficients. The length L should be chosen large enough that the periodic tiling isn't too conspicuous, but not too large relative to the simulation grid spacing Δx—after all, we won't be able to afford to take m too large, and we want the Fourier grid spacing L/m (the smallest details we'll procedurally add) to be a lot smaller than Δx.

Shinya and Fournier [SF92] and Stam and Fiume [SF93] introduced to graphics perhaps the simplest physically reasonable turbulence model, the Kolmogorov "5/3-law." This states that for fully developed steady-state turbulence, the kinetic energy contained in all the Fourier modes of spatial frequency around ω should scale like $\omega^{-5/3}$. This means that the (i, j, k) Fourier coefficient (with spatial frequency $\omega = \sqrt{i^2 + j^2 + k^2}$) should have magnitude on the order of

$$\|\hat{u}_{ijk}\| \sim (i^2 + j^2 + k^2)^{-11/12}$$

for i, j, k large enough (the low spatial frequencies are assumed to not belong to the isotropic turbulence regime.) We can take it, in fact, to be a random vector uniformly sampled from a ball of radius $C(i^2+j^2+k^2)^{-11/12}$, for some user-tunable constant C. The cut-off frequency, below which we keep $\hat{u}_{ijk}$ zero, should be on the order of $L/\Delta x$ or more, so that we don't add procedural details at scales that were captured in the simulation.

The divergence of velocity becomes a simple algebraic operation on the Fourier series:

$$\nabla \vec{u}(\vec{x}) = \sum_{i,j,k=-\infty}^{\infty} \frac{\sqrt{-1}2\pi}{L} \left[(i, j, k) \cdot \hat{u}_{ijk} \right] e^{\sqrt{-1}2\pi(ix+jy+kz)/L}.$$

Therefore, $\nabla \cdot \vec{u} = 0$ is equivalent to requiring that each Fourier coefficient $\hat{u}_{ijk}$ is perpendicular to its **wave vector** (i, j, k). Making a velocity field divergence-free then simplifies to just fixing each coefficient individually, subtracting off their component in the radial direction—a simple 3D projection.

Finally, once the Fourier coefficients have been determined, an inverse FFT can be applied on each of the u-, $v-$, and w-components to get a grid of plausible velocities. Note that the velocity vectors are sampled at the grid points, all components together—this is not a staggered MAC grid. Trilinear interpolation can be used between grid points for particle advection.

To animate this velocity field in time, the simplest technique (proposed by Rasmussen et al. [RNGF03]) is just to construct two such velocity fields and then cross-fade back and forth between them. The key observation is that while on its own this method of animation falls short of plausibility (and for that matter, the periodicity of the field is objectionable too), this only is added on top of an already detailed simulation. The extra detail is just needed to break up the smooth interpolation between simulation grid points, not to behave perfectly.

11.3.2   Noise

While Fourier synthesis has many advantages—it's fairly efficient and has a nice theoretical background—it has a few problems too, chief among them being the problem of how to control it in space. If you want the turbulence to be stronger in one region than another, or to properly handle a solid wall somewhere in the flow, simultaneously meeting the divergence-free constraint becomes difficult.

An alternative is to forget about Fourier transforms and instead directly construct divergence-free velocity fields from building blocks such as Perlin noise. We get the divergence-free condition by exploiting vector calculus identities. For example, the divergence of the curl of a vector field is always zero:

$$\nabla \cdot (\nabla \times \vec{\psi}) = 0 \quad \text{for all vector fields } \vec{\psi}$$

and the cross-product of two gradients is always divergence free as well:

$$\nabla \cdot (\nabla \phi \times \nabla \psi) = 0 \quad \text{for all scalar fields } \phi \text{ and } \psi.$$

Kniss and Hart [KH04] and Bridson et al. [BHN07] used the first of these formulas, with $\vec{\psi}$ a vector-valued noise function, and DeWolf [DeW05] used the second with ϕ and possibly ψ scalar noise functions (see also von Funck et al. [vFTS06] for an application of this identity in geometric modeling).

To get full turbulence, several octaves of noise can be added in either formula, with an appropriate power-law scaling of magnitudes. For example, using the first formula, **curl-noise**, we might take for the vector potential

$$\vec{\psi}(\vec{x}) = \sum_{p=1}^{m} A_p \vec{N} \left(\frac{C2^p \vec{x}}{\Delta x} \right)$$

and then get the velocity field as

$$\vec{u} = \nabla \times \vec{\psi}.$$

The curl here can be approximated with finite differences for convenience, rather than evaluated exactly. The simulation grid Δx appears here to emphasize that this should be done only for length scales below the simulation.

In addition, the amplitude A_p of each octave of noise can be modulated in space, allowing full control over where turbulence should appear. Bridson et al. [BHN07] in addition show that ramping A_p down to zero at the boundary of a solid causes the velocity field to meet the solid wall boundary condition.

All of these noise formulations can be animated in time, either using 4D noise functions or, more intriguingly, the FlowNoise method of Perlin and Neyret [PN01].

11.4   Simulating Sub-Grid Turbulence

The previous section gives us some tools to add extra turbulent detail beyond the resolution of the core simulation. However, it relies on artistic intervention to decide how much to add. With Fourier synthesis, it is added globally which only really helps if all of the domain should have uniform extra turbulent noise and solid boundaries aren't important. With curl-noise the artist has very detailed control, allowing them to modulate the amplitude of noise, include different scales in varying amounts, and respect solid boundaries with control over the bandwidth of the their effect—but all this control can be overwhelming! Ideally we want a way to automatically modulate the curl-noise, simulating the turbulence we expect should be present in a flow beneath the grid resolution.

This is by no means a solved problem, and in fact touches on a very hard topic in computational fluid dynamics, Large Eddy Simulation (LES), which attempts to model the effect of unresolved small turbulent scales on the fluid simulated on a grid. At this point in time, we just don't know how to do this, and for the most part rely on heuristic formulas backed up by experimental validation, both measured in real fluids and also tested with extremely high resolution, fully resolved computer simulations which go by the name "Direct Numerical Simulation" (DNS).

The two main ideas in sub-grid turbulence modeling are:

- nonlinear effects in the Navier-Stokes equations, like vortex-stretching, cause small grid-scale vortices to evolve at least partly into even smaller vortices below the scale of the grid;

- turbulence below the scale of the grid mostly effects grid-scale features by mixing them up in space, like viscosity would, but at a rate derived from the amplitude of turbulence which is much larger than the fluid's true viscosity.

The last point is sometimes called **turbulent mixing**, and modeling its effect on the grid by a viscosity-like term leads to something called **effective viscosity**. Unfortunately the truth is that while these two effects are important, turbulence can also work the other way: sub-grid vortices can evolve into grid-scale features, and turbulent mixing doesn't always diffuse grid-scale features like viscosity would. However, engineers and scientists regularly get good-enough results with these sorts of subgrid models.

In graphics, there have been a few attempts at simulating turbulence with this. At the simplest end of the spectrum, Kim et al. [KTJG08] modulate several octaves of wavelet-noise-based curl-noise with amplitudes scaled through the octaves like the Kolmogorov fully-developed turbulence spectrum (used above for Fourier synthesis). The amplitudes are chosen automatically by estimating the rate of transfer of energy from the grid-scale simulation into sub-grid modes. Other researchers have looked at tracking and evolving the sub-grid energy as extra fields in the simulation (e.g. [SB08, NSCL08, PTC$^+$10]), drawing inspiration from $k - \epsilon$ models in computational fluid dynamics [JL72, LS74]. A good book (albeit not for the faint of engineering heart) to get up to speed on turbulence is Pope's *Turbulent Flows* [Pop00]. This is an ongoing area of research, both in CFD and graphics; there's a lot to read, a lot still to do, and this is where we will leave it.

Shallow Water

In this chapter and the next we will turn to special cases of water simulation that allow much faster and simpler algorithms. In both cases, we will use the simplifying assumption that the water surface can be represented as a **height field** $y = h(x, z)$: the water region is all of the points where $y < h(x, z)$, excluding solids. The most important solid is of course the bottom, which we also represent as a height field $y = b(x, z)$, giving a water region defined by

$$b(x, z) < y < h(x, z),$$

and thus the water depth is $d(x, z) = h(x, z) - b(x, z)$. We will actually use depth d as a primary simulation variable, reconstructing the height $h = b+d$ as needed. This geometric simplification rules out many interesting effects such as convincing splashes, breaking waves, droplets or sprays, but still allows many interesting wave motions.[1] For the purposes of the book, we'll also restrict the bottom to be stationary—$b(x, z)$ remains constant— though allowing it to move is a fairly easy generalization if you follow the modeling steps in this chapter.

For the height field assumption to remain a good approximation for the water throughout the simulation, we also need to restrict our attention to height fields that aren't too steep and velocities which aren't too extreme: mainly we will be looking at fairly calm waves. For example, a tall column of water can be represented with a height field in the first frame, but when it starts to collapse it is almost bound to start splashing around in more general ways that will rule it out.

While you can of course use the height field representation to track the water surface in conjunction with a full three-dimensional solver as detailed earlier in the book—see Foster and Metaxas [FM96]—we'll make some further approximations to reduce the complexity of the equations. In this chapter we'll look at the case where the water is shallow, i.e., the depth $d = h - b$ is very small compared to the horizontal length scale of waves

---

[1]Many authors have worked out ways to bring back some of these features, usually by way of adding a particle system for the extra effects. For example, see the articles by O'Brien and Hodgins [OH95] and Thürey et al. [TMSG07].

or other flow features, and in the next chapter we'll instead consider the water very deep relative to this scale.

12.1   Deriving the Shallow Water Equations

12.1.1   Assumptions

The shallowness assumption means essentially that we can ignore vertical variations in the velocity field: the fluid doesn't have "room" for vertical features like vortices stacked on top of each other. We'll then just track the **depth-averaged** horizontal velocities, $u(x, z)$ and $w(x, z)$, which are the average of u and w for y varying along the depth of the water. For the inviscid flow we're modeling in this chapter, you can think of u and w as constant along y; for viscous flow a better model would be that u and w vary linearly from zero at the bottom to some maximum velocity at the free surface.

Just as an interjection: the process of depth averaging is used in many more contexts than the one here. For example, avalanches have been modeled this way (the snow layer is thin compared to the extent of the mountainside it flows along) as well as large-scale weather patterns (the atmosphere and oceans are extremely thin compared to the circumference of the Earth). The resulting systems of equations are still commonly called "shallow water equations," even if referring to fluids other than water.

The other fundamental simplification we'll make is assuming hydrostatic pressure. That is, if we look at the vertical component of the momentum equation

$$\frac{\partial v}{\partial t} + u\frac{\partial v}{\partial x} + v\frac{\partial v}{\partial y} + w\frac{\partial v}{\partial z} + \frac{1}{\rho}\frac{\partial p}{\partial y} = -g,$$

(where $g \approx 9.81\text{m/s}$ is the magnitude of acceleration due to gravity) we will assume that the dominant terms are the pressure gradient and gravity, with the rest much smaller. This is consistent with the requirement that the water is shallow and relatively calm, with accelerations in the fluid much smaller than g. Dropping the small terms gives the equation for hydrostatic pressure:

$$\frac{1}{\rho}\frac{\partial p}{\partial y} = -g.$$

Combining that with the free surface boundary condition $p = 0$ at $y = h$ gives

$$p(x, y, z, t) = \rho g \left(h(x, z, t) - y \right). \tag{12.1}$$

Again, this isn't strictly true if the water is moving, but it's a good approximation. The fact that we can directly write down the pressure in the shallow water case, as opposed to solving a big linear system for pressure as we had to in fully three-dimensional flow, is one of the key speed-ups.

12.1.2 Velocity

Assuming that u and w are constant along y means $\partial u / \partial y = \partial w / \partial y = 0$, which means the horizontal parts of the momentum equation are reduced to

$$\frac{\partial u}{\partial t} + u \frac{\partial u}{\partial x} + w \frac{\partial u}{\partial z} + \frac{1}{\rho} \frac{\partial p}{\partial x} = 0,$$

$$\frac{\partial w}{\partial t} + u \frac{\partial w}{\partial x} + w \frac{\partial w}{\partial z} + \frac{1}{\rho} \frac{\partial p}{\partial z} = 0.$$

This is just two-dimensional advection along with the horizontal parts of the pressure gradient. Note that although pressure varies linearly in y, the horizontal components of its gradient are in fact constant in y; substituting in Equation (12.1) gives

$$\frac{\partial u}{\partial t} + u \frac{\partial u}{\partial x} + w \frac{\partial u}{\partial z} + g \frac{\partial h}{\partial x} = 0,$$

$$\frac{\partial w}{\partial t} + u \frac{\partial w}{\partial x} + w \frac{\partial w}{\partial z} + g \frac{\partial h}{\partial z} = 0. \tag{12.2}$$

That is, the horizontal velocity components are advected in the plane as usual, with an additional acceleration proportional to gravity that pulls water down from higher regions to lower regions.

What about vertical velocity v? It turns out this is fully determined from the "primary" shallow water variables (u, w and d) that we will be simulating. We won't actually need v in the simulation, unless for some reason you need to evaluate it for, say, particle advection in the flow, but it will come in handy to figure out how the surface height evolves in a moment.

First take a look at the incompressibility condition:

$$\frac{\partial u}{\partial x} + \frac{\partial v}{\partial y} + \frac{\partial w}{\partial z} = 0 \tag{12.3}$$

$$\Leftrightarrow \quad \frac{\partial v}{\partial y} = -\frac{\partial u}{\partial x} - \frac{\partial w}{\partial z}. \tag{12.4}$$

The right-hand side of this equation doesn't depend on y, so $\partial v/\partial y$ must be a constant along the y-direction too—which implies v has to be a linear function of y. It's fully determined from its value at the bottom $y = b(x, z)$ and the gradient we just derived.

The bottom velocity comes from the boundary condition $\vec{u} \cdot \hat{n} = 0$, remembering again that we're assuming the bottom is stationary. Recalling some basic calculus, the normal at the bottom is proportional to $(-\partial b/\partial x, 1, -\partial b/\partial z)$, so at the bottom $y = b(x, z)$:

$$-u\frac{\partial b}{\partial x} + v - w\frac{\partial b}{\partial z} = 0$$

$$\Leftrightarrow \quad v = u\frac{\partial b}{\partial x} + w\frac{\partial b}{\partial z}.$$

Note that if the bottom is flat, so the partial derivatives of b are zero, this reduces to $v = 0$ as expected. Combined with Equation (12.3) we get the following vertical velocity at any point in the fluid:

$$v(x, y, z, t) = u\frac{\partial b}{\partial x} + w\frac{\partial b}{\partial z} - \left(\frac{\partial u}{\partial x} + \frac{\partial w}{\partial z}\right)(y - b). \qquad (12.5)$$

In other words, for shallow water we take v to be whatever it requires for the flow to be incompressible and to satisfy the bottom solid boundary condition, given the horizontal velocity.

12.1.3   Height

We can also describe the vertical velocity at the free surface, in a different way. Note that the function $\phi(x, y, z) = y - h(x, z)$ implicit defines the free surface as its zero isocontour—similar to how we tracked general liquid surfaces back in Chapter 8. We know that the free surface, i.e., the zero isocontour, moves with the velocity of the fluid, and so ϕ should satisfy an advection equation

$$\frac{D\phi}{Dt} = 0$$

$$\Leftrightarrow \quad \frac{\partial \phi}{\partial t} + u\frac{\partial \phi}{\partial x} + v\frac{\partial \phi}{\partial y} + w\frac{\partial \phi}{\partial z} = 0$$

$$\Leftrightarrow \quad -\frac{\partial h}{\partial t} + u\left(-\frac{\partial h}{\partial x}\right) + v(1) + w\left(-\frac{\partial h}{\partial z}\right) = 0$$

at least at the surface $y = h$ itself. Plugging in what we derived for the velocity in Equation (12.5) at $y = h$ gives us an equation for the rate of change of height:

$$-\frac{\partial h}{\partial t} - u\frac{\partial h}{\partial x} + \left[u\frac{\partial b}{\partial x} + w\frac{\partial b}{\partial z} - \left(\frac{\partial u}{\partial x} + \frac{\partial w}{\partial z}\right)(h-b)\right] - w\frac{\partial h}{\partial z} = 0,$$

$$\frac{\partial h}{\partial t} + u\frac{\partial(h-b)}{\partial x} + w\frac{\partial(h-b)}{\partial z} = -(h-b)\left(\frac{\partial u}{\partial x} + \frac{\partial w}{\partial z}\right). \tag{12.6}$$

Using the depth $d = h - b$, and remembering that b is stationary, this can be simplified to

$$\frac{\partial d}{\partial t} + u\frac{\partial d}{\partial x} + w\frac{\partial d}{\partial z} = -d\left(\frac{\partial u}{\partial x} + \frac{\partial w}{\partial z}\right). \tag{12.7}$$

That is, the water depth is advected by the horizontal velocity and, in addition, increased or decreased proportional to the depth and the two-dimensional divergence.

We can simplify Equation (12.7) even further, putting it into what's called **conservation law form**:

$$\frac{\partial d}{\partial t} + \frac{\partial}{\partial x}(ud) + \frac{\partial}{\partial z}(wd) = 0. \tag{12.8}$$

This can in fact be directly derived from conservation of mass, similar to the approach in Appendix B. It's significant here because it leads to numerical methods that exactly conserve the total volume of water in the system—avoiding the mass-loss problems we saw earlier with three-dimensional free surface flow.[2] However, discretizing this accurately enough (to avoid numerical dissipation) is a topic that lies outside the scope of this book.

12.1.4 Boundary Conditions

Equations (12.2) and (12.7) or (12.8) also need boundary conditions, where the water ends (in the x–z horizontal plane) or the simulation domain ends. The case of a solid wall is simplest: if $\hat{n}$ is the two-dimensional normal to the wall in the x–z plane, then we require

$$(u, w) \cdot \hat{n} = 0.$$

---

[2]This conservation law form can also be applied in three dimensions, leading to a **volume-of-fluid** or **VOF** simulation that exactly conserves volume as well. However, in three dimensions, VOF techniques have their own share of problems in terms of accurately localizing the surface of the fluid and requiring small time steps.

Of course, for a moving solid wall, this should instead be $(u_{solid}, w_{solid}) \cdot \hat{n}$. To maintain that velocity in the normal direction, following the velocity equations (12.2), we also need

$$\left(\frac{\partial h}{\partial x}, \frac{\partial h}{\partial z} \right) \cdot \hat{n} = 0.$$

This also applies at an inflow/outflow boundary, where we pump water in or out of the simulation. The utility of such a boundary may be enhanced by adding a source term to the height equation, directly adding (or subtracting) water in some regions; such source terms are also perfect for modeling vertical sinks or sources of water (such as a drop falling from above, perhaps in a particle system, or a drainage hole).

It's much more difficult dealing with the edge of the simulation domain, if it's assumed that the water continues on past the edge. If you expect all the waves in the system to travel parallel to the edge, it's perfectly reasonable to put an invisible solid wall boundary there. If you determine waves should be entering along one edge, perhaps from a simple sinusoid model (see the next section for how to choose such a wave), you can further specify normal velocity and height. However, if you also expect waves to leave through the edge, things are much, much trickier: solid walls, even if invisible or specifying fancy normal velocities and heights, reflect incoming waves. Determining a **non-reflecting** (or **absorbing**) boundary condition is not at all simple and continues as a subject of research in numerical methods. The usual approach taken is to gradually blend away the simulated velocities and heights with a background field (such as a basic sinusoid wave, or flat water at rest), over the course of many grid cells: if the blend is smooth and gradual enough, reflections should be minimal.

Finally one boundary condition of prime importance for many shallow water simulations is at the **moving contact line**: where the depth of the water drops to zero, such as where the water ends on a beach. In fact, no boundary conditions need to be applied in this case: if desired for a numerical method, the velocity can be extrapolated to the dry land as usual, and the depth is zero ($h = b$).

12.2   The Wave Equation

Before jumping to numerical methods for solving the shallow water equations, it's worth taking a quick look at a further simplification. For very calm water we can completely neglect the advection terms, leaving us with

$$\frac{\partial u}{\partial t} + g\frac{\partial h}{\partial x} = 0,$$

$$\frac{\partial w}{\partial t} + g\frac{\partial h}{\partial z} = 0,$$

$$\frac{\partial h}{\partial t} = -d\left(\frac{\partial u}{\partial x} + \frac{\partial w}{\partial z}\right).$$

Divide the height equation through by the depth d and differentiate in time:

$$\frac{\partial}{\partial t}\left(\frac{1}{d}\frac{\partial h}{\partial t}\right) = -\frac{\partial}{\partial x}\frac{\partial u}{\partial t} - \frac{\partial}{\partial z}\frac{\partial w}{\partial t}.$$

Then substitute in the simplified velocity equations to get

$$\frac{\partial}{\partial t}\left(\frac{1}{d}\frac{\partial h}{\partial t}\right) = \frac{\partial}{\partial x}\left(g\frac{\partial h}{\partial x}\right) + \frac{\partial}{\partial z}\left(g\frac{\partial h}{\partial z}\right).$$

Expanding the left-hand side, but further neglecting the quadratic term as being much smaller, gives

$$\frac{\partial^2 h}{\partial t} = gd\nabla \cdot \nabla h,$$

where the Laplacian $\nabla \cdot \nabla$ here is just in two dimensions (x and z). Finally, with the assumption that the depth d in the right-hand side remains near enough constant, this is known as the **wave equation**.

The wave equation also pops up naturally in many other phenomena—elastic waves in solid materials, electromagnetic waves, acoustics (sound waves), and more—and has been well studied. Fourier analysis can provide a full solution, but to keep things simple let's just try a single sinusoid wave.[3] Take a unit-length vector $\hat{k}$ (in two dimensions) which will represent the direction of wave motion; the peaks and troughs of the waves will lie on lines perpendicular to $\hat{k}$. Let λ be the wavelength, A the amplitude, and c the speed of the wave. Putting this all together gives

$$A\sin\left(\frac{2\pi(\hat{k} \cdot (x, z) - ct)}{\lambda}\right).$$

---

[3]In fact, any wave shape will do—we pick sinusoids simply out of convention and to match up with the ocean wave modeling in the next chapter where sinusoids are critical.

If you plug this in as a possible $h(x, z, t)$ in the wave equation, we get the following equation:

$$-A\frac{4\pi^2 c^2}{\lambda^2}\sin\left(\frac{2\pi(\hat{k}\cdot(x,z)-ct)}{\lambda}\right) = -gdA\frac{4\pi^2}{\lambda^2}\sin\left(\frac{2\pi(\hat{k}\cdot(x,z)-ct)}{\lambda}\right).$$

This reduces to

$$c^2 = gd.$$

In other words, the wave equation has solutions corresponding to waves moving at speed $\sqrt{gd}$. Yuksel et al. [YHK07] directly made a very fast wave solver from this observation, using "wave particles" traveling at this speed which locally change the height of the water.

The key insight to glean from all these simplifications and models is that shallow water waves move at a speed related to the depth: the deeper the water, the faster the waves move. For example as a wave approaches the shore, the depth decreases and the wave slows down. In particular, the front of the wave slows down earlier, and so water from the back of the wave starts to pile up as the wave front slows down. Waves near the shore naturally get bigger and steeper, and if conditions are right, they will eventually crest and overturn. The shallow water equations we've developed in this chapter do contain this feature, though of course the height field assumption breaks down at the point of waves breaking: we won't be able to quite capture that look, but we'll be able to come close.

12.3 Discretization

There are many possibilities for discretizing the shallow water equations, each with its own strengths and weaknesses. You might in particular take a look at Kass and Miller's introduction of the equations to animation [KM90], and Layton and van de Panne's unconditionally stable method [LvdP02]. Here we'll provide a small variation on the Layton and van de Panne method that avoids the need for a linear solver at the expense of having a stability restriction on the time step.

We begin with the two-dimensional staggered MAC grid as usual, storing the velocity components u and w at the appropriate edge midpoints and the depth d at the cell centers. Where needed, the height h is reconstructed from the depth as $h = b + d$. We also use the usual time-splitting approach of handling advection in an initial stage, perhaps with the semi-Lagrangian method we've been using so far:

$$u^A = \text{advect}(\vec{u}^n, \Delta t, u^n),$$
$$w^A = \text{advect}(\vec{u}^n, \Delta t, w^n),$$
$$d^A = \text{advect}(\vec{u}^n, \Delta t, d^n).$$

We then compute the intermediate height field $h^A = b + d^A$ and extrapolate it to non-fluid cells, i.e., setting h equal to the value in the nearest fluid cell. Note that it is important to extrapolate height h, not depth d, as we want to make sure water sitting still on a sloped beach, for example, will remain still. We then update the velocities with the pressure acceleration:

$$u^{n+1}_{i+1/2,k} = u^A_{i+1/2,k} - \Delta t\, g\, \frac{h^A_{i+1,k} - h^A_{i,k}}{\Delta x},$$

$$w^{n+1}_{i,k+1/2} = w^A_{i,k+1/2} - \Delta t\, g\, \frac{h^A_{i,k+1} - h^A_{i,k}}{\Delta x}.$$

We extrapolate these velocities to non-fluid cells as usual and finally update the depth with the divergence term:

$$d^{n+1}_{i,k} = d^A_{i,k} - \Delta t d^A_{i,k} \left(\frac{u^{n+1}_{i+1/2,k} - u^{n+1}_{i-1/2,k}}{\Delta x} + \frac{w^{n+1}_{i,k+1/2} - w^{n+1}_{i,k-1/2}}{\Delta x} \right).$$

That's all there is to it!

There is a stability time-step restriction here, however. A simple analysis in the same vein as the approximations made in Section 12.2 to get to the wave equation can be made, showing that for stability we require

$$\Delta t \lesssim \frac{\Delta x}{\sqrt{gD}},$$

where D is the maximum depth value in the simulation. For safety a fraction of this quantity, such as 0.2, should be used.

13

Ocean Modeling

Simulating the ocean is an ongoing challenge in computer animation. This chapter will demonstrate a series of simplifications that allow relatively calm ocean surfaces to be efficiently simulated; efficiently handling rough oceans, or large-scale interactions between the ocean and solid objects immersed or floating in it, is still an open research problem. The chief resource in graphics for relatively calm ocean waves is by Tessendorf [Tes04].

The main difficulty in the ocean setting is scale. Essential to the look of waves are both large-scale swells and small ripples, and as we'll see in a moment, to get the relative speeds of these different sizes of waves correct, a simulation needs to take into account the true depth of the water. (In particular, the shallow water model of the previous chapter is completely wrong.) A naïve brute-force approach of just running a 3D fluid simulator like the ones we've looked at so far would result in an excessively and impractically large grid. Therefore we'll take a look at changing the equations themselves.

13.1 Potential Flow

Recall the vorticity equation (11.1) from Chapter 11, and since we're dealing with large-scale water, drop the small viscosity term:

$$\frac{\partial \vec{\omega}}{\partial t} + \vec{u} \cdot \nabla \vec{\omega} = -\omega \cdot \nabla \vec{u}.$$

It's not hard to see that if vorticity starts at exactly zero in a region, it has to stay zero unless modified by boundary conditions. Since the ocean at rest (with zero velocity) has zero vorticity, it's not too much of a stretch to guess that vorticity should stay nearly zero once calm waves have developed, as long as boundaries don't become too important—i.e., away from the shoreline or large objects, and assuming the free surface waves don't get too violent. That is, we will model the ocean as **irrotational**, meaning the vorticity is zero: $\nabla \times \vec{u} = \vec{\omega} = 0$.

A basic theorem of vector calculus tells us that if a smooth vector field has zero curl in a simply-connected region, it must be the gradient of some scalar potential:

$$\vec{u} = \nabla \phi.$$

Note that the ϕ used here has nothing to do with the signed distance function or any other implicit surface function we looked at earlier. Combining this with the incompressibility condition, $\nabla \cdot \vec{u} = 0$, indicates that the potential ϕ must satisfy Laplace's equation:

$$\nabla \cdot \nabla \phi = 0.$$

This is the basis of **potential flow**: instead of solving the full non-linear Navier-Stokes equations, once we know the fluid is irrotational and the region is simply-connected, we only need solve a single linear PDE.

The boundary conditions for potential flow are where it gets interesting. For solid walls the usual $\vec{u} \cdot \hat{n} = \vec{u}_{\text{solid}} \cdot \hat{n}$ condition becomes a constraint on $\nabla \phi \cdot \hat{n}$. Free surfaces, where before we just said $p = 0$, are a bit trickier: pressure doesn't enter into the potential flow equation directly. However, there is a striking resemblance between the PDE for the potential and the PDE for pressure in the projection step: both involve the Laplacian $\nabla \cdot \nabla$. We'll use this as a clue in a moment.

The equation that pressure does appear in is momentum: let's substitute $\vec{u} = \nabla \phi$ into the inviscid momentum equation and see what happens:

$$\frac{\partial \nabla \phi}{\partial t} + (\nabla \phi) \cdot (\nabla \nabla \phi) + \frac{1}{\rho} \nabla \phi = \vec{g}.$$

Exchanging the order of the space and time derivatives in the first term, and assuming ρ is constant so it can be moved inside the gradient in the pressure term, takes us to

$$\nabla \frac{\partial \phi}{\partial t} + (\nabla \phi) \cdot (\nabla \nabla \phi) + \nabla \frac{p}{\rho} = \vec{g}.$$

Seeing a pattern start to form, we can also write the gravitational acceleration as the gradient of the gravity potential, $\vec{g} \cdot \vec{x} = -gy$ where $g = 9.81 \text{ m/s}^2$ and y is height (for concreteness, let's take $y = 0$ at the average sea level).

$$\nabla \frac{\partial \phi}{\partial t} + (\nabla \phi) \cdot (\nabla \nabla \phi) + \nabla \frac{p}{\rho} + \nabla(gy) = 0.$$

Only the advection term is left. Writing it out in component form

$$(\nabla \phi) \cdot (\nabla \nabla \phi) = \begin{pmatrix} \frac{\partial \phi}{\partial x} \frac{\partial^2 \phi}{\partial x^2} + \frac{\partial \phi}{\partial y} \frac{\partial^2 \phi}{\partial x \partial y} + \frac{\partial \phi}{\partial z} \frac{\partial^2 \phi}{\partial x \partial z} \\ \frac{\partial \phi}{\partial x} \frac{\partial^2 \phi}{\partial x \partial y} + \frac{\partial \phi}{\partial y} \frac{\partial^2 \phi}{\partial y^2} + \frac{\partial \phi}{\partial z} \frac{\partial^2 \phi}{\partial y \partial z} \\ \frac{\partial \phi}{\partial x} \frac{\partial^2 \phi}{\partial x \partial z} + \frac{\partial \phi}{\partial y} \frac{\partial^2 \phi}{\partial y \partial z} + \frac{\partial \phi}{\partial z} \frac{\partial^2 \phi}{\partial z^2} \end{pmatrix},$$

and it becomes clear that this is actually the same as

$$(\nabla\phi)\cdot(\nabla\nabla\phi) = \begin{pmatrix} \frac{\partial}{\partial x}\frac{1}{2}\left(\frac{\partial\phi}{\partial x}\right)^2 + \frac{\partial}{\partial x}\frac{1}{2}\left(\frac{\partial\phi}{\partial y}\right)^2 + \frac{\partial}{\partial x}\frac{1}{2}\left(\frac{\partial\phi}{\partial z}\right)^2 \\ \frac{\partial}{\partial y}\frac{1}{2}\left(\frac{\partial\phi}{\partial x}\right)^2 + \frac{\partial}{\partial y}\frac{1}{2}\left(\frac{\partial\phi}{\partial y}\right)^2 + \frac{\partial}{\partial y}\frac{1}{2}\left(\frac{\partial\phi}{\partial z}\right)^2 \\ \frac{\partial}{\partial z}\frac{1}{2}\left(\frac{\partial\phi}{\partial x}\right)^2 + \frac{\partial}{\partial z}\frac{1}{2}\left(\frac{\partial\phi}{\partial y}\right)^2 + \frac{\partial}{\partial z}\frac{1}{2}\left(\frac{\partial\phi}{\partial z}\right)^2 \end{pmatrix}$$

$$= \nabla\left(\tfrac{1}{2}\|\nabla\phi\|^2\right).$$

Using this now brings the momentum equation to

$$\nabla\frac{\partial\phi}{\partial t} + \nabla\left(\tfrac{1}{2}\|\nabla\phi\|^2\right) + \nabla\frac{p}{\rho} + \nabla(gy) = 0$$

$$\Rightarrow \quad \nabla\left[\frac{\partial\phi}{\partial t} + \left(\tfrac{1}{2}\|\nabla\phi\|^2\right) + \frac{p}{\rho} + gy\right] = 0.$$

The only function whose gradient is everywhere zero is a constant, and since constants added to ϕ (a theoretical abstraction) have no effect on the velocity field (the real physical thing), we can assume that the constant is just zero for simplicity. This gives **Bernoulli's equation**:

$$\frac{\partial\phi}{\partial t} + \left(\tfrac{1}{2}\|\nabla\phi\|^2\right) + \frac{p}{\rho} + gy = 0.$$

You may have already heard of this. For example, in the steady-state case, where $\partial\phi/\partial t = 0$, and after subtracting out the hydrostatic component of pressure, we end up with the pressure variation $\Delta p = -\tfrac{1}{2}\rho\|\vec{u}\|^2$. Many simple experiments, such as blowing over the top of a sheet of paper held along one edge, verify how fast-moving air can induce a pressure drop which sucks things toward it.[1]

Bernoulli's equation gives us a relationship, admittedly non-linear, between pressure and the potential ϕ. In the interior of the fluid this can be used to get pressure from our solution for ϕ. At a free surface where $p = 0$ is known, we can instead use it as a boundary condition for ϕ:

$$\frac{\partial\phi}{\partial t} + \left(\tfrac{1}{2}\|\nabla\phi\|^2\right) + gy = 0.$$

---

[1] It also unfortunately figures in a bogus explanation of the lift on an airplane wing, namely that due to the curved shape of the airfoil the air has to go faster over the top than over the bottom to meet at the other side; hence there is lower pressure on the top surface, which gives lift. It's not hard to see this is almost completely wrong: angle of attack is the biggest factor in determining lift, allowing airplanes to fly even when upside-down, and allowing flat fan blades with no fancy curvature to effectively push air around.

Well, almost—this is more of a boundary condition on $\partial\phi/\partial t$, not ϕ itself. But it's not hard to see that as soon as we discretize in time, this will end up as a boundary condition on the new value of ϕ that happens to also depend on old values of ϕ.

13.2 Simplifying Potential Flow for the Ocean

Unfortunately as it stands we still have to solve a three-dimensional PDE for the potential ϕ, and though it's a much simpler linear problem in the interior of the water, it now has a fairly nasty non-linear boundary condition at the free surface. In this section we'll go through a series of simplifications to make it solvable in an efficient way. The critical assumption underlying all the simplifications is that we're only going to look at fairly calm oceans.

The first step is to rule out breaking waves so the geometry of the free surface can be described by a height field, just like the previous chapter:

$$y = h(x, z).$$

Of course h is also a function of time, $h(x, z, t)$, but we'll omit the t to emphasize the dependence on just two of the spatial variables. For a perfectly calm flat ocean we'll take $h(x, z) = 0$; our chief problem will be to solve for h as a function of time. In fact, given the velocity field $\vec{u}$ we know that the free surface should follow it—and in fact viewing the surface as implicit defined as the zero level set of $h(x, z) - y$, we already know the advection equation it should satisfy:

$$\frac{D}{Dt}(h(x, z) - y) = 0$$

$$\Rightarrow \quad \frac{\partial h}{\partial t} + u\frac{\partial h}{\partial x} - v + w\frac{\partial h}{\partial z} = 0$$

$$\Leftrightarrow \quad \frac{\partial h}{\partial t} + (u, w) \cdot \left(\frac{\partial h}{\partial x}, \frac{\partial h}{\partial z}\right) = v.$$

Just as with shallow water, this looks like a two-dimensional material derivative of height, with vertical velocity v as an additional term.

We'll also make the assumption that the ocean floor is flat, at depth $y = -H$ for some suitably large H. While this is almost certainly false, the effect of variations in the depth will not be apparent for the depths and the wavelengths we're considering.[2] The solid "wall" boundary condition at the bottom, where the normal is now $(0, 1, 0)$, becomes $\partial\phi/\partial y = 0$.

---

[2]Once you get to truly big waves, tsunamis, variation in ocean depth becomes important: for a tsunami the ocean looks shallow, and so the previous chapter actually

We can now write down the exact set of differential equations we want to solve:

$$\nabla \cdot \nabla \phi = 0 \qquad\qquad \text{for } -H \leq y \leq h(x, z),$$

$$\frac{\partial \phi}{\partial y} = 0 \qquad\qquad \text{at } y = -H,$$

$$\frac{\partial \phi}{\partial t} + \left(\tfrac{1}{2}\|\nabla\phi\|^2\right) + gh(x, z) = 0 \quad \text{at } y = h(x, z),$$

$$\frac{\partial h}{\partial t} + (u, w) \cdot \left(\frac{\partial h}{\partial x}, \frac{\partial h}{\partial z}\right) = v.$$

This is still hard to deal with, thanks to the non-linear terms at the free surface. We will thus use the clever mathematical trick of ignoring them—in effect, assuming that $\vec{u}$ is small enough and h is smooth enough that all the quadratic terms are negligible compared to the others. This cuts them down to

$$\frac{\partial \phi}{\partial t} = -gh(x, z) \qquad \text{at } y = h(x, z),$$

$$\frac{\partial h}{\partial t} = v.$$

However, it's still difficult to solve since the location at which we are applying the free surface boundary condition moves according to the solution of h. Assuming that the waves aren't too large, i.e., h is small, we can cheat and instead put the boundary condition at $y = 0$, leading to a new simplified problem:

$$\nabla \cdot \nabla \phi = 0 \qquad\qquad \text{for } -H \leq y \leq 0,$$

$$\frac{\partial \phi}{\partial y} = 0 \qquad\qquad \text{at } y = -H,$$

$$\frac{\partial \phi}{\partial t} = -gh(x, z) \qquad \text{at } y = 0,$$

$$\frac{\partial h}{\partial t} = \frac{\partial \phi}{\partial y} \qquad\qquad \text{at } y = 0.$$

This now is a perfectly linear PDE on a simple slab $-H \leq y \leq 0$. (We also swapped in $\partial\phi/\partial y$ for v, to make it clear how h and ϕ are coupled.) One of the great properties we now have is that we can add (superimpose) two solutions to get another solution, which we'll exploit to write the general exact solution as a linear combination of simpler solutions.

---

provides a better model. However, in the deep ocean these waves are practically invisible, since they tend to have wavelengths of tens or hundreds of kilometers but very small heights on the order of a meter.

We haven't yet touched on boundary conditions along x and z: we've implicitly assumed so far that the ocean is infinite, stretching out forever horizontally. We can actually solve this analytically, using Fourier integrals, but clearly this raises some problems when it comes to implementation on a finite computer. Instead we will assume the ocean is *periodic* in x and z, with some suitably large length L being the period. From a graphics stand-point, L should be large enough that the periodicity is inconspicuous—an $L \times L$ ocean "tile" should probably fill a reasonable fraction of the screen. (We'll later discuss a few other tricks to further obscure periodicity.) Any reasonable periodic function can be represented as a Fourier series, which for computer implementation we'll simply truncate to a finite number of terms.

Before jumping to the full Fourier series, let's take a look at a single Fourier mode. Though it may be a little mind-bending to try and visualize it, we'll actually use a complex exponential for this: ultimately this is more convenient mathematically and corresponds best to what a typical Fast Fourier transform library offers in its API, even though the PDE as we have written it only involves real numbers.

Let's start with a generic Fourier component of the height field:

$$h(x, z, t) = \hat{h}_{ij}(t) e^{\sqrt{-1} 2\pi (ix + jz)/L}.$$

The **Fourier coefficient** is $\hat{h}_{ij}(t)$; the t is included to emphasize that it depends on time, but not on spatial variables. In general $\hat{h}_{ij}(t)$ will be a complex number, even though in the end we'll construct a real-valued height field—more on this in a minute. I use the notation $\sqrt{-1}$ instead of the usual i (for mathematicians) or j (for engineers) since i and j are reserved for integer indices. Speaking of which, the integers i and j are the indices of this Fourier component—they may be negative or zero as well as positive. The vector $(i, j)/L$ gives the spatial frequency, and the vector $\vec{k} = 2\pi(i, j)/L$ is called the **wave vector**. Define the **wave number** k as

$$k = \|\vec{k}\| = \frac{2\pi \sqrt{i^2 + j^2}}{L}.$$

The **wavelength** is $\lambda = 2\pi/k = L/\sqrt{i^2 + j^2}$. As you can probably guess, this corresponds precisely to what we would physically measure as the length of a set of waves that this Fourier mode represents.

We'll now make the guess, which will prove to be correct, that when we plug this in for the height field, the corresponding solution for $\phi(x, y, z, t)$ will be in the following form:

$$\phi(x, y, z, t) = \hat{\phi}_{ij}(t) e^{\sqrt{-1} 2\pi (ix + jz)/L} d_{ij}(y).$$

We don't yet know what the depth function $d_{ij}(y)$ should be. Let's first try this guess in the interior of the domain, where $\nabla \cdot \nabla \phi = 0$ should hold:

$$\nabla \cdot \nabla \phi = 0$$

$$\Leftrightarrow \quad \frac{\partial^2 \phi}{\partial x^2} + \frac{\partial^2 \phi}{\partial y^2} + \frac{\partial^2 \phi}{\partial z^2} = 0$$

$$\Leftrightarrow \quad \frac{-4\pi^2 i^2}{L^2}\phi + \frac{d_{ij}''}{d_{ij}}\phi + \frac{-4\pi^2 j^2}{L^2}\phi = 0$$

$$\Leftrightarrow \quad \frac{d_{ij}''}{d_{ij}}\phi = k^2\phi$$

$$\Leftrightarrow \quad d_{ij}'' = k^2 d_{ij}.$$

We now have an ordinary differential equation for d_{ij}, with the general solution being a linear combination of e^{ky} and e^{-ky}. Note that the bottom boundary condition, $\partial \phi/\partial y = 0$ at $y = -H$, reduces to $d_{ij}'(-H) = 0$. Since our guess at ϕ already has a yet-to-be-determined factor $\hat{\phi}_{ij}(t)$ built in, we take

$$d_{ij}(y) = e^{ky} + e^{-2kH}e^{-ky}.$$

With this choice, ϕ now satisfies the Laplace equation in the interior of the fluid and the bottom boundary condition. Let's write out what we have for this Fourier mode so far:

$$\phi(x, y, z, t) = \hat{\phi}_{ij}(t)e^{\sqrt{-1}2\pi(ix+jz)/L}\left(e^{ky} + e^{-2kH}e^{-ky}\right) \quad (13.1)$$

All that's left to determine is the time dependence of the potential $\hat{\phi}_{ij}(t)$ and the height field $\hat{h}_{ij}(t)$, and the only equations we have left are the boundary conditions at $y = 0$: $\partial\phi/\partial t = -gh$ and $\partial h/\partial t = \partial\phi/\partial y$. These two boundary equations at the free surface become (after cancelling out the common $e^{\sqrt{-1}2\pi(ix+jz)/L}$ factor):

$$\frac{\partial\hat{\phi}_{ij}}{\partial t}(1 + e^{-2kH}) = -g\hat{h}_{ij}$$

$$\frac{\partial\hat{h}_{ij}}{\partial t} = \hat{\phi}_{ij}(k - ke^{-2kH}) \quad (13.2)$$

Now, differentiate the second equation with respect to time, and replace the $\partial\hat{\phi}_{ij}/\partial t$ term with the first equation, to get:

$$\frac{\partial^2\hat{h}_{ij}}{\partial t^2} = -kg\frac{1 - e^{-2kH}}{1 + e^{-2kH}}\hat{h}_{ij} \quad (13.3)$$

This is another simple ordinary differential equation, with general solution consisting of yet more Fourier sinusoids, $e^{\sqrt{-1}\omega_k t}$ and $e^{-\sqrt{-1}\omega_k t}$ where the wave frequency ω_k (how fast the wave is going up and down, no relation at all to vorticity) is given by:

$$\omega_k = \sqrt{kg\frac{1 - e^{-2kH}}{1 + e^{-2kH}}} \tag{13.4}$$

Before going on to the full solution, and accompanying numerical method, it's instructive to pause a moment and reinterpret this height field solution.

Writing out the one of the components of the height field gives:

$$\begin{aligned} h(x, z, t) &= e^{-\sqrt{-1}\omega_k t}e^{\sqrt{-1}2\pi(ix+jz)/L} \\ &= e^{\sqrt{-1}(\vec{k}\cdot(x,z)-\omega_k t)} \tag{13.5} \\ &= e^{\sqrt{-1}\vec{k}\cdot[(x,z)-c_k t\hat{k}]} \end{aligned}$$

where $\hat{k} = \vec{k}/k$ is the unit-length direction of the wave (normal to the crests and troughs) and c_k is the wave speed, defined as:

$$\begin{aligned} c_k &= \frac{\omega_k}{k} \\ &= \sqrt{\frac{g(1 - e^{-2kH})}{k(1 + e^{-2kH})}} \tag{13.6} \end{aligned}$$

Equation (13.5) tells us that the value at a horizontal position (x, z) and time t is the same as the initial wave form at time t and position $(x, z) - c_k t\hat{k}$. It's a lot like the advection equations we have seen over and over again, only this time it's just the wave moving at that speed, not the individual molecules of water. Equation (13.6) is called the **dispersion relation**, giving the speed of a wave as a function of its wave number k. Remembering that wavelength is inversely proportional to k, the dispersion relation shows that waves of different sizes will travel at different speeds—in particular if they all start off in the same patch of ocean, as time progresses they will disperse apart, hence the name. This fact is probably the most crucial visual element in a convincing ocean: it's what communicates to the audience that there is significant depth below the water, whether or not they know the physics underlying it.

In fact, what we have derived so far is just as valid for shallow water (H small) as deep water (H big). If the waves are shallow, i.e. H is small compared to the wavelength so that kH is small, then asymptotically $c \sim \sqrt{gH}$. That is, the speed depends on gravity and depth but not wavelength, which is exactly what we saw for shallow water in chapter 12. On the other hand, for deep water and moderate sized waves, i.e. where kH is very large, to a very good approximation we have

$$c_k \approx \sqrt{\frac{g}{k}}, \qquad \omega_k \approx \sqrt{gk} \qquad (13.7)$$

which is in fact the simplified formula normally used in the ocean—beyond a certain depth the dependence on H doesn't really matter. This form makes it clear that longer waves (k small) move faster than short waves (k large) in the ocean, which again is a very characteristic look: big swells rushing past underneath slow moving ripples.[3]

13.3 Evaluating the Height Field Solution

We derived the wave speed using only one component of the general solution in time for the height field. You can double check that the other component gives a wave moving at the same speed, but in the opposite direction $-\hat{k}$. This leads to some redundancy with the Fourier mode associated with wave vector $-\vec{k}$, which has the same wave number k, the same wave speed, and the same directions. We'll sort this out now, and also clean up the issue of how to make sure the height field is only real-valued despite all the complex numbers flying around. We now build the general real-valued solution from a collection of real cosine waves:

$$h(x, z, t) = \sum_{i,j} A_{ij} \cos(\vec{k} \cdot (x, z) - \omega_k t + \theta_{ij}) \qquad (13.8)$$

Here A_{ij} is the real-valued constant amplitude of the wave, $\vec{k} = 2\pi(i, j)/L$ is the wave vector as before and now points in the direction of the wave's motion, ω_k is the time frequency of the wave from equation (13.7), and θ_{ij} is a constant phase shift. We'll get to picking A_{ij} and θ_{ij} later on in the chapter.

Equation (13.8) can be used directly to evaluate the height field at any point in space and time, but if a lot of waves are involved the summation becomes expensive. However, a cheaper alternative exists by way of the Fast Fourier Transform (FFT). Let $n = 2^m$ be a power of two—this isn't essential as FFT algorithms exist for any n, but typically the transform is fastest for powers of two—and restrict the wave indices to

$$-n/2 + 1 \le i, j \le n/2 \qquad (13.9)$$

---

[3]Incidentally, the full spectrum of dispersion is also very easily seen in boat wakes: if you look far enough away from the boat, the wake will have separated into big wavelengths at the leading edge and smaller scale stuff behind.

We thus have an $n \times n$ grid of wave parameters. We'll additionally specify that the constant term is zero, $A_{00} = 0$, as this is not a wave but the average sea level, and to simplify life also zero out the highest positive frequency (which doesn't have a matching negative frequency): $A_{n/2,j} = A_{i,n/2} = 0$. The sum will then actually only be up to $i = n/2 - 1$ and $j = n/2 - 1$.

We'll now show how to evaluate $h(x, z, t)$ for any fixed time t on the $n \times n$ regular grid of locations $0 \le x, z < L$, i.e. where $x_p = pL/n$ and $z_q = qL/n$ for integer indices p and q. This grid of h values can then be fed directly into a renderer. Note that this in fact gives an $L \times L$ tile which can be periodically continued in any direction: we'll talk more about that at the end of the chapter.

The problem is to determine, for a fixed time t and all integer indices $0 \le p, q < n$, the height values as specified by:

$$h_{pq} = \sum_{i=-n/2+1}^{n/2-1} \sum_{j=-n/2+1}^{n/2-1} A_{ij} \cos(\vec{k} \cdot (x_p, z_q) - \omega_k t + \theta_{ij}) \qquad (13.10)$$

This is not quite in the form that an FFT code can handle, so we will need to manipulate it a little, first by substituting in the wave vector $\vec{k} = 2\pi(i, j)/L$ and the coordinates of the grid $x_p = pL/n$, $z_q = qL/n$:

$$h_{pq} = \sum_{i=-n/2+1}^{n/2-1} \sum_{j=-n/2+1}^{n/2-1} A_{ij} \cos(2\pi(ip + jq)/n - \omega_k t + \theta_{ij}) \qquad (13.11)$$

Next we write the cosine in terms of complex exponentials:

$$
\begin{aligned}
h_{pq} &= \sum_{i=-n/2+1}^{n/2-1} \sum_{j=-n/2+1}^{n/2-1} \tfrac{1}{2} A_{ij} e^{\sqrt{-1}(2\pi(ip+jq)/n - \omega_k t + \theta_{ij})} \\
&\qquad + \tfrac{1}{2} A_{ij} e^{-\sqrt{-1}(2\pi(ip+jq)/n - \omega_k t + \theta_{ij})} \\
&= \sum_{i=-n/2+1}^{n/2-1} \sum_{j=-n/2+1}^{n/2-1} \tfrac{1}{2} e^{\sqrt{-1}(\theta_{ij} - \omega_k t)} A_{ij} e^{\sqrt{-1}(2\pi(ip+jq)/n)} \\
&\qquad + \tfrac{1}{2} e^{-\sqrt{-1}(\theta_{ij} - \omega_k t)} A_{ij} e^{\sqrt{-1}(2\pi(-ip-jq)/n)}
\end{aligned}
\qquad (13.12)
$$

Finally we shuffle terms around in the sum to get

$$h_{pq} = \sum_{i=-n/2+1}^{n/2-1} \sum_{j=-n/2+1}^{n/2-1} \left[\tfrac{1}{2} e^{\sqrt{-1}(\theta_{ij} - \omega_k t)} A_{ij} \right.$$

$$\left. + \tfrac{1}{2} e^{-\sqrt{-1}(\theta_{-i,-j} - \omega_k t)} A_{-i,-j} \right] e^{\sqrt{-1}(2\pi(ip+jq)/n)} \quad (13.13)$$

$$= \sum_{i=-n/2+1}^{n/2-1} \sum_{j=-n/2+1}^{n/2-1} Y_{ij}(t) e^{\sqrt{-1}(2\pi(ip+jq)/n)}$$

where the complex Fourier coefficients $Y_{ij}(t)$ are defined as:

$$Y_{ij}(t) = \tfrac{1}{2} e^{\sqrt{-1}(\theta_{ij} - \omega_k t)} A_{ij} + \tfrac{1}{2} e^{-\sqrt{-1}(\theta_{-i,-j} - \omega_k t)} A_{-i,-j}$$

$$= \tfrac{1}{2} \left[\cos(\theta_{ij} - \omega_k t) + \sqrt{-1} \sin(\theta_{ij} - \omega_k t) \right] A_{ij}$$

$$+ \tfrac{1}{2} \left[\cos(\theta_{-i,-j} - \omega_k t) - \sqrt{-1} \sin(\theta_{ij} - \omega_k t) \right] A_{-i,-j}$$

$$= \left[\tfrac{1}{2} \cos(\theta_{ij} - \omega_k t) A_{ij} + \tfrac{1}{2} \cos(\theta_{-i,-j} - \omega_k t) A_{-i,-j} \right]$$

$$+ \sqrt{-1} \left[\tfrac{1}{2} \sin(\theta_{ij} - \omega_k t) A_{ij} - \tfrac{1}{2} \sin(\theta_{-i,-j} - \omega_k t) A_{-i,-j} \right]$$

$$(13.14)$$

In the last line it's spelled out in real and imaginary parts. Evaluating Equation (13.13) is exactly what FFT software is designed to do: all you need to do is evaluate $Y_{ij}(t)$ for each i and j and pass in that 2D array of Y values, getting back the heights. The results should be real, up to round-off errors—you can safely ignore the imaginary parts, though a good bug check is to make sure they all are zero or very close to zero. Some FFT libraries allow you to specify that the result should be real-valued, and then allow you to define and pass in only half the Y coefficients: this can certainly be a worthwhile optimization, but the specifics of how to do it vary from library to library.

13.4 Unsimplifying the Model

We made a lot of simplifying assumptions to get to an easily solved fully linear PDE. Unfortunately, the resulting height field solution isn't terribly convincing beyond very small amplitudes. In this section we'll try to boost our solution to look better even at larger amplitudes, by compensating for some of the terms we dropped earlier.

The first order of business is looking at the solution for the potential ϕ that accompanies our height field solution in Equation (13.8). We left this hanging before, rushing on to the height field instead, but ϕ offers some extremely useful information: in particular, $\nabla \phi$ gives us the implied

velocity field. As we'll see in a moment, the plain height field solution is
what you get when you ignore horizontal motion, letting the water bob
up and down but not side to side; the characteristic look of larger waves,
with wide flat troughs and sharper peaks, is largely due to this horizontal
motion so we will bring it back.

It's not hard to verify that the potential ϕ which matches the height
field in Equation (13.8) is as follows, building on our earlier incomplete
form and taking the limit as $H \to \infty$ as we did for the wave speed c_k and
time frequency ω_k:

$$\phi(x, y, z, t) = \sum_{i,j} \frac{A_{ij}\omega_k}{k} \sin(\vec{k} \cdot (x, z) - \omega_k t + \theta_{ij})e^{ky} \qquad (13.15)$$

Taking the gradient gives us the complete velocity field, both at the surface
($y \approx 0$) and even far below:

$$u(x, y, z, t) = \frac{\partial \phi}{\partial x} = \sum_{i,j} \frac{A_{ij}\omega_k 2\pi i}{kL} \cos(\vec{k} \cdot (x, z) - \omega_k t + \theta_{ij})e^{ky}$$

$$v(x, y, z, t) = \frac{\partial \phi}{\partial y} = \sum_{i,j} A_{ij}\omega_k \sin(\vec{k} \cdot (x, z) - \omega_k t + \theta_{ij})e^{ky} \qquad (13.16)$$

$$w(x, y, z, t) = \frac{\partial \phi}{\partial z} = \sum_{i,j} \frac{A_{ij}\omega_k 2\pi j}{kL} \cos(\vec{k} \cdot (x, z) - \omega_k t + \theta_{ij})e^{ky}$$

These formulas are themselves fairly useful if you want velocity vectors at
arbitrary points, say to aid in simulating the motion of a small solid in the
water.

However we'll go one step further. Imagine tracking a blob of water
starting at some initial position. The velocity field implied by a single
wave, evaluated at that fixed point in space, is just a periodic sinusoid in
time. As long as these velocities are small enough, the particle can't stray
too far, so to a good approximation the velocity of the particle itself will
be that periodic sinusoid. This means its position, the integral of velocity,
will also be a periodic sinusoid: the particle will follow an elliptic orbit
round and round as waves pass by. Experimental observation confirms this
is a fairly accurate description of the motion; it's not perfect—there is a
very small net movement in the direction of the wave propagation, termed
Stokes drift—but it's pretty good.

Solving for the motion of a blob of water starting at position $\vec{x}_0$, from
the simplified equation $d\vec{x}/dt = \vec{u}(\vec{x}_0, t)$, gives this general solution for the

displacement from $\vec{x}_0$:

$$\Delta x = \sum_{i,j} \frac{-2\pi A_{ij} i}{kL} \sin(\vec{k} \cdot (x_0, z_0) - \omega_k t + \theta_{ij}) e^{ky_0}$$

$$\Delta y = \sum_{i,j} A_{ij} \cos(\vec{k} \cdot (x_0, z_0) - \omega_k t + \theta_{ij}) e^{ky_0} \qquad (13.17)$$

$$\Delta z = \sum_{i,j} \frac{-2\pi A_{ij} j}{kL} \sin(\vec{k} \cdot (x_0, z_0) - \omega_k t + \theta_{ij}) e^{ky_0}$$

This displacement field can be evaluated anywhere for $y_0 \leq 0$ to give a particle that's moving with the water should be displaced to at any given time. For example, for a solid floating on the surface of the water you can get its position at any time by plugging in $y_0 = 0$ and its "resting" horizontal x_0 and z_0 coordinates. Objects suspended underneath the surface are the same, just with an exponential reduction of the motion by e^{ky_0} for each component. (Note that the components with large k will be nearly zero deep enough down, so they can be dropped for more efficient evaluation—as you go deeper, only the large wavelength, small wave number k, waves have an effect.)

In fact this displacement field also tells us how to get a more accurate free surface: we use it to deform the $y = 0$ plane. The technical term for this, when applied to enrich a single Fourier component, is a **Gerstner wave**, first introduced to graphics by Fournier and Reeves [FR86]. Our earlier height field solution only included the vertical displacement (notice $h(x, z, t)$ and Δy at $y = 0$ are identical), and now we will add in the matching horizontal displacement. Just as with the height field vertical displacement, we can evaluate this horizontal displacement on a regular grid efficiently with the FFT. Using the same process as we did before with the height field to reduce it the desired complex exponential form, we get

$$\Delta x_{pq} = \sum_{i=-n/2+1}^{n/2-1} \sum_{j=-n/2+1}^{n/2-1} X_{ij}(t) e^{\sqrt{-1}(2\pi(ip+jq)/n)}$$

$$\qquad (13.18)$$

$$\Delta z_{pq} = \sum_{i=-n/2+1}^{n/2-1} \sum_{j=-n/2+1}^{n/2-1} Z_{ij}(t) e^{\sqrt{-1}(2\pi(ip+jq)/n)}$$

where the Fourier coefficients are defined from

$$
X_{ij}(t) = \left[-\frac{\pi A_{ij}i}{kL} \sin(\theta_{ij} - \omega_k t) + \frac{\pi A_{-i,-j}i}{kL} \sin(\theta_{-i,-j} - \omega_k t) \right]
$$
$$
+ \sqrt{-1} \left[\frac{\pi A_{ij}i}{kL} \cos(\theta_{ij} - \omega_k t) + \frac{\pi A_{-i,-j}i}{kL} \cos(\theta_{-i,-j} - \omega_k t) \right]
$$
$$
Z_{ij}(t) = \left[-\frac{\pi A_{ij}j}{kL} \sin(\theta_{ij} - \omega_k t) + \frac{\pi A_{-i,-j}j}{kL} \sin(\theta_{-i,-j} - \omega_k t) \right]
$$
$$
+ \sqrt{-1} \left[\frac{\pi A_{ij}j}{kL} \cos(\theta_{ij} - \omega_k t) + \frac{\pi A_{-i,-j}j}{kL} \cos(\theta_{-i,-j} - \omega_k t) \right]
$$

$$(13.19)$$

or more simply:

$$
(X_{ij}(t),\, Z_{ij}(t)) = \sqrt{-1}\frac{\vec{k}}{k} Y_{ij}(t). \tag{13.20}
$$

These can be evaluated just like the vertical component Fourier coefficients $Y_{ij}(t)$, and for each component a call to the FFT library will then return that component of the displacement evaluated on a regular grid. Adding this fully 3D displacement to the coordinates of a regular grid at $y = 0$ gives a much more convincing ocean surface. Tessendorf recommends including a tunable choppiness parameter $\lambda \in [0, 1]$ to scale down the horizontal displacement, allowing more range in the look: $\lambda = 0$ gives the soft look of the pure height field solution, and $\lambda = 1$ the choppy full displacement solution. We can go even further, in fact, getting a bit of a wind-blown look by displacing in the horizontal direction of the wind, by a small amount proportional to the height—more tunable parameters.

However, all the approximations we've taken to get to this point aren't entirely self-consistent. If the amplitudes A_{ij} are too large the full displacement field might actually cause self-intersections, giving strange loopy inside-out artifacts. This is fairly easy to detect—if a surface normal is pointing downwards (has a negative y component) anywhere, it's a self-intersection. These spots could be interpreted as points where the waves got so steep and pointed that this solution breaks down, i.e. the wave is breaking; the problem can then be plausible covered up with a procedural foam shader, or used as an emitter for a spray and mist particle system.

13.5   Wave Parameters

We turn now to the selection of the wave parameters, the amplitudes A_{ij} and phase shifts θ_{ij}, which so far have been left as unspecified constants. The phase shifts are straightforward: they have no special significance, and so each θ_{ij} may be chosen as an independent uniform random number from $[0, 2\pi]$. The amplitudes, however, are a little more interesting.

The first point to make follows from the nature of the solution method itself: if the ratio of amplitude to wavelength is too large, the approximations we made are unjustifiable and the result looks unconvincing—real waves simply don't get that steep, and simulating very rough violent oceans is a continuing research problem beyond this method. Therefore it makes sense to put a limit of, say, $A_{ij} \lesssim O(1/k)$. However, beyond this our physical model doesn't give us much guidance for automatically picking a convincing set of amplitudes; ultimately waves are driven by the wind or by ocean currents which we are not even considering. Tessendorf recommends instead turning to phenomological models garnered from observations, such as the **Phillips spectrum**, which biases waves to align with some chosen wind direction, but there is a lot of freedom to experiment. The FFTs can run fast enough to give interactive feedback even on half-decent grids (say 128^2), allowing you to tune the amplitudes effectively. Horvath recently gave an excellent review of existing models and further synthesized a highly usable model to easily get good looking waves [Hor15].

13.6 Eliminating Periodicity

The ocean model we've defined so far often works just fine for ocean shots. However, it is periodic: if the perspective of a shot allows the audience to see many of these tiles, there is a chance the periodicity will be visible and distracting. One way of overcoming this, which in fact is a simple trick to turn any unstructured periodic texture into a nonperiodic pattern, is to superimpose two repeating tiles of different sizes. That is, add to our $L \times L$ repeating ocean tile another one of dimension $\alpha L \times \alpha L$. (In practice, this means evaluating both tiles, then interpolating values from both onto one master grid.) If α is an irrational number, the sum of the two is nonperiodic. You can see if α is rational, it's not hard to prove the sum *is* periodic, in fact if $\alpha = r/s$ for integers r and s then the period is L times the least common multiple of r and s, divided by s. If α is irrational but very close to a rational number r/s with small integers r and s, the sum will not be exactly periodic but look very close to it, which still might appear objectionable. One of the best choices then is the golden ratio $(\sqrt{5} + 1)/2 = 1.61803\ldots$ which (in a sense we will not cover in this book) is as far as possible from small integer fractions.

Other possible techniques involve layering in further effects based on nonperiodic noise. For example, combinations of upwelling currents in the sea and wind gusts above often give the ocean a patchy look, where in some regions there are lots of small ripples to reflect light but in others the surface is much smoother. This can be modeled procedurally, but here we stop as it lies outside the realm of simulation.

14

Vortex Methods

Chapter 11 began with a discussion of vorticity, and highlighted its importance for turbulent, lively detail, especially in smoke and fire simulations. We will focus just on these scenarios in this chapter, looking at alternative simulation methods which directly work with vorticity. While some of this work is equally applicable to water simulation, experience shows most water simulations don't involve a lot of vorticity, or at least vorticity variation, in the fluid (e.g. the last chapter on ocean waves used the assumption of zero vorticity in the water), and the free surface boundary condition is considerably trickier when working with vorticity. Compared to other topics in this book, this chapter is also a bit less "finished": I'm including some basics on vortex methods because they show incredible promise for smoke, but there are still tricky issues left to work out for practical fluid simulation in graphics.

Readers interested in going further with vortex methods may want to follow up with Chorin's paper which started it all [Cho73], some of the graphics papers on this topic (e.g. [YUM86, GLG95, AN05, PK05, ANSN06, ETK+07, WP10, BKB12, PTG12, ZB14]), the somewhat-harder-to-crack but authoritative book by Cottet and Koumoutsakos [CK08], the SIGGRAPH course notes by Koumoutsakos et al. [KCR08], or Mark Stock's summary [Sto07].

Recall again that vorticity is defined as the curl of velocity,

$$\vec{\omega} = \nabla \times \vec{u},$$

and measures locally how much the flow is rotating. For a rigid body motion, it is exactly twice the angular velocity. It also can be directly extracted from the skew-symmetric part of the velocity gradient $\nabla \vec{u}$.

Slightly differently from Chapter 11, we take the vorticity equation with a body force $\vec{b}$ included:

$$\frac{\partial \vec{\omega}}{\partial t} + \vec{u} \cdot \nabla \vec{\omega} = -\vec{\omega} \cdot \nabla \vec{u} + \nu \nabla \cdot \nabla \vec{\omega} + \nabla \times \vec{b}.$$

If we are going to work primarily with vorticity for smoke, then $\vec{g}$ won't represent gravity but instead buoyancy, which is mostly zero but shows up at hot sources. Assuming negligible viscosity, the vorticity equation simplifies further,

$$\frac{\partial \vec{\omega}}{\partial t} + \vec{u} \cdot \nabla \vec{\omega} = -\vec{\omega} \cdot \nabla \vec{u} + \nabla \times \vec{b},$$

and in two-dimensions (where vorticity is just a scalar) even further:

$$\frac{D\vec{\omega}}{Dt} = \nabla \times \vec{b}.$$

Particularly given just how simple this last form is—tracking it almost perfectly with particles is nearly trivial—and knowing that vorticity is essential to the look of detailed smoke, it is only natural to ask if we can directly track vorticity as a primary fluid variable.

The major problem to overcome with this, however, is that we still need to know the fluid velocity $\vec{u}$ to move vorticity, not to mention smoke concentration, temperature, etc. Luckily, if we know vorticity (the curl of velocity), it is possible to solve for the velocity whose curl matches that as closely as possible. Let's see how.

14.1 Velocity from Vorticity

As a first attempt, we could consider the definition of vorticity $\vec{\omega} = \nabla \times \vec{u}$ as an equation to solve for velocity given vorticity. However, life is not so simple. First of all, even if we directly discretized this on a grid to form a system of linear equations, the matrix we would be solving with is pretty horrible: PCG definitely can't work. However, more importantly, given an arbitrary velocity field $\vec{\omega}$, which might have resulted from approximately solving the vorticity equation forward in time, there is no guarantee that it is exactly the curl of *any* velocity field. For example, the divergence of the curl of a vector field is always zero (a fact we used in Chapter 11 for curl-noise) so if $\nabla \cdot \vec{\omega} \neq 0$, it cannot be exactly the curl of any velocity field. Unfortunately, most of our methods for solving the vorticity equation forward in time will not exactly keep a zero divergence vorticity field, due to numerical errors.

Instead, we can ask for the velocity field $\vec{u}$ whose curl is as close as possible to the given vorticity ω. Ignoring boundaries for now, and assuming the fields all decay to zero far enough from the origin, we can express this by integrating the squared magnitude of the difference between $\nabla \times \vec{u}$ and $\vec{\omega}$ over all space:

$$\vec{u} = \arg\min_{\vec{u}} \iiint \|\nabla \times \vec{u} - \vec{\omega}\|^2$$

If you followed the calculus of variations derivation in Chapter 10, you can guess what's coming next. We'll use the same approach to get a handle on what equation $\vec{u}$ actually solves.

Suppose $\vec{u}$ is the optimal velocity field to match up against the given vorticity $\vec{\omega}$, and let $\vec{p}$ be any other smooth function which decays to zero far enough from the origin. Then define the regular function of one variable, $g(s)$, as

$$g(s) = \iiint \|\nabla \times (\vec{u} + s\vec{p}) - \vec{\omega}\|^2.$$

Since $\vec{u}$ is optimal, $g(s)$ must have a minimum at $s = 0$. Therefore $g'(0) = 0$.

In fact, $g(s)$ is actually just a quadratic! We can expand it out to see:

$$g(s) = \iiint \left(\nabla \times (\vec{u} + s\vec{p}) - \vec{\omega}\right) \cdot \left(\nabla \times (\vec{u} + s\vec{p}) - \vec{\omega}\right)$$

$$= \iiint \|\nabla \times \vec{u} - \vec{\omega}\|^2 + 2\left(\nabla \times \vec{u} - \vec{\omega}\right) \cdot \left(\nabla \times \vec{p}\right)s + \|\nabla \times \vec{p}\|^2 s^2$$

The condition $g'(0) = 0$ is equivalent to the middle term, the linear coefficient, being zero:

$$\iiint 2\left(\nabla \times \vec{u} - \vec{\omega}\right) \cdot \left(\nabla \times \vec{p}\right) = 0$$

Dividing by two and using a generalized integration-by-parts, this is equivalent to

$$-\iiint \nabla \times \left(\nabla \times \vec{u} - \vec{\omega}\right) \cdot \vec{p} = 0$$

This integral should be exactly zero no matter which smooth vector field $\vec{p}$ (that decays to zero) we use. Therefore, it must be the case that

$$\nabla \times \left(\nabla \times \vec{u} - \vec{\omega}\right) = 0$$

everywhere in space. We have an equation for $\vec{u}$ again:

$$\nabla \times \nabla \times \vec{u} = \nabla \times \vec{\omega}.$$

This one should always have a solution.

However, it turns out we still have a problem: there are many different solutions! In fact, if you take any solution $\vec{u}$, and add the gradient of any scalar function ∇f to it, the curl is unchanged, since $\nabla \times \nabla f = 0$. (As a reminder, this and other vector calculus identities are reviewing in Appendix A.) This is actually a fundamental point about reconstructing velocity from vorticity: the answer is not unique. In fact, we will exploit this a little bit later.

For now we really would like to pin down one particular solution among the infinitely many. We can start by rewriting the $\nabla \times \nabla \times$ operator, which a little bit of differentiation reveals is the same as:

$$-\nabla \cdot \nabla \vec{u} + \nabla(\nabla \cdot \vec{u}) = \nabla \times \vec{\omega}.$$

That is, curl-curl is the same thing as the negative Laplacian (applied to each component of $\vec{u}$ separately) plus the gradient of the divergence of $\vec{u}$. Well, we know the velocity field we want at the end should be incompressible, i.e. divergence-free, so the second term should just be zero. (We had better check this later, of course!) Throwing it away, we are left with a much nicer problem:

$$-\nabla \cdot \nabla \vec{u} = \nabla \times \vec{\omega}.$$

This is our dear old Poisson problem yet again! It's actually three independent Poisson problems, one for each component of velocity.

In this case, since we don't have boundaries, we can actually write down the solution by way of the **fundamental solution**. The fundamental solution of the Laplacian is a radially symmetric function Φ whose Laplacian is zero everywhere except at the origin, where it is singular—in fact, so singular it is the Dirac delta δ. Without going through the pain of deriving it, the fundamental solution in 2D is

$$\Phi_2(\vec{x}) = \frac{1}{2\pi} \log \|\vec{x}\|,$$

and in 3D it is

$$\Phi_3(\vec{x}) = -\frac{1}{4\pi\|\vec{x}\|}.$$

You can easily check, albeit with some heavy-duty differentiation, that the Laplacian of each, in their respective dimension, is indeed zero when $\vec{x} \neq 0$. Obviously they are not differentiable in the usual sense at $\vec{x} = 0$: in a fuzzy sense their Laplacian at the origin is so infinitely huge that if you integrated around it you would get the value 1 instead of 0. You can check this relatively easily too, say in 3D, by integrating the fundamental solution over the sphere S of radius one centered at the origin:

$$\iiint_S \nabla \cdot \nabla \Phi_3(\vec{x}).$$

First use the divergence theorem (fundamental theorem of calculus) to convert this into an integral over the surface of the sphere:

$$\iiint_S \nabla \cdot \nabla \Phi_3(\vec{x}) = \iint_{\partial S} \nabla \Phi_3(\vec{x}) \cdot \hat{n}.$$

A little bit of calculation shows the gradient of $\Phi_3(\vec{x})$ is just

$$\nabla\Phi_3(\vec{x}) = \nabla\left(-\frac{1}{4\pi\|\vec{x}\|}\right) = \frac{\vec{x}}{4\pi\|\vec{x}\|^3}.$$

On the surface of the unit sphere, $\|vec x\| = 1$, so this simplifies, and in fact the normal $\hat{n}$ is the same as the position $\vec{x}$. Our integral becomes:

$$\iiint_S \nabla\cdot\nabla\Phi_3(\vec{x}) = \iint_{\partial S} \frac{\vec{x}}{4\pi}\cdot\vec{x}.$$

But $\vec{x}\cdot\vec{x}$ is just $\|\vec{x}\|$ on the surface of the unit sphere, which again is 1. So we have

$$\iiint_S \nabla\cdot\nabla\Phi_3(\vec{x}) = \iint_{\partial S} \frac{1}{4\pi}.$$

The surface area of the unit sphere is 4π, so integrating the constant $1/4\pi$ over it gives us the answer 1:

$$\iiint_S \nabla\cdot\nabla\Phi_3(\vec{x}) = 1.$$

This is exactly what defines the Dirac delta, which technically is a "distribution" rather than a normal function:

$$\nabla\cdot\nabla\Phi(\vec{x}) = \delta(\vec{x})$$

It is zero everywhere except at 0, but it's so singular at the origin that its integral over a region containing the origin is 1.

The fundamental solution is called fundamental because it gives us an easy way to write down the solution for any Poisson problem, modulo boundary conditions. For our problem, that solution is

$$\vec{u}(\vec{x}) = \iiint \Phi(\vec{x}-\vec{p})\nabla\times\vec{\omega}(\vec{p})\,d\vec{p}.$$

That is, the velocity at a point $\vec{x}$ is a weighted integral of $\nabla\times\omega(\vec{p})$ over all of space, where the weight comes from the fundamental solution applied to the vector between them $\vec{x}-\vec{p}$.

Let's check this actually is a solution, by taking the Laplacian with respect to $\vec{x}$:

$$\nabla_x\cdot\nabla_x\vec{u}(\vec{x}) = \nabla_x\cdot\nabla_x\iiint \Phi(\vec{x}-\vec{p})\nabla\times\vec{\omega}(\vec{p})\,d\vec{p}.$$

Differentiating with $\vec{x}$ can be brought inside the integral with $\vec{p}$:

$$\nabla_x\cdot\nabla_x\vec{u}(\vec{x}) = \iiint \nabla_x\cdot\nabla_x\Phi(\vec{x}-\vec{p})\nabla\times\vec{\omega}(\vec{p})\,d\vec{p}$$
$$= \iiint \delta(\vec{x}-\vec{p})\nabla\times\vec{\omega}(\vec{p})\,d\vec{p}.$$

This integral with the Dirac delta is special. Since $\delta(\vec{x} - \vec{p})$ is zero except at $\vec{x} - \vec{p} = 0$, i.e. except when $\vec{x} = \vec{p}$, only $\nabla \times \vec{\omega}(\vec{x})$ can contribute to the answer. Since the integral of the Dirac delta over the origin is one, the contribution is direct:

$$\nabla \cdot \nabla \vec{u}(\vec{x}) = \nabla \times \vec{\omega}(\vec{x}).$$

So we know this is the solution we want.

Let's massage the expression just a little bit, using integration-by-parts:

$$\vec{u}(\vec{x}) = \iiint \Phi(\vec{x} - \vec{p}) \nabla \times \vec{\omega}(\vec{p}) \, d\vec{p}$$

$$= - \iiint \nabla_p \Phi(\vec{x} - \vec{p}) \times \vec{\omega}(\vec{p}) \, d\vec{p}$$

Now, since $\Phi(\vec{x} - \vec{p}) = \Phi(\vec{p} - \vec{x})$, the gradient with resepct to $\vec{p}$ is the same as the gradient with respect to $\vec{x}$:

$$\vec{u}(\vec{x}) = - \iiint \nabla_x \Phi(\vec{x} - \vec{p}) \times \vec{\omega}(\vec{p}) \, d\vec{p}$$

$$= - \iiint \nabla_x \times \left(\Phi(\vec{x} - \vec{p}) \vec{\omega}(\vec{p}) \right) d\vec{p}$$

$$= -\nabla_x \times \iiint \Phi(\vec{x} - \vec{p}) \vec{\omega}(\vec{p}) \, d\vec{p}$$

$$= \nabla_x \times \vec{\psi}(\vec{x})$$

In the last line we introduce a new function $\vec{\psi}$ defined by the integral of the fundamental solution with $\vec{\omega}$. Our velocity is the curl of $\vec{\psi}$ so it has to divergence-free, justifying our step way back at the beginning of this odyssey.

14.2   Biot-Savart and Streamfunctions

Our last little derivation actually breezed through two very important equations. The first is called the Biot-Savart law:

$$\vec{u}(\vec{x}) = \iiint -\nabla \Phi(\vec{x} - \vec{p}) \times \vec{\omega} \, d\vec{p}.$$

This gives the velocity at any point in space given the vorticity, or at least (as we saw from our derivation in the last section) the velocity whose curl is as close as possible to the given $\vec{\omega}$ in a least-squares sense.

The other equation expresses the velocity as the curl of a function $\vec{\psi}$. The definition of this function is

$$\vec{\psi}(\vec{x}) = -\iiint \Phi(\vec{x} - \vec{p})\vec{\omega}(\vec{p})\, d\vec{p},$$

which you can recognize, since it's an integral with the fundamental solution, as really saying that $\vec{\psi}$ is the solution to this Poisson problem:

$$\nabla \cdot \nabla \vec{\psi} = -\vec{\omega}.$$

This gives an alternative interpretation of the velocity we reconstructed from $\vec{\omega}$: we first solve a Poisson problem for $\vec{\psi}$, then take its curl to get the velocity. In fact, if $\vec{\omega}$ happened to be divergence-free itself (so it could possibly be the curl of some velocity), a little effort can show that $\nabla \times \nabla \vec{\psi} = \vec{\omega}$ exactly, and likewise $\nabla \times \vec{u} = \vec{\omega}$.

In 2D, this function like the vorticity is actually just a scalar, ψ, and has a special name: the **streamfunction**. The name derives from the fact that its level set isocontours are in fact the streamlines of the velocity field. This isn't hard to see: the curl in 2D is just the gradient rotated by 90° (see Appendix A), and the gradient points 90° out from the level set isocontours, therefore the velocity is parallel to the level sets.

In 3D, there isn't such a nice geometric property for $\vec{\psi}$, but some people still call it the streamfunction. Others prefer to describe it as a vector-valued potential, but streamfunction is easier to say, so I will go with that.

14.3 Vortex Particles

At last, we can arrive at an interesting numerical method. Let's begin in 2D. We know there that the inviscid vorticity equation is especially simple, even more so if we drop buoyancy for now:

$$\frac{D\omega}{Dt} = 0.$$

Solving this with particles is as easy as it gets! Suppose we approximate the vorticity of the flow as being zero everywhere except at a set of points (our particles), where it's concentrated. Each particle at position $\vec{x}_i$ will have vorticity ω_i, and the above equation says the particles should just flow through the velocity field while never changing their vorticity values.

How do we get the velocity? More precisely we will model the vorticity field as a sum of weighted Dirac delta spikes:

$$\omega(\vec{x}) = \sum_{i=1}^{n} \omega_i \delta(\vec{x} - \vec{x}_i).$$

Such singularities can't exist in reality, of course, so think of each particle as a simplifying approximation to a vortex where the total integral of its vorticity is ω_i, concentrated in a small region of space around $\vec{x}_i$.

The Biot-Savart law then allows us to compute the velocity at any point in space (written here in 2D with $\nabla\Phi^{\perp}$ meaning the 90° rotation of the gradient, in lieu of a 3D cross-product):

$$\vec{u}(\vec{x}) = \iiint -\nabla\Phi(\vec{x} - \vec{p})^{\perp} \left(\sum_{i=1}^{n} \omega_i \delta(\vec{p} - \vec{x}_i) \right) d\vec{p}.$$

Integrals with Dirac deltas simplify:

$$\vec{u}(\vec{x}) = \sum_{i=1}^{n} -\nabla\Phi(\vec{x} - \vec{x}_i)^{\perp} \omega_i.$$

We can evaluate this at each particle itself to find the velocity there, with the proviso that $\nabla\Phi(\vec{x} - \vec{x}_i)$ isn't yet defined at $\vec{x} = \vec{x}_i$: we set the value to be zero, so a particle's own vorticity does not influence its velocity.

With this simple formula, we have a 2D smoke simulator of surprising power. It has zero dissipation, zero numerical viscosity: the only numerical error arises from the choice of time integrator to update positions, and rounding error in the calculations. There is also modeling error, of course: real fluids don't have vorticity concentrated in Dirac deltas, and real fluids generally have some nonzero viscosity. It still gives amazingly good results with surprisingly few vortex particles—for a simple 2D smoke simulation, this is a far more effective approach than what we took earlier in the book.

But wait, if it's so good, why did we even bother with solving pressure on grids and all that earlier in the book? Well, there are a few flies in the ointment. For one, we're still in 2D and we also haven't seen how to incorporate solid boundaries, or even buoyancy. The Biot-Savart formula above is also a bit scary: to find the velocity of one particle, we have to sum over all n particles, and therefore the cost of evaluating all velocities is $O(n^2)$, which doesn't scale well. Unlike our solvers up to this point, it turns out the inviscid assumption together with the Dirac deltas takes us into dangerous ill-posed territory: if two particles get close to each other, their velocities can blow up. And finally, tracking vorticity on a few scattered particles doesn't give us detailed smoke concentration, temperature, etc.

14.3.1 Tracking Smoke

Let's start with the easiest issue, the last. Part of the power of vortex particle methods is that relatively few particles are needed to generate very rich motion for a large region of space—in fact, unlike grid methods with velocity and pressure, by default our simulation is running in all of space without any artificial domain boundaries! However, this does mean the few vortex particles we have are not going to cut it for tracking smoke, temperature, and other related fields. The vortex particles and the Biot-Savart formula can provide us velocity anywhere, however, so we can track other fields with that however we want—on grids with semi-Lagrangian advection, on particles, or with particle-grid hybrids where we splat values down on to the grid for further processing.

14.3.2 Buoyancy

Buoyancy is also simple. Recall the 2D vorticity equation with body force $\vec{b}$ included is

$$\frac{D\vec{\omega}}{Dt} = \nabla \times \vec{b}.$$

We need to estimate the curl of the buoyancy vector field at the particles to see how to update their vorticity. This could be as simple as specifying a buoyancy field and taking its curl. For example, you could specify an upward buoyancy in a region around where smoke is being emitted, possibly with an animated volumetric texture to make it more interesting, modeling the idea that the air will cool off to ambient temperature by the time it leaves that region, more or less. If we are tracking temperature on a grid (or splatting it from particles to a grid), we can also compute buoyancy on the grid and then use finite differences to estimate the curl, interpolating that curl at our vortex particles.

14.3.3 Mollification

Dealing with the blow-up when particles get close is a little more involved. Instead of insisting ω is concentrated in unrealistic Dirac delta spikes, we can instead assume it is spread out more smoothly. Coming up with a smoothed kernel function, like a Gaussian, and then computing the integral with the fundamental solution is usually intractable, but instead we can just directly "mollify" the fundamental solution itself, avoiding the singularity. There's no single correct way to do this. The guiding principle is to keep the asymptotic behavior the same, i.e. the mollified version should converge to the true fundamental solution as you go far away from the origin. This will keep the implied vorticity distribution concentrated around the particle, and it also makes sure that the Laplacian of the mollified version still integrates to 1. For example, one might use

$$\tilde{\Phi}_2(\vec{x}) = \frac{1}{2\pi} \log\left(\|\vec{x}\| + he^{-\|\vec{x}\|/h} \right),$$

where h is a small length which you can think of as the characteristic radius of the particles.

14.3.4 Undoing the inviscid assumption

Accurately simulating viscous diffusion of vorticity is hard with just the particle representation. However, we can at least hack in a very simple dissipation of vorticity. Assume that the sum of all the vorticities stored on the particles is zero, so there isn't a net rotation for the entire gas—indeed it could be useful to check this in the simulation, and if the sum is nonzero, subtract the mean vorticity from each particle to bring it back to zero. A very simple model of viscously transferring vorticity to the rest of the fluid averaged out over all of space is then to use a simple exponential decay. In each time step, reduce the vorticity of each particle by the factor $e^{-k\Delta t}$, where k controls the speed of dissipation.

14.3.5 Jumping to 3D

Switching all of this to three dimensions is straightforward: just swap in the 3D fundamental solution, or a mollified version like

$$\tilde{\Phi}_3(\vec{x}) = -\frac{1}{4\pi(\|\vec{x}\| + he^{-\|\vec{x}\|/h})}.$$

However, the vortex-stretching term in the 3D vorticity equation needs careful treatment:

$$\frac{D\vec{\omega}}{Dt} = -\vec{\omega} \cdot \nabla\vec{u}.$$

Trying to directly evaluate the gradient of velocity and plugging it in is not a good idea—most schemes that start out that way tend to be vulnerable to instability.

It's better to begin by understanding the physical meaning of this term. In 3D, rotations don't just exist around a point, but instead are always around an axis. Likewise, it turns out that vorticity in 3D can never actually be isolated to separate points, but always is arranged in at least "filaments" (curves), if not vortex sheets (surfaces) or spread across volumes. Even if we take isolated vortex particles as our approximate representation, the velocity field produced by Biot-Savart must have a true vorticity which is nonzero along curves though the space. Perhaps a better model to have in mind for a vortex particle in 3D is that it (approximately) represents a little portion of a longer vortex filament, like a segment, aligned in the direction of $\vec{\omega}$. In a sense, it is almost a rotating cylinder of fluid of very small radius, spinning around its axis with angular velocity proportional to $\vec{\omega}$.

The vortex filaments, made up of these tiny rotating cylinders, are advected by the velocity field. The velocity field can deform them, if the velocity field varies along the tangential direction of the filament, as measured by the directional derivative of $\vec{u}$ in the direction of $\vec{\omega}$, namely $\vec{\omega} \cdot \nabla \vec{u}$. In particular, the tangential direction along the filament has to change accordingly, i.e. $\vec{\omega}$ has to change direction.

Thinking again of just one spinning cylinder of fluid, if the velocity field moves its endpoints at different speeds, the cylinder can change direction and/or change its length. If it gets stretched longer, it has to get thinner (since the flow is incompressible, conserving volume). If it gets thinner, it has to spin faster, by conservation of angular momentum—just like ice skaters will spin faster if they bring their limbs in close to their body.

The vortex stretching term exactly accounts for both of these effects: the axis of vorticity changing direction as the velocity field deforms the vortex filaments, and the magnitude of vorticity changing to preserve angular momentum if the filament is stretched or compressed in length.

This suggests that perhaps instead of vortex particles, for 3D we should instead use vortex filaments or vortex sheets, whose deformation under the flow can be tracked exactly, and using conservation of angular momentum and their geometry to avoid needing to directly approximate the vortex-stretching term—and indeed, many graphics papers do just this. However, there are then heavier geometric problems.

If we stick to plain vortex particles it's still not clear what the best way to handle vortex-stretching is. Geometric approaches which take into account exactly how the time integrator would deform a cylinder lined up with $\vec{\omega}$, then appealing to conservation of angular momentum, are probably the best bet.

14.3.6 Speeding up Biot-Savart

For a very detailed simulation with tens of thousands of vortex particles, or more, and perhaps also orders of magnitude more smoke particles to track as well for rendering, the cost of the Biot-Savart summation over particles is huge. The main saving grace is that it at least is embarrassingly parallel: evaluating the velocity at one point in space can be computed completely independently of any other point. However, it's still worrisome.

There are several algorithms available to speed this up. Two of the most famous, in the "tree code" family, are the Barnes-Hut algorithm [BH86] and the Fast Multipole Method [GR87]. These are complicated algorithms, particularly the latter, and I won't dive into a full explanation here. But let's look at an outline of these methods.

Suppose k of the particles, $\vec{x}_1, \ldots, \vec{x}_k$, are in a cluster. For example, they all lie inside a sphere of radius R with center $\vec{x}_C$. Look at evaluting the velocity at some point $\vec{x}$ far away from the cluster, i.e. with $\|\vec{x} - \vec{x}_C\| \gg R$. The regular Biot-Savart formula would include their contribution with this sum:

$$\sum_{i=1}^{k} -\nabla\Phi(\vec{x} - \vec{x}_i) \times \vec{\omega}_i.$$

However, $\nabla\Phi$ decays rapidly and smoothly to zero at distances like this, and is basically almost the same for all of the particles in this sum. Therefore we would not commit very much error if we changed the sum to just use the center point of the cluster:

$$\sum_{i=1}^{k} -\nabla\Phi(\vec{x} - \vec{x}_C) \times \vec{\omega}_i.$$

In fact, a little math with a Taylor series can give us a good bound of the worst-case error involved, but I will spare you that detour. The main thing is that we can now factor out the fundamental solution from the sum like this:

$$-\nabla\Phi(\vec{x} - \vec{x}_C) \times \left(\sum_{i=1}^{k} \vec{\omega}_i \right).$$

If we compute and store the sum of vorticity in the cluster just once, then finding the cluster's contribution to velocity far away drops to $O(1)$ time from $O(k)$ time.

This idea can be taken several steps further, for example approximating the contribution of one cluster on another well-separated cluster all in one go, by considering just the separation of the cluster centers, or using a more accurate approximation (akin to taking more terms in a Taylor series).

The next big idea is to construct a bounding-volume hierarchy around the particles, for example using octrees or kd-trees to divide up the space and cluster nearby particles together in the tree. Each node in the tree then becomes a candidate cluster. We can efficiently compute the vorticity sums and so forth in each tree node (for the particles contained in that branch of the tree) bottom-up from the leaves. Then when we need to evaluate velocity, we can traverse the tree starting at the root, and stop traversal as soon as we find a cluster that is tight enough and far enough away from the evaluation point that we can get a good approximation without descending further.

14.3.7   Solid Boundaries

Finally we turn to solid boundaries. There are actually two solid boundary conditions we have seen so far:

- no-stick $\vec{u} \cdot \hat{n} = \vec{u}_{\text{solid}} \cdot \hat{n}$, and

- no-slip $\vec{u} = \vec{u}_{\text{solid}}$.

The first is natural for inviscid flow, the second for viscous flow.

Let's look at no-stick first, because it is a bit simpler. The key thing to remember is that when we reconstructed velocity from vorticity, you may recall we computed only one of infinitely many possible velocities whose curls are as close as possible to a given $\vec{\omega}$. Call that choice, from the Biot-Savart law, $\vec{u}_0$. For any scalar field ϕ, the velocity field

$$\vec{u} = \vec{u}_0 + \nabla\phi$$

will have exactly the same curl, so is just as good a solution. We can use this freedom to enforce no-stick boundaries with the right choice of ϕ.[1]

As we saw, the Biot-Savart velocity $\vec{u}_0$ is automatically divergence-free, because it is the curl of the streamfunction. Even if we use a mollified fundamental solution, this will still be true—it will be the curl of a somewhat blurred streamfunction instead. However, $\nabla\phi$ isn't necessarily divergence-free. We can actually use this freedom to inject nonzero divergence into the flow (e.g. an expansion in a combustion region), but for now we will want to impose zero divergence as a constraint:

$$\nabla \cdot \nabla\phi = 0.$$

Surprise! Here's yet another Laplacian popping up. This equation is another way of saying ϕ has to be a **harmonic** function.

At any point on a solid boundary with normal $\hat{n}$, we want to impose the no-stick condition,

$$(\vec{u}_0 + \nabla\phi) \cdot \hat{n} = \vec{u}_{\text{solid}} \cdot \hat{n},$$

which we can rearrange as a boundary condition on ϕ:

$$\nabla\phi \cdot \hat{n} = (\vec{u}_{\text{solid}} - \vec{u}_0) \cdot \hat{n}.$$

At each solid boundary, we can evaluate the Biot-Savart velocity, subtract it from the solid velocity, and the dot-product with the normal gives us the boundary condition for ϕ.

This may seem a little familiar: it's actually just like the potential flow we saw in Chapter 13. There we imposed a similar Neumann boundary condition on the bottom of the ocean, while using Bernoulli's theorem to get the boundary condition at the free surface.

---

[1]Incidentally, this also closely relates to the famous Helmholtz decomposition; many people prefer to start from Helmholtz to get into vortex methods.

Writing down the PDE for ϕ is a far cry from solving for it, and then evaluating $\nabla \phi$ wherever we need it, of course. There are at least two interesting possibilities for general solid geometry. The first is to actually use the fundamental solution and summation again, but with "particles" embedded on the solid boundary: this leads to Boundary Integral Equations a.k.a. the Boundary Element Method. Brochu et al. [BKB12] used this approach together with vortex sheets for the flow, if you want to read more on that. The other approach to consider is to discretize the problem onto a grid. We already know how to solve the Poisson problem for pressure, with Neumann solid boundary conditions, on a grid quite well: this is hardly any different.

Let's now turn to no-slip viscous boundaries. Given that we are ostensibly looking at inviscid flow, it may be mysterious why we even consider them. However, remember that air really does have a small amount of viscosity, so no-slip is correct at some level. Moreover, inviscid no-stick boundaries have some strange, even paradoxical features. It can be shown that, with truly inviscid flow and boundaries, it is impossible for a solid object to experience lift or drag or any interesting net force in the air if it starts at rest—and yet we are all familiar with lift and drag, not the least in airplanes which can in fact fly. With our earlier velocity-pressure solvers, we always had enough numerical dissipation in the system that this theoretical problem doesn't bother us, but vortex particles eliminate numerical dissipation to the extent that we have to worry about it here.

In reality, the flow near a solid tends to exhibit "boundary layers," where the velocity changes from matching the solid at its surface to slipping past tangentially a very short distance away. That kind of layer with rapidly changing tangential velocity naturally has very strong vorticity. This guides us to the idea that to enforce no-slip boundaries, we should add vortex particles (or similar vortex sources) on the surface of the solid. Where it gets particularly interesting is in deciding when and where the vorticity computed at the solid can detach from the solid and flow into the air as more vortex particles. This is critical to the right look for flow past solids, but is still very much an active area of research: I refer you to the papers and books mentioned above to learn more.

14.3.8 Vortex-in-Cell

Continuing with the idea of solving for ϕ on a grid to enforce no-stick solid boundaries, also remember the Biot-Savart velocity itself is derived from solving a Poisson problem (either directly from the curl of vorticity, or through a streamfunction): why not solve it on a grid too? This leads to the Vortex-in-Cell (VIC) method (begun by Christiansen [Chr73]).

The essence of VIC, much like PIC and FLIP, is to transfer vorticity stored on particles to a background grid of the whole domain, solve for the velocity field on the grid, and then interpolate back to the particles. This immediately avoids the cost of Biot-Savart summation—instead we just need to solve a few Poisson problems on a grid, which we can do very efficiently already, plus some cheap finite differences and interpolation. No complicated tree codes are needed.

The main downside to VIC, compared to Biot-Savart-based methods, is that we lose some of the extraordinary detail which vortex particles can provide. To match the same detail requires a very fine grid, which may end up being more expensive again.

15

Coupling Fluids and Solids

We have covered in some detail earlier (Chapter 5) how to incorporate moving solid-wall boundary conditions in a simulation. The assumption there was that the solids followed an immutable scripted path: the fluid can't push back on them to change their motion. This chapter is focused on providing this two-way coupling.

15.1 One-Way Coupling

However, before going into two-way coupling, let's take a quick look at the other one-way coupling: solids that take their motion from the fluid, but don't affect it. This is particularly useful for solids that are much lighter than the fluid or much smaller than the features of the flow. In fact we have already seen this, tracing marker particles in the velocity field of the fluid for smoke animation. Here the position $\vec{x}_i$ of each particle simply followed the fluid velocity field:

$$\frac{d\vec{x}_i}{dt} = \vec{u}(\vec{x}_i, t). \tag{15.1}$$

This is also useful for small objects, or even particle systems representing foam, drifting in water, perhaps with a step projecting them to stay on the water surface.

One step up from marker particles are rigid bodies that take their motion from the fluid. In addition to moving their centers of mass with Equation (15.1), we need to update their orientations. Recalling that the vorticity of the flow $\vec{\omega} = \nabla \times \vec{u}$ is twice the angular velocity of the fluid at any given point, we simply integrate the rigid body position using $\frac{1}{2}\vec{\omega}$. For example, using a unit-length quaternion $\hat{q}_i$ to represent the orientation, we could update it over a time step Δt with

$$\tilde{q}_i = \left(1, \tfrac{1}{4}\Delta t \vec{\omega}\right) \hat{q}_i^n,$$

$$\hat{q}_i^{n+1} = \frac{\tilde{q}_i}{\|\tilde{q}_i\|}.$$

Take note of the factor of $\frac{1}{4}$: this is $\frac{1}{2}$ from the quaternion integration formula and another $\frac{1}{2}$ to get angular velocity from vorticity. Advancing orientations in this manner is useful not just for actual rigid bodies but also for oriented particles that carry a local coordinate system—see Rasmussen et al. [RNGF03] for an example in constructing highly detailed smoke plumes from explosions, where each particle carries a volumetric texture.

More generally, we might want solids to have some inertia, with the effect of the fluid felt in terms of force, not velocity. As we know, there are two forces in effect in a fluid: pressure and viscous stress. The second is perhaps more important for very small objects.

The net force due to viscosity is the surface integral of viscous traction, the viscous stress tensor times the surface normal:

$$\vec{F} = -\iint_{\partial S} \tau \hat{n}.$$

Here I take S to be the volume of the solid and ∂S to be its boundary—this is a slight change of notation from earlier chapters where S represented the solid surface. The normal here points *out* of the solid and *into* the fluid, leading to the negative sign. In one-way coupling, the viscous boundary condition $\vec{u} = \vec{u}_{\text{solid}}$ isn't present in the simulation and thus the fluid's viscous stress tensor isn't directly usable. Indeed, the assumption underlying one-way coupling is that the solid objects don't have an appreciable effect on the fluid at the resolution of the simulation. However, we can imagine that *if* the solid were in the flow, there would be a small **boundary layer** around it in which the velocity of the fluid rapidly alters to match the solid velocity: the gradient of velocity in this region gives us the viscous stress tensor. The actual determination of this boundary layer and exactly what average force results is in general unsolved. We instead boil it down to simple formulas, with tunable constants. For small particles in the flow, we posit a simple drag force of the form:

$$\vec{F}_i = D(\vec{u} - \vec{u}_i).$$

Here D is proportional to the fluid's dynamic viscosity coefficient, and might be a per-particle constant, or involve the radius or cross-sectional area of the object, or might even introduce a non-linearity such as being proportional to $\|\vec{u} - \vec{u}_i\|$—in various engineering contexts all of these have been found to be useful. For flatter objects, such as leaves or paper, we might constrain the normal component of the velocity to match the fluid and only apply a weak (if not zero) viscous force in the tangential direction.

If we are further interested in solids with orientation, the net torque on an object due to viscosity is likewise

$$\vec{T} = -\iint_S (\vec{x} - \vec{x}_i) \times (\tau \hat{n}),$$

where $\vec{x}_i$ is the center of mass of the object, and similarly we can't hope to derive a perfect physical formula for it. Instead we can posit simple formulas now based on the difference between the angular velocity of the solid and half the vorticity of the fluid:

$$\vec{T} = E\left(\tfrac{1}{2}\vec{\omega} - \vec{\Omega}\right).$$

The proportionality E can be tuned similar to D and may even be generalized to a matrix incorporating the current rotation matrix of the object if the solids are far from round.

The effect of pressure is a little simpler. The net force in this case is

$$\vec{F} = -\iint_{\partial S} p\hat{n} = -\iiint_S \nabla p,$$

where we have used the divergence theorem to convert it into an integral of the pressure gradient over the volume occupied by the solid. For small objects, we can evaluate ∇p from the simulation at the center of mass and multiply by the object's volume to get the force. Note that for water sitting still (and assuming a free surface pressure of zero), the hydrostatic pressure is equal to $\rho_{\text{water}}|g|d$ where d is depth below the surface, giving a gradient of $-\rho_{\text{water}}\vec{g}$. Multiplying this by the volume that the object displaces, we get the mass of displaced water, leading to the usual buoyancy law.

The torque due to pressure is

$$T = -\iint_{\partial S} (\vec{x} - \vec{x}_i) \times (p\hat{n}).$$

If p is smooth enough throughout the volume occupied by the solid—say it is closely approximated as a constant or even linear function—this integral vanishes, and there is no torque on the object; we needn't model it. Do note that in the case of water sitting still, the pressure is *not* smooth across the surface—it can be well approximated as a constant zero above the surface, compared to the steep linear gradient below—and thus a partially submerged object can experience considerable torque from pressure. In the partially submerged case, the integral should be taken (or approximated) over the part of the solid below the water surface.

15.2 Weak Coupling

For objects large or heavy enough to significantly affect the fluid flow, but light enough to be affected in turn by the fluid, we need methods for simulating both in tandem. One common approach to implementing this two-way coupling is sometimes termed **weak coupling**. In this scheme, we interleave the solid- and fluid-simulation steps. At its simplest, we get the following algorithm for each time step:

- Advect the fluid, and update the solid positions (and orientations if relevant).

- Integrate non-coupled forces into all velocities (e.g., gravity, internal elasticity forces).

- Solve for the pressure to make the fluid incompressible, enforcing the solid-wall boundary condition with the current solid velocities held fixed.

- Update the solid velocities from forces due to the new fluid pressure and from contact/collision.

More complicated schemes are of course possible, e.g., with repeated alternations between fluid and solid or with substeps to get higher accuracy for the internal elastic forces, but the essence of weak coupling remains: one pressure solve for fluid treats the solid velocities as fixed, and one update to solid velocities treats the fluid pressure as fixed.

In terms of implementation, we have already covered the fluid aspect of this problem since, from the point of view of the fluid solver, the solid is always treated as fixed as before.[1] All that needs to be added is the fluid-to-solid stage, where fluid forces are applied to the solid.

For a rigid object, the fluid-to-solid coupling amounts to finding the net force and torque due to the fluid, which we have seen in surface integral form in the previous section. If the geometry of the solid objects is tesselated finely enough (i.e., on a scale comparable to the grid spacing Δx) these surface integrals can be directly approximated with numerical quadrature. For example, if the object surface is represented by a triangle mesh, the force could be as simple as summing over the triangles the product of triangle area with pressure interpolated at the centroid of the triangle, and if relevant, the viscous stress tensor times the triangle normal. The torque can similarly be approximated. However, in other circumstances (e.g., objects tesselated at a very different scale) directly approximating these surface integrals can be inconvenient. Luckily the face area fractions we compute for the pressure solve can directly be used here too with a little effort.

---

[1]Though as Guendelman et al. [GSLF05] point out, if the solids are thin, care must be taken in advection—in the semi-Lagrangian approach, if a particle trajectory is traced back *through* a solid, the fluid velocity at the interfering solid wall should be used, interpolated in a one-sided way only from the correct side of the solid; for particle methods, collision detection should be used to ensure particles don't pass through solid walls.

For example, the net pressure force is

$$\vec{F} = -\iint_{\partial S} p\hat{n}.$$

Breaking this up into a sum over grid cells intersected by the surface of the solid, and assuming pressure is constant in each such cell, gives

$$\vec{F} = -\sum_{i,j,k} p_{i,j,k} \iint_{\partial S_{i,j,k}} \hat{n}.$$

Consider one such grid cell, and suppose the fluid volume in the cell is $F_{i,j,k}$, while the parts of the cell faces in the fluid are $\partial F_{i,j,k}$. The Fundamental Theorem of Calculus applied to the constant 1 shows that

$$0 = \iiint_{F_{i,j,k}} \nabla 1 = \iint_{\partial F_{i,j,k}} 1\hat{n} + \iint \partial S_{i,j,k} 1\hat{n},$$

or rearranged,

$$-\iint_{\partial S_{i,j,k}} \hat{n} = \iint_{\partial S_{i,j,k}} \hat{n}.$$

The latter is just an easy sum over the face fractions we compute for our accurate pressure solve anyhow, scaled by Δx^2.

Likewise the net torque is

$$\vec{T} = -\iint_{\partial S} (\vec{x} - \vec{x}_C) p\hat{n},$$

where $\vec{x}_C$ is the center of mass. The same approach can be taken to compute this in terms of face area fractions of grid cells..

This general approach has met with success in many graphics papers (e.g., [THK02,GSLF05]) and is quite attractive from a software architecture point of view—the internal dynamics of fluids and solids remain cleanly separated, with new code only for integrating fluid forces applied to solids—but does suffer from a few problems that may necessitate smaller than desirable time steps. For example, if we start with a floating solid initially resting at equilibrium: after adding acceleration due to gravity all velocities are $\Delta t \vec{g}$, the fluid pressure solve treats this downward velocity at the solid surface as a constraint and thus leads to non-zero fluid velocities, and finally the pressure field (perturbed from hydrostatic equilibrium) doesn't quite cancel the velocity of the solid; the solid sinks to some extent, and the water starts moving. These errors are proportional to the time-step size and thus of course can be reduced, but at greater expense.

15.3   The Immersed Boundary Method

A somewhat stronger coupling scheme is epitomized by the immersed boundary method (the classic reference is the review article by Peskin [Pes02]). Here we give the fluid pressure solve leeway to change the solid velocity by, in effect, momentarily pretending the solid is also fluid (just of a different density). In particular, rather than impose the solid velocity as boundary conditions for the fluid pressure solve, we add the mass and velocity of the solid to the fluid grid and then solve for pressure throughout the whole domain. The usual fluid fractions are used as weights in determining the average density and average velocity in each u-, v-, and w-cell, and then the fractions actually used in determining the pressure equations are full. (Incidentally, this approach was in fact combined with the approach of the previous section in the paper of Guendelman et al. [GSLF05], where this pressure is used instead of the less accurate pressure of the classic voxelized pressure solve to update the solid's velocity.)

A related method, the rigid fluid approach of Carlson et al. [CMT04], simplifies the solve somewhat by moreover assuming the density of the solid to be the same as the fluid and adding a corrective buoyancy force as a separate step, recovering a rigid body's velocity directly from averaging the velocity on the grid after the pressure solve (i.e., finding the average translational and angular velocity of the grid cells the solid occupies) rather than integrating pressure forces over the surface of the body. This can work extremely well if the ratio of densities isn't too large.

For inviscid flow, simply averaging the solid and fluid velocities in mixed cells as is typically done in the immersed boundary method may lead to excessive numerical dissipation. Recall that the tangential velocity of the solid is not coupled to the tangential velocity of the fluid: only the normal components are connected for inviscid flows. When averaging the full velocities together we are, in essence, constraining the fluid to the viscous boundary condition $\vec{u} = \vec{u}_{\text{solid}}$. Therefore it is recommended if possible to extrapolate the tangential component of fluid velocity into the cells occupied by the solid and only average the normal component of the solid's velocity onto the grid. For very thin solids, such as cloth, this is particularly simple since extrapolation isn't required—just a separation of the solid velocities into normal and tangential components.

This approach helps reduce some of the artifacts of the previous weak-coupling method, but it doesn't succeed in all cases. For example, starting a simulation with a floating object resting at equilibrium still ends up creating false motion, since in the pressure solve the solid object appears to be an odd-shaped wave on the fluid surface.

15.4   General Sparse Matrices

Before getting into strong coupling, where we compute fluid and solid forces simultaneously, we need to take a brief diversion to generalize our sparse matrix capabilities: the regular structure of the matrices used up until now will not accommodate the addition of solids.

There are several possible data structures for storing and manipulating general sparse matrices. The one we will focus on is sometimes called the **compressed sparse row** (or CSR) format. Here each row of the matrix is stored as an array of non-zero values and their associated column indices. We'll actually use two variations of CSR, a simple dynamic version (that makes adding new non-zeros when dynamically constructing a matrix fairly efficient) and a static version that gives better performance in PCG.

In dynamic CSR, the array for each sparse row is stored independently with an associated length. To support adding new non-zeros relatively efficiently, we may allocate extra storage for these arrays and keep track of the total available; when the extra space runs out, we can reallocate the array with double the size (or some other multiplier). This is the strategy taken in the C++ STL `vector` container for example. Often people will further maintain the arrays in order sorted by column index, making it more efficient to find entries or add two sparse rows together.

However, the core of PCG, multiplying the sparse matrix and a dense vector, loses some efficiency with this approach: each sparse row might be scattered in memory leading to poor cache usage. Therefore, after constructing a matrix using the dynamic CSR structure, we convert it to a static CSR structure. Here just three arrays are defined, ensuring that all matrix non-zeros are contiguous in memory:

- a floating-point array `value` containing all non-zero values ordered row by row,

- an integer array `colindex` of the same length containing the corresponding column indices, and

- an integer array `rowstart` of length $n+1$ (for an $n \times n$ matrix) indicating where each sparse row begins in `value` and `colindex`—an extra entry at the end points just past the end of the `value` and `colindex` arrays (i.e., contains the number of non-zeros in the matrix).

The small overhead of converting a dynamic CSR matrix to the static format is generally well worth it for PCG, bringing the cost back in line with our earlier grid-based method.

You may recall that with our grid version of the matrix we optimized the storage by exploiting symmetry, in some sense just storing the upper

```
for i = 0 to n-1
  y(i) = 0
  for j = rowstart(i) to rowstart(i+1)-1
    y(i) += value(j)*x(colindex(j))
```

Figure 15.1. Pseudocode for multiplying an $n \times n$ static CSR matrix with a dense vector, $y = Ax$.

(or lower) triangle of the matrix. This is generally not worthwhile with CSR: it considerably complicates matrix operations.

It is fairly straightforward to multiply a static CSR sparse matrix with a dense vector; see Figure 15.1 for pseudocode. It's another matter to generalize the incomplete Cholesky preconditioner and associated triangular solves. It turns out, for general sparsity patterns, that the previous simplification of only having to compute diagonal entries (and reusing the off-diagonal entries of A) doesn't hold, and furthermore the modified incomplete Cholesky factorization cannot be computed with the same loop-ordering presented earlier. It is more natural, in fact, to compute $R = L^T$ in CSR format (or equivalently, L in a compressed sparse column format). All that said, we can still define the regular incomplete factor from the previous properties:

- R is upper triangular, and $R_{i,j} = 0$ wherever $A_{i,j} = 0$,

---

- Set tuning constant $\tau = 0.97$ and safety constant $\sigma = 0.25$.
- Copy the upper triangle of A into R (including the diagonal).
- For $k = 0$ to $n - 1$ where $R_{k,k} \neq 0$:
  - If $R_{k,k} < \sigma A_{k,k}$ then set $R_{k,k} \leftarrow \sqrt{A_{k,k}}$, otherwise set $R_{k,k} \leftarrow \sqrt{R_{k,k}}$.
  - Rescale the rest of the k'th row of R: $R_{k,j} \leftarrow \frac{R_{k,j}}{R_{k,k}}$ for stored entries with $j > k$.
  - Loop over $j > k$ where $R_{k,j}$ is stored:
    - Set $\delta = 0$ (where we keep a sum of the elements we drop).
    - Loop over $i > k$ where $R_{k,i}$ is stored:
      - If $R_{j,i}$ is stored, set $R_{j,i} \leftarrow R_{j,i} - R_{k,i}R_{k,j}$, otherwise $\delta \leftarrow \delta + R_{k,i}R_{k,j}$.
    - Set $R_{j,j} \leftarrow R_{j,j} - \tau\delta$.

Figure 15.2. The calculation of the MIC(0) preconditioner R for general matrices A, using CSR format.

- (First solve $R^T z = r$).
- Copy $z \leftarrow r$.
- For $i = 0$ to $n - 1$ where $R_{i,i} \neq 0$:
  - Set $z_i \leftarrow \frac{z_i}{R_{i,i}}$.
  - Loop over $j > i$ where $R_{i,j}$ is stored:
    - Set $z_j \leftarrow z_j - R_{i,j} z_i$.
- (Next solve $R z^{\text{new}} = z$ in place).
- For $i = n - 1$ down to 0, where $R_{i,i} \neq 0$:
  - Loop over $j > i$ where $R_{i,j}$ is stored:
    - Set $z_i \leftarrow z_i - R_{i,j} z_j$.
  - Set $z_i \leftarrow \frac{z_i}{R_{i,i}}$.

Figure 15.3. Applying the MIC(0) preconditioner in CSR format to get $z = (R^T R)^{-1} r$.

- $(R^T R)_{i,j} = A_{i,j}$ wherever $A_{i,j} \neq 0$,

and the modified factor from:

- R is upper triangular, and $R_{i,j} = 0$ wherever $A_{i,j} = 0$,
- $(R^T R)_{i,j} = A_{i,j}$ wherever $A_{i,j} \neq 0$ with $i < j$ (i.e. off the diagonal),
- each row sum $\sum_j (R^T R)_{i,j}$ matches the row sum $\sum_j A_{i,j}$ of A.

Without going into the picky but obvious details of using the format, Figure 15.2 presents pseudocode to construct R, with the same parameters as before, and Figure 15.3 demonstrates how to apply the preconditioner by solving with R and R^T.

15.5 Strong Coupling

Strong coupling has been most thoroughly worked out for the rigid body case, with an inviscid fluid (just pressure); this is where we will end the chapter. Let's work out the equations for the continuous case before proceeding to discretization.

First we'll define some notation for a rigid body:

- $\vec{X}$ the center of mass of the rigid body,
- $\vec{V}$ its translation velocity,

- $\vec{\Omega}$ its angular velocity,

- $\vec{L}$ its angular momentum,

- m its mass, and

- I its inertia tensor.

(Extending this to multiple rigid bodies is straightforward.) We saw the net force and torque on the body due to pressure above, which gives us the following updates:

$$\vec{V}^{n+1} = \vec{V} - \frac{\Delta t}{m} \iint_{\partial S} p\hat{n}, \tag{15.2}$$

$$\vec{\Omega}^{n+1} = \vec{\Omega} - \Delta t I^{-1} \iint_{\partial S} \left(\vec{x} - \vec{X} \right) \times p\hat{n}. \tag{15.3}$$

The velocity of the solid at a point $\vec{x}$ on the surface is

$$\vec{u}_{\text{solid}}(\vec{x}) = \vec{V} + \Omega \times \left(\vec{x} - \vec{X} \right),$$

which then appears in the boundary conditions for the usual pressure problem:

$$\nabla \cdot \frac{\Delta t}{\rho} \nabla p = \nabla \cdot \vec{u} \qquad \text{in the fluid,}$$

$$\left(\vec{u} - \frac{\Delta t}{\rho} \nabla p \right) \cdot \hat{n} = \vec{u}_{\text{solid}}^{n+1} \cdot \hat{n} \qquad \text{on } \partial S.$$

A free surface boundary condition $p = 0$ may also be included.

As an aside, though not immediately apparent in this form, the linear operator that maps $(\vec{V}, \vec{\Omega})$ to the normal velocity field on the boundary can be shown to be the adjoint[2] of the operator that maps pressures on the boundary to net force and torque on the solid. It's this property that will end up, after discretization, giving us a symmetric matrix to solve for pressure.

A simpler form of the equations are given by Batty et al. [BBB07]. We keep the rigid body update Equations (15.2) and (15.3), but avoid the boundary conditions by instead seeking a pressure that minimizes the kinetic energy of the entire system. This is quite compatible with the more accurate FVM pressure solve in this book, only where Batty et al. use

---

[2]Adjoint simply means transpose when talking about matrices but is also used for operators involving infinite-dimensional spaces such as the space of normal velocity fields here.

volume fractions as coefficients in the matrix, we use face fractions. Recall that the kinetic energy of the rigid body is just $\frac{1}{2}m\|\vec{V}\|^2 + \frac{1}{2}\vec{\Omega}^T I\vec{\Omega}$.

It is this variational form of the equations that we choose to discretize. We already have discussed how to approximate the pressure update to the rigid body (i.e., the net force and torque) in the earlier weak-coupling section; we need only make this concrete with a sparse matrix J which, when multiplied with a vector containing the grid pressure values yields the force and torque. Examine the first three rows of J that correspond to the net force. For example, the x-component F_1 (the first row) is determined, with a little rearrangement of the summation, from

$$F_1 = \sum_{i,j,k} \Delta x^2 (V_{i+1/2,j,k} - V_{i-1/2,j,k}) p_{i,j,k},$$

where $V_{i+1/2,j,k}$ is the face area fraction of the solid in u-cell $(i+1/2, j, k)$—note that this is the complement of the face area fractions for the fluid! This gives us

$$J_{1,(i,j,k)} = \Delta x^2 (V_{i+1/2,j,k} - V_{i-1/2,j,k}),$$

Similarly, the next two rows of J, corresponding to the y- and z-components of net force, are

$$J_{2,(i,j,k)} = \Delta x^2 (V_{i,j+1/2,k} - V_{i,j-1/2,k}),$$
$$J_{3,(i,j,k)} = \Delta x^2 (V_{i,j,k+1/2} - V_{i,j,k-1/2}).$$

Similarly we can get the other three rows of J that correspond to the net torque. The first component T_1 is approximated by

$$T_1 = \sum_{i,j,k} \Delta x^2 V_{i,j+1/2,k}(z_k - Z)(p_{i,j+1,k} - p_{i,j,k})$$
$$- \sum_{i,j,k} \Delta x^2 V_{i,j,k+1/2}(y_j - Y)(p_{i,j,k+1} - p_{i,j,k}),$$

where x_i, y_j and z_k give the coordinates of the center of grid cell (i, j, k). From this we see that the fourth row of J is given by

$$J_{4,(i,j,k)} = - \Delta x^2 (z_k - Z)(V_{i,j+1/2,k} - V_{i,j-1/2,k})$$
$$+\Delta x^2 (y_j - Y)(V_{i,j,k+1/2} - V_{i,j,k-1/2}).$$

Similarly, the last two rows of J, corresponding to the second and third components of net torque, are

$$J_{5,(i,j,k)} = -\Delta x^2 (x_i - X)(V_{i,j,k+1/2} - V_{i,j,k-1/2})$$
$$+ \Delta x^2 (z_k - Z)(V_{i+1/2,j,k} - V_{i-1/2,j,k}),$$
$$J_{6,(i,j,k)} = -\Delta x^2 (y_j - Y)(V_{i+1/2,j,k} - V_{i-1/2,j,k})$$
$$+ \Delta x^2 (x_i - X)(V_{i,j+1/2,k} - V_{i,j-1/2,k}).$$

Note that away from the boundary of the solid, all of these differences are just zero, so J is quite sparse: it has non-zero columns only for cells near the boundary of the solid.

To be perfectly consistent, and thus be able to get exact hydrostatic rest for neutrally buoyant bodies fully immersed in fluid, we can also use the same fractions to approximate the rigid body's inertia tensor—however, outside of this particular scenario this is probably unnecessary work, and thus we leave it to the reader to derive it if interested.

For notational convenience, we'll put the rigid body's translational velocity $\vec{V}$ and angular velocity Ω together into one six-dimensional vector $\vec{U}$. Similarly we can construct a 6×6 mass matrix M from the mass and inertia tensor:

$$M = \begin{pmatrix} m & 0 & 0 & \vec{0} \\ 0 & m & 0 & \vec{0} \\ 0 & 0 & m & \vec{0} \\ \vec{0} & \vec{0} & \vec{0} & I \end{pmatrix}.$$

Then the kinetic energy of the body is $\frac{1}{2}\vec{U}^T M \vec{U}$ and the pressure update is $\vec{U}^{n+1} = \vec{U} + \Delta t M^{-1} J p$.

Finally, we are ready for the discrete minimization. Taking the gradient of the new kinetic energy with respect to pressure gives

$$\frac{\partial}{\partial p}\left[\frac{1}{2}\left(\vec{U} + \Delta t M^{-1} J p \right)^T M \left(\vec{U} + \Delta t M^{-1} J p \right) \right] = \\ \Delta t^2 J^T M^{-1} J p + \Delta t J^T \vec{U}.$$

Batty et al. show how to rephrase the pressure solve as a kinetic energy minimization; without going into those details, the upshot is we just add $\Delta t J^T M^{-1} J$ to the appropriately scaled pressure matrix and $-J^T \vec{U}$ to the right-hand side.

This is precisely where we need more general sparse matrices: $\Delta t J^T M^{-1} J$ doesn't correspond to a simple grid structure. In fact, it forms a dense submatrix, connecting up all the cells near the boundary of the object. If you're interested in the linear algebra, it's also simple to see that it is (at most) rank six and must be symmetric positive semi-definite—so PCG still works! The density may, however, cause memory and performance problems: these can mostly be overcome by keeping the extra terms separate in factored form. The matrix-vector multiplies in PCG can be significantly accelerated then by multiplying $J^T M^{-1} J s$ as $J^T (M^{-1}(J^T s))$ and, since they are only rank six, can be ignored in constructing the preconditioner without too big a penalty.

For large objects, which overlap many grid cells, this is actually a considerable problem: a large amount of memory will be required to store it, and PCG will run slowly due to all the work multiplying with this dense submatrix. One possibility for improvement is to add the new rigid body velocity $\vec{U}^{n+1}$ as an auxiliary variable in the pressure solve, giving the following slightly larger but much sparser system:

$$\begin{pmatrix} A & J^T \\ J & -\frac{1}{\Delta t}M \end{pmatrix} \begin{pmatrix} p \\ \vec{U}^{n+1} \end{pmatrix} = \begin{pmatrix} -d \\ -\frac{1}{\Delta t}M\vec{U} \end{pmatrix}.$$

While this still leads to a symmetric matrix, it is unfortunately now indefinite, which means PCG no longer can work. Nevertheless, this is in a well-studied class of matrices, sometimes termed "saddle-point" matrices (in fact, apart from the constant pressure null-space, it would be a "symmetric quasi-definite" matrix), and it seems promising to solve it as such. For example, it would be worthwhile trying an iterative method such as MINRES in conjunction with an incomplete Cholesky preconditioner in LDL^T form (where L has unit diagonal, and D is a diagonal matrix with positive entries for the pressure unknowns and negative entries for the rigid body unknowns). For more on solving this class of matrix problems, see the review article by Benzi et al. [BGL05] for example.

Another interesting direction to consider is to generalize this approach to include strong coupling of articulated rigid bodies: for example, the Lagrange multiplier approach to constraints can also be phrased as a minimization of kinetic energy. Frictional contact forces fall in the same category, albeit with inequality constraints that complicate the minimization considerably.

Turning to deformable objects, the energy minimization framework falters. Strong coupling in this context means combining an implicit time step of the internal dynamics of the deformable object with the pressure solve; however, implicitly advancing elastic forces (involving potential energy) apparently cannot be interpreted as a minimization of energy with respect to forces. At the time of writing, within graphics only the work of Chentanez et al. [CGFO06] has tackled this problem, discretizing the fluid on an unstructured tetrahedral mesh that conforms to the boundary mesh of the deformable object; so far the generalization to regular grids with volume fractions hasn't been made. We thus end the chapter here.

A

Background

A.1 Vector Calculus

The following three differential operators are fundamental to vector calculus: the gradient ∇, the divergence $\nabla\cdot$, and the curl $\nabla\times$. They occasionally are written in equations as grad, div, and curl instead.

A.1.1 Gradient

The gradient simply takes all the spatial partial derivatives of the function, returning a vector. In two dimensions,

$$\nabla f(x, y) = \left(\frac{\partial f}{\partial x}, \quad \frac{\partial f}{\partial y}\right),$$

and in three dimensions,

$$\nabla f(x, y, z) = \left(\frac{\partial f}{\partial x}, \quad \frac{\partial f}{\partial y}, \quad \frac{\partial f}{\partial z}\right).$$

It can sometimes be helpful to think of the gradient operator as a symbolic vector, e.g., in three dimensions:

$$\nabla = \left(\frac{\partial}{\partial x}, \quad \frac{\partial}{\partial y}, \quad \frac{\partial}{\partial z}\right).$$

The gradient is often used to approximate a function locally:

$$f(\vec{x} + \Delta\vec{x}) \approx f(\vec{x}) + \nabla f(\vec{x}) \cdot \Delta\vec{x}.$$

In a related vein we can evaluate the **directional derivative** of the function; that is, how fast the function is changing when looking along a particular vector direction, using the gradient. For example, if the direction is $\hat{n}$,

$$\frac{\partial f}{\partial n} = \nabla f \cdot \hat{n}.$$

Occasionally we will take the gradient of a vector-valued function, which results in a matrix (sometimes called the **Jacobian**). For example, in three dimensions,

$$\nabla \vec{f} = \nabla(f, g, h) = \begin{pmatrix} \frac{\partial f}{\partial x} & \frac{\partial f}{\partial y} & \frac{\partial f}{\partial z} \\ \frac{\partial g}{\partial x} & \frac{\partial g}{\partial y} & \frac{\partial g}{\partial z} \\ \frac{\partial h}{\partial x} & \frac{\partial h}{\partial y} & \frac{\partial h}{\partial z} \end{pmatrix}.$$

Note that each *row* is the gradient of one component of the function. One way to remember that it's the rows and not the columns is that it should work with the approximation

$$\vec{f}(\vec{x} + \Delta \vec{x}) \approx \vec{f}(\vec{x}) + \nabla \vec{f}(\vec{x})\Delta \vec{x}.$$

The matrix-vector product is just computing the dot-product of each row of the matrix with the vector, and so each row should be a gradient of the function:

$$\nabla(f, g, h) = \begin{pmatrix} \nabla f \\ \nabla g \\ \nabla h \end{pmatrix}.$$

An alternative notation for the gradient that is sometimes used is

$$\nabla f = \frac{\partial f}{\partial \vec{x}}.$$

Using a vector in the denominator of the partial derivative indicates we're taking derivatives with respect to each component of $\vec{x}$.

A.1.2 Divergence

The divergence operator only is applied to vector fields and measures how much the vectors are converging or diverging at any point. In two dimensions it is

$$\nabla \cdot \vec{u} = \nabla \cdot (u, v) = \frac{\partial u}{\partial x} + \frac{\partial v}{\partial y},$$

and in three dimensions,

$$\nabla \cdot \vec{u} = \nabla \cdot (u, v, w) = \frac{\partial u}{\partial x} + \frac{\partial v}{\partial y} + \frac{\partial w}{\partial z}.$$

Note that the input is a vector and the output is a scalar.

The notation $\nabla \cdot$ is explained by thinking of it as symbolically taking a dot-product between the gradient operator and the vector field, e.g., in three dimensions,

$$\nabla \cdot \vec{u} = \left(\frac{\partial}{\partial x}, \frac{\partial}{\partial y}, \frac{\partial}{\partial z} \right) \cdot (u, v, w)$$

$$= \frac{\partial}{\partial x}u + \frac{\partial}{\partial y}v + \frac{\partial}{\partial z}w.$$

A.1.3   Curl

The curl operator measures how much a vector field is rotating around any point. In three dimensions this is a vector:

$$\nabla \times \vec{u} = \nabla \times (u, v, w) = \left(\frac{\partial w}{\partial y} - \frac{\partial v}{\partial z}, \; \frac{\partial u}{\partial z} - \frac{\partial w}{\partial x}, \; \frac{\partial v}{\partial x} - \frac{\partial u}{\partial y} \right).$$

We can reduce this formula to two dimensions in two ways. The curl of a two-dimensional vector field results in a scalar, the third component of the expression above, as if we were looking at the three-dimensional vector field $(u, v, 0)$:

$$\nabla \times \vec{u} = \nabla \times (u, v) = \frac{\partial v}{\partial x} - \frac{\partial u}{\partial y}.$$

The curl of a two-dimensional scalar field results in a vector field, as if we were looking at the three-dimensional field $(0, 0, w)$:

$$\nabla \times w = \left(\frac{\partial w}{\partial y}, \; -\frac{\partial w}{\partial x} \right).$$

The simple way to remember these formulas is that the curl is taking a symbolic cross-product between the gradient operator and the function. For example, in three dimensions,

$$\nabla \times \vec{u} = \left(\frac{\partial}{\partial x}, \; \frac{\partial}{\partial y}, \; \frac{\partial}{\partial z} \right) \times (u, v, w)$$

$$= \left(\frac{\partial}{\partial y} w - \frac{\partial}{\partial z} v, \; \frac{\partial}{\partial z} u - \frac{\partial}{\partial x} w, \; \frac{\partial}{\partial x} v - \frac{\partial}{\partial y} u \right).$$

The curl is a way of measuring how fast (and in three dimensions along what axis) a vector field is rotating locally. If you imagine putting a little paddle wheel in the flow and letting it be spun, then the curl is twice the angular velocity of the wheel. You can check this by taking the curl of the velocity field representing a rigid rotation.

   A vector field whose curl is zero is called curl-free, or **irrotational** for obvious reasons.

A.1.4   Laplacian

The Laplacian is usually formed as the divergence of the gradient (as it repeatedly appears in fluid dynamics). Sometimes it is written as ∇^2 or

Δ, but since these symbols are occasionally used for other purposes, I will stick to writing it as $\nabla \cdot \nabla$. In two dimensions,

$$\nabla \cdot \nabla f = \frac{\partial^2 f}{\partial x^2} + \frac{\partial^2 f}{\partial y^2}$$

and in three dimensions,

$$\nabla \cdot \nabla f = \frac{\partial^2 f}{\partial x^2} + \frac{\partial^2 f}{\partial y^2} + \frac{\partial^2 f}{\partial z^2}.$$

The Laplacian can also be applied to vector or even matrix fields, and the result is simply the Laplacian of each component.

Incidentally, the partial differential equation $\nabla \cdot \nabla f = 0$ is called Laplace's equation, and if the right-hand side is replaced by something non-zero, $\nabla \cdot \nabla f = q$ we call it the Poisson equation. More generally, you can multiply the gradient by a scalar field a (such as $1/\rho$), like $\nabla \cdot (a\nabla f) = q$ and still call it a Poisson problem.

A.1.5   Differential Identities

There are several identities based on the fact that changing the order of mixed partial derivatives doesn't change the result (assuming reasonable smoothness), e.g.,

$$\frac{\partial}{\partial x}\frac{\partial}{\partial y}f = \frac{\partial}{\partial y}\frac{\partial}{\partial x}f.$$

Armed with this, it's simple to show that for any smooth function,

$$\nabla \cdot (\nabla \times \vec{u}) \equiv 0,$$
$$\nabla \times (\nabla f) \equiv 0.$$

Another identity that shows up in vorticity calculations is

$$\nabla \times (\nabla \times \vec{u}) \equiv \nabla(\nabla \cdot \vec{u}) - \nabla \cdot \nabla\vec{u}.$$

The Helmholtz or Hodge decomposition is the result that any smooth vector field $\vec{u}$ can be written as the sum of a divergence-free part and a curl-free part. In fact, referring back to the first two identities above, the divergence-free part can be written as the curl of something and the curl-free part can be written as the gradient of something else. In three dimensions,

$$\vec{u} = \nabla \times \vec{\psi} - \nabla\phi,$$

where $\vec{\psi}$ is a vector-valued potential function and ϕ is a scalar potential function. In two dimensions this reduces to ψ being a scalar potential function as well:

$$\vec{u} = \nabla \times \psi - \nabla\phi.$$

This decomposition is highly relevant to incompressible fluid flow, since we can interpret the pressure projection step as decomposing the intermediate velocity field $\vec{u}^{n+1}$ into a divergence-free part and something else which we throw away, just keeping the divergence-free part. When we express a divergence-free velocity field as the curl of a potential ψ, we call ψ the **streamfunction**.

Some more useful identities are generalizations of the product rule:

$$\nabla(fg) = (\nabla f)g + f\nabla g,$$
$$\nabla \cdot (f\vec{u}) = (\nabla f) \cdot \vec{u} + f\nabla \cdot \vec{u}.$$

A.1.6 Integral Identities

The Fundamental Theorem of Calculus (that the integral of a derivative is the original function evaluated at the limits) can be generalized to multiple dimensions in a variety of ways.

The most common generalization is the divergence theorem discovered by Gauss:

$$\iiint_\Omega \nabla \cdot \vec{u} = \iint_{\partial\Omega} \vec{u} \cdot \hat{n}.$$

That is, the volume integral of the divergence of a vector field $\vec{u}$ is the boundary integral of $\vec{u}$ dotted with the unit outward normal $\hat{n}$. This actually is true in any dimension (replacing volume with area or length or hypervolume as appropriate). This provides our intuition of the divergence measuring how fast a velocity field is expanding or compressing: the boundary integral above measures the net speed of fluid entering or exiting the volume.

Stokes' Theorem applies to the integral of a curl. Suppose we have a bounded surface S with normal $\hat{n}$ and with boundary curve Γ whose tangent vector is τ. Then,

$$\iint_S (\nabla \times \vec{u}) \cdot \hat{n} = \int_\Gamma \vec{u} \cdot \tau.$$

This can obviously be restricted to two dimensions with $\hat{n} = (0, 0, 1)$. The curve integral is called the **circulation** in the context of a fluid velocity field.

We can also integrate a gradient:

$$\iiint_\Omega \nabla f = \iint_{\partial\Omega} f\hat{n}.$$

Some of the most useful identities of all are ones called **integration by parts**, which is what we get when we combine integration identities based on the Fundamental Theorem of Calculus with the product rule for derivatives. They essentially let us move a differential operator from one factor in a product to the other. Here are some of the most useful:

$$\iiint_\Omega (\nabla f)g = \iint_{\partial\Omega} fg\hat{n} - \iiint_\Omega f(\nabla g),$$

$$\iiint_\Omega f\nabla \cdot \vec{u} = \iint_{\partial\Omega} f\vec{u} \cdot \hat{n} - \iiint_\Omega (\nabla f) \cdot \vec{u},$$

$$\iiint_\Omega (\nabla f) \cdot \vec{u} = \iint_{\partial\Omega} f\vec{u} \cdot \hat{n} - \iiint_\Omega f\nabla \cdot \vec{u}.$$

Replacing $\vec{u}$ by ∇g in the last equation gives us one of Green's identities:

$$\iiint_\Omega (\nabla f) \cdot (\nabla g) = \iint_{\partial\Omega} f\nabla g \cdot \hat{n} - \iiint_\Omega f\nabla \cdot \nabla g$$

$$= \iint_{\partial\Omega} g\nabla f \cdot \hat{n} - \iiint_\Omega g\nabla \cdot \nabla f.$$

A.1.7   Basic Tensor Notation

When you get into two or three derivatives in multiple dimensions, it can get very confusing if you stick to using the ∇ symbols. An alternative is to use tensor notation, which looks a little less friendly but makes it trivial to keep everything straight. Advanced differential geometry is almost impossible to do without this notation. We'll present a simplified version that is adequate for most of fluid dynamics.

The basic idea is to label the separate components of a vector with subscript indices 1, 2, and in three dimensions, 3. Usually we'll use variables i, j, k, etc., for these indices. Note that this can get very confusing if you also are thinking of discretizing on a grid—if you want to avoid that confusion, it's often a good idea to only use Greek letters for your tensor indices, e.g., α, β, γ instead.

The gradient of a function is $(\partial f/\partial x_1, \partial f/\partial x_2, \partial f/\partial x_3)$. This is still a bit longwinded, so we instead use the generic $\partial f/\partial x_i$ without specifying what i is: it's a "free" index.

We could then write the divergence, for example, as

$$\sum_i \frac{\partial u_i}{\partial x_i}.$$

This brings us to the **Einstein summation convention**. It's tedious to have to write the sum symbol Σ again and again. Thus we just won't bother writing it: instead, we will assume that in any expression that contains the index i twice, there is an implicit sum over i in front of it. If we don't want a sum, we use different indices, like i and j. For example, the dot-product of two vectors $\vec{u}$ and $\hat{n}$ can be written very succinctly as

$$u_i n_i.$$

Note that by expression I mean a single term or a product—it does not include addition. So this

$$u_i + r_i$$

is a vector, $\vec{u} + \vec{r}$, not a scalar sum.

Einstein notation makes it very simple to write a matrix-vector product, such as $A\vec{x}$:

$$A_{ij} x_j.$$

Note that the free index in this expression is j: this is telling us the jth component of the result. This is also an introduction to second-order tensors, which really are a fancy name for matrices: they have two indices instead of the one for a vector (which can be called a first-order tensor). We can write matrix multiplication just as easily: the product AB is

$$A_{ij} B_{jk}$$

with free indices i and k: this is the i, k entry of the result. Similarly, the outer-product matrix of vectors $\vec{u}$ and $\hat{n}$ is

$$u_i n_j.$$

Other useful symbols for tensor expressions are the Kronecker delta δ_{ij} and the Levi-Civita symbol ϵ_{ijk}. The Kronecker delta is δ_{ij}, which is actually just the identity matrix in disguise: $\delta_{ij} x_j = x_i$. The Levi-Civita symbol has three indices, making it a third-order tensor (kind of like a three-dimensional version of a matrix!). It is zero if any of the indices are repeated, $+1$ if (i, j, k) is just a rotation of $(1, 2, 3)$, and -1 if (i, j, k) is a rotation of $(3, 2, 1)$. What this boils down to is that we can write a cross-product using it: $\vec{r} \times \vec{u}$ is just

$$\epsilon_{ijk} r_j u_k,$$

which is a vector with free index i.

Putting all this together, we can translate the definitions, identities and theorems from before into very compact notation. Furthermore, just by keeping our indices straight, we won't have to puzzle over what an expression like $\nabla \nabla \vec{u} \cdot \hat{n} \times \nabla f$ might actually mean. Here are some of the translations that you can check:

$$(\nabla f)_i = \frac{\partial f}{\partial x_i},$$

$$\nabla = \frac{\partial}{\partial x_i},$$

$$f(x_i + \Delta x_i) \approx f(x_i) + \frac{\partial f}{\partial x_i} \Delta x_i,$$

$$\frac{\partial f}{\partial n} = \frac{\partial f}{\partial x_i} n_i,$$

$$(\nabla \vec{f})_{ij} = \frac{\partial f_i}{\partial x_j},$$

$$\nabla \cdot \vec{u} = \frac{\partial u_i}{\partial x_i},$$

$$(\nabla \times \vec{u})_i = \epsilon_{ijk} \frac{\partial u_k}{\partial x_j},$$

$$\nabla \cdot \nabla f = \frac{\partial^2 f}{\partial x_i \partial x_i},$$

$$\frac{\partial}{\partial x_i} \epsilon_{ijk} \frac{\partial u_k}{\partial x_j} = 0,$$

$$\epsilon_{ijk} \frac{\partial}{\partial x_j} \frac{\partial f}{\partial x_k} = 0.$$

The different versions of the product rule for differentiation, in tensor notation, all just fall out of the regular single-variable calculus rule. For example,

$$\frac{\partial}{\partial x_i}(fg) = \frac{\partial f}{\partial x_i}g + f\frac{\partial g}{\partial x_i},$$

$$\frac{\partial}{\partial x_i}(fu_i) = \frac{\partial f}{\partial x_i}u_i + f\frac{\partial u_i}{\partial x_i}.$$

The integral identities also simplify. For example,

$$\iiint_\Omega \frac{\partial u_i}{\partial x_i} = \iint_{\partial\Omega} u_i n_i,$$

$$\iiint_\Omega \frac{\partial f}{\partial x_i} = \iint_{\partial\Omega} f n_i,$$

$$\iiint_\Omega \frac{\partial f}{\partial x_i}g = \iint_{\partial\Omega} f g n_i - \iiint_\Omega f\frac{\partial g}{\partial x_i}.$$

A.2 Numerical Methods

This book concentrate on methods based on finite differences, which themselves boil down simply to applications of the Taylor series.

Assuming a function f has at least k smooth derivatives, then

$$f(x + \Delta x) = f(x) + \frac{\partial f}{\partial x}(x)\Delta x + \frac{1}{2}\frac{\partial^2 f}{\partial x^2}(x)\Delta x^2 + \frac{1}{6}\frac{\partial^3 f}{\partial x^3}(x)\Delta x^3 + \cdots$$
$$+ \frac{1}{(k-1)!}\frac{\partial^{k-1} f}{\partial x^{k-1}}(x)\Delta x^{k-1} + R_k.$$

The remainder term R_k can be expressed in several ways, for example,

$$R_k = \int_x^{x+\Delta x} \frac{1}{k!}\frac{\partial^k f}{\partial x^k}(s)s^{k-1}ds,$$

$$R_k = \frac{1}{k!}\frac{\partial^k f}{\partial x^k}(s)\Delta x^k \quad \text{for some } s \in [x, x+\Delta x],$$

$$R_k = O(\Delta x^k).$$

Note that Δx could be negative, in which case the second form of the remainder uses the interval $[x + \Delta x, x]$. We'll generally stick with the last form, using the simple $O()$ notation, but do remember that the hidden constant is related to the kth derivative of f—and if f isn't particularly smooth, that could be huge and the Taylor series (taken up to that term) isn't particularly useful.

A.2.1   Finite Differences in Space

Partial derivatives of smooth functions sampled on a grid can be estimated using Taylor's theorem. For example, for a function $q(x)$ sampled at grid points spaced Δx apart, i.e., $q_i = q(x_i) = q(i\Delta x)$, Taylor's theorem gives

$$q_{i+1} = q_i + \Delta x \frac{\partial q}{\partial x}(x_i) + O(\Delta x^2).$$

We can rearrange this to get an estimate of $\partial q/\partial x$ at x_i:

$$\frac{\partial q}{\partial x}(x_i) = \frac{q_{i+1} - q_i}{\Delta x} + O(\Delta x).$$

Note that after dividing through by Δx, the error term was reduced to **first order**, i.e., the exponent of Δx in the $O()$ notation is one.

Of course, you can also estimate the same derivative from q_{i-1}, using Taylor's theorem for $q_{i-1} = q(x_{i-1})$:

$$\frac{\partial q}{\partial x}(x_i) = \frac{q_i - q_{i-1}}{\Delta x} + O(\Delta x).$$

This is also only first-order accurate. Both this and the previous finite difference are **one-sided**, since values of q only to one side of the approximation point are used.

We can get second-order accuracy by using both q_{i+1} and q_{i-1}, for a **centered** or **central** finite difference: the value we're approximating lies in the center of the points we use. Write down the Taylor series for both these points:

$$q_{i+1} = q_i + \Delta x \frac{\partial q}{\partial x}(x_i) + \frac{\Delta x^2}{2} \frac{\partial^2 q}{\partial x^2}(x_i) + O(\Delta x^3),$$

$$q_{i-1} = q_i - \Delta x \frac{\partial q}{\partial x}(x_i) + \frac{\Delta x^2}{2} \frac{\partial^2 q}{\partial x^2}(x_i) + O(\Delta x^3).$$

Now subtract them to get, after cancellation,

$$q_{i+1} - q_{i-1} = 2\Delta x \frac{\partial q}{\partial x}(x_i) + O(\Delta x^3).$$

Dividing through gives the second-order accurate central finite difference:

$$\frac{\partial q}{\partial x}(x_i) = \frac{q_{i+1} - q_{i-1}}{2\Delta x} + O(\Delta x^2).$$

Similar reasoning also shows that the first formula we saw is a second-order accurate central finite difference for the point $x_{i+1/2} = (i + 1/2)\Delta x$:

$$\frac{\partial q}{\partial x}(x_{i+1/2}) = \frac{q_{i+1} - q_i}{\Delta x} + O(\Delta x^2).$$

Throughout this book we also deal with functions sampled at midpoints, $q_{i+1/2} = q(x_{i+1/2})$, for which we can similarly write down

$$\frac{\partial q}{\partial x}(x_i) = \frac{q_{i+1/2} - q_{i-1/2}}{\Delta x} + O(\Delta x^2).$$

Higher derivatives can also be estimated. In particular, we can get a second-order accurate central finite difference for the second derivative $\partial^2 q/\partial x^2$ by writing down the Taylor series yet again:

$$q_{i+1} = q_i + \Delta x \frac{\partial q}{\partial x}(x_i) + \frac{\Delta x^2}{2}\frac{\partial^2 q}{\partial x^2}(x_i) + \frac{\Delta x^3}{6}\frac{\partial^3 q}{\partial x^3}(x_i) + O(\Delta x^4),$$

$$q_{i-1} = q_i - \Delta x \frac{\partial q}{\partial x}(x_i) + \frac{\Delta x^2}{2}\frac{\partial^2 q}{\partial x^2}(x_i) + \frac{\Delta x^3}{6}\frac{\partial^3 q}{\partial x^3}(x_i) + O(\Delta x^4).$$

The following combination cancels out most of the terms:

$$q_{i+1} - 2q_i + q_{i-1} = \Delta x^2 \frac{\partial^2 q}{\partial x^2}(x_i) + O(\Delta x^4).$$

Dividing through by Δx^2 gives the finite difference formula,

$$\frac{\partial^2 q}{\partial x^2}(x_i) = \frac{q_{i+1} - 2q_i + q_{i-1}}{\Delta x^2} + O(\Delta x^2).$$

A.2.2   Time Integration

Solving differential equations in time generally revolves around the same finite difference approach. For example, to solve the differential equation

$$\frac{\partial q}{\partial t} = f(q)$$

with initial conditions $q(0) = q^0$, we can approximate q at discrete times t^n, with $q^n = q(t^n)$. The **time step** Δt is simply the length of time between these discrete times: $\Delta t = t^{n+1} - t^n$. This time-step size may or may not stay fixed from one step to the next. The process of **time integration** is determining the approximate values $q^1, q^2, \ldots$ in sequence; it's called integration since we are approximating the solution

$$q(t) = \int_0^t f(q(\tau))\, d\tau,$$

which has an integral in it.

The simplest time integration method is **forward Euler**, based on the first one-sided finite difference formula we saw:

$$\frac{q^{n+1} - q^n}{\Delta t} = \frac{\partial q}{\partial t}(t^n) + O(\Delta t).$$

Plugging in the differential equation and rearranging gives the formula for the new value q^{n+1} based on the previous value q^n:

$$q^{n+1} = q^n + \Delta t f(q^n)$$

This is only first-order accurate, however.

This book makes use of a few more advanced time integration schemes, such as Runge-Kutta methods. The Runge-Kutta family gets higher-order accuracy and other numerical advantages by evaluating f at several points during a time step. For example, one of the classic second-order accurate Runge-Kutta methods can be written as

$$q^{n+1/2} = q^n + \tfrac{1}{2}\Delta t f(q^n),$$
$$q^{n+1} = q^n + \Delta t f(q^{n+1/2}).$$

Probably the best third-order accurate Runge-Kutta formula is due to Ralston [Ral62]:

$$k_1 = f(q^n),$$
$$k_2 = f(q^n + \tfrac{1}{2}\Delta t k_1),$$
$$k_3 = f(q^n + \tfrac{3}{4}\Delta t k_2),$$
$$q^{n+1} = q^n + \tfrac{2}{9}\Delta t k_1 + \tfrac{3}{9}\Delta t k_2 + \tfrac{4}{9}\Delta t k_3.$$

These schemes are not easy to derive in general!

Many time integration schemes come with a caveat that unless Δt is chosen small enough, the computed solution exponentially blows up despite the exact solution staying bounded. This is termed a **stability time-step restriction**. For some problems, a time integration scheme may even be unstable no matter how small Δt is: both forward Euler and the second-order accurate Runge-Kutta scheme above suffer from this flaw in some cases. The third-order accurate Runge-Kutta scheme may be considered the simplest general-purpose method as a result.

B

Derivations

B.1 The Incompressible Euler Equations

The classic derivation of the incompressible Euler equations is based on conservation of mass and momentum. Consider an arbitrary but fixed region of space Ω, in the fluid. The mass of the fluid in Ω is

$$M = \iiint_\Omega \rho,$$

and the total momentum of the fluid in Ω is

$$\vec{P} = \iiint_\Omega \rho\vec{u}.$$

The rate of change of M, as fluid flows in or out of Ω, is given by the integral around the boundary of the speed at which mass is entering or exiting, since mass cannot be created or destroyed inside Ω:

$$\frac{\partial M}{\partial t} = -\iint_{\partial\Omega} \rho\vec{u} \cdot \hat{n}.$$

Here $\hat{n}$ is the outward-pointing normal. We can transform this into a volume integral with the divergence theorem:

$$\frac{\partial M}{\partial t} = -\iiint_\Omega \nabla \cdot (\rho\vec{u}).$$

Expanding M and differentiating with respect to time (recalling that Ω is fixed) gives

$$\iiint_\Omega \frac{\partial \rho}{\partial t} = -\iiint_\Omega \nabla \cdot (\rho\vec{u}).$$

Since this is true for any region Ω, the integrands must match:

$$\frac{\partial \rho}{\partial t} + \nabla \cdot (\rho\vec{u}) = 0.$$

This is called the **continuity equation**. For an incompressible fluid the material derivative of density $D\rho/Dt$ is zero, i.e.,

$$\frac{\partial \rho}{\partial t} + \vec{u} \cdot \nabla \rho = 0.$$

Subtracting this from the continuity equation gives $\rho \nabla \cdot \vec{u} = 0$, or more simply

$$\nabla \cdot \vec{u} = 0,$$

which is termed the **incompressibility condition**. Note that this is independent of density, even for problems where fluids of different densities mix together.

We can apply the same process to the rate of change of momentum:

$$\frac{\partial \vec{P}}{\partial t} = \iiint_\Omega \frac{\partial(\rho\vec{u})}{\partial t}.$$

Momentum can change in two ways: the transport of fluid across the boundary and a net force $\vec{F}$ applied to region. The transport of momentum with the fluid is the boundary integral of momentum $\rho\vec{u}$ times the speed of the fluid through the boundary:

$$-\iint_{\partial\Omega} (\rho\vec{u})\vec{u} \cdot \hat{n}.$$

(The negative sign comes from the fact that the normal is outward-pointing.) There are two forces in play for an inviscid fluid: pressure p on the boundary and gravity ρg throughout the region:

$$\vec{F} = -\iint_{\partial\Omega} p\hat{n} + \iiint_\Omega \rho g.$$

(Again, we get a negative sign in front of the pressure integral since the normal is outward-pointing.) Combining all these terms we get

$$\iiint_\Omega \frac{\partial(\rho\vec{u})}{\partial t} = -\iint_{\partial\Omega} (\rho\vec{u})\vec{u} \cdot \hat{n} - \iint_{\partial\Omega} p\hat{n} + \iiint_\Omega \rho g.$$

Transforming the boundary integrals into volume integrals with the Fundamental Theorem of Calculus and rearranging gives

$$\iiint_\Omega \frac{\partial(\rho\vec{u})}{\partial t} + \iiint_\Omega \nabla \cdot (\rho\vec{u} \otimes \vec{u}) + \iiint_\Omega \nabla p = \iiint_\Omega \rho g.$$

Here $\vec{u} \otimes \vec{u}$ is the 3×3 outer-product matrix. Again, since this is true for any arbitrary region Ω, the integrands must be equal:

$$\frac{\partial(\rho\vec{u})}{\partial t} + \nabla \cdot (\rho\vec{u} \times \vec{u}) + \nabla p = \rho g.$$

This is the **conservation law** form of the **momentum equation**. Using the product rule of differentiation, exploiting $D\rho/Dt = 0$ for an incompressible fluid, and dividing through by ρ, this can readily be reduced to the form of the momentum equation used in the rest of this book.

Bibliography

[AN05]   A. Angelidis and F. Neyret. Simulation of smoke based on vortex filament primitives. In *Proc. ACM SIGGRAPH/Eurographics Symp. Comp. Anim.*, 2005.

[ANSN06]   A. Angelidis, F. Neyret, K. Singh, and D. Nowrouzezahrai. A controllable, fast and stable basis for vortex based smoke simulation. In *Proc. ACM SIGGRAPH/Eurographics Symp. Comp. Anim.*, 2006.

[APKG07]   B. Adams, M. Pauly, R. Keiser, and L. Guibas. Adaptively sampled particle fluids. *ACM Trans. Graph. (SIGGRAPH Proc.)*, 26(3), 2007.

[BB06]   T. Brochu and R. Bridson. Fluid animation with explicit surface meshes. In *Proc. ACM SIGGRAPH/Eurographics Symp. Comp. Anim. (posters)*, 2006.

[BB08]   Christopher Batty and Robert Bridson. Accurate viscous free surfaces for buckling, coiling, and rotating liquids. In *Proc. ACM SIGGRAPH/Eurographics Symp. Comp. Anim.*, SCA '08, pages 219–228, 2008.

[BB09]   Tyson Brochu and Robert Bridson. Robust topological operations for dynamic explicit surfaces. *SIAM J. Sci. Comput.*, 31(4):2472–2493, 2009.

[BB10]   Christopher Batty and Robert Bridson. A simple finite difference method for time-dependent, variable coefficient stokes flow on irregular domains. Technical report, arXiv:1010.2832, 2010.

[BB12]   Landon Boyd and Robert Bridson. Multiflip for energetic two-phase fluid simulation. *ACM Trans. Graph.*, 31(2):16:1–16:12, 2012.

[BBB07]   C. Batty, F. Bertails, and R. Bridson. A fast variational framework for accurate solid-fluid coupling. *ACM Trans. Graph. (Proc. SIGGRAPH)*, 26(3), 2007.

[BBB10]   Tyson Brochu, Christopher Batty, and Robert Bridson. Matching fluid simulation elements to surface geometry and topology. *ACM Trans. Graph. (Proc. SIGGRAPH)*, 29(4):47:1–47:9, 2010.

[BGL05]   M. Benzi, G. H. Golub, and J. Liesen. Numerical solution of saddle point problems. *Acta Numerica*, pages 1–137, 2005.

[BH86]   J. Barnes and P. Hut. A hierarchical O(N log N) force-calculation algorithm. *Nature*, 324(4):446–449, 1986.

[BHN07]   R. Bridson, J. Hourihan, and M. Nordenstam. Curl-noise for procedural fluid flow. *ACM Trans. Graph. (Proc. SIGGRAPH)*, 26(3), 2007.

[BKB12]   Tyson Brochu, Todd Keeler, and Robert Bridson. Linear-time smoke animation with vortex sheet meshes. In *Proc. ACM SIGGRAPH/Eurographics Symp. Comp. Anim.*, SCA '12, pages 87–95, 2012.

[Bli82]   J. Blinn. A generalization of algebraic surface drawing. *ACM Trans. Graph.*, 1(3):235–256, 1982.

[Bon07]   M. Bonner. Compressible subsonic flow on a staggered grid. Master's thesis, UBC Dept. Computer Science, 2007.

[BR86]   J. U. Brackbill and H. M. Ruppel. FLIP: a method for adaptively zoned, particle-in-cell calculuations of fluid flows in two dimensions. *J. Comp. Phys.*, 65:314–343, 1986.

[Bri02]   Robert Bridson. Digital sculpture. Cs348b course project, Stanford University, 2002. http://graphics.stanford.edu/courses/cs348b-competition/cs348b-02/bridson/.

[Bri03]   R. Bridson. *Computational Aspects of Dynamic Surfaces*. PhD thesis, Stanford University, June 2003.

[BT00]   Robert Bridson and Wei-Pai Tang. A structural diagnosis of some ic orderings. *SIAM J. Sci. Comput.*, 22(5):1527–1532, May 2000.

[CFL28]   R. Courant, K. Friedrichs, and H. Lewy. Über die partiellen differenzengleichungen der mathematischen physik. *Mathematische Annalen*, 100(1):32–74, 1928.

[CGFO06]   N. Chentanez, T. G. Goktekin, B. E. Feldman, and J. F. O'Brien. Simultaneous coupling of fluids and deformable bodies. In *Proc. ACM SIGGRAPH/Eurographics Symp. Comp. Anim.*, pages 83–89, 2006.

[Cho73]   A. J. Chorin. Numerical study of slightly viscous flow. *J. Fluid Mechanics*, 57(4):785–796, 1973.

[Chr73]   I. P. Christiansen. Numerical simulation of hydrodynamics by the method of point vortices. *J. Comp. Phys.*, 13(3):363–379, 1973.

[CK08]   Georges-Henri Cottet and Petros D. Koumoutsakos. *Vortex Methods: Theory and Practice*. Cambridge University Press, 2008.

[CMF12]   Nuttapong Chentanez and Matthias Mueller-Fischer. A multigrid fluid pressure solver handling separating solid boundary conditions. *IEEE Trans. Vis. Comp. Graph.*, 18(8):1191–1201, 2012.

[CMIT02]   M. Carlson, P. Mucha, R. Van Horn III, and G. Turk. Melting and flowing. In *Proc. ACM SIGGRAPH/Eurographics Symp. Comp. Anim.*, pages 167–174, 2002.

[CMT04]   M. Carlson, P. J. Mucha, and G. Turk. Rigid fluid: animating the interplay between rigid bodies and fluid. *ACM Trans. Graph. (Proc. SIGGRAPH)*, 23:377–384, 2004.

[Cor05]   R. Corbett. Point-based level sets and progress towards unorganised particle based fluids. Master's thesis, UBC Dept. Computer Science, 2005.

[DBG14]   Fang Da, Christopher Batty, and Eitan Grinspun. Multimaterial mesh-based surface tracking. *ACM Trans. Graph. (Proc. SIGGRAPH)*, 33(4):112:1–112:11, 2014.

[DC96]   M. Desbrun and M.-P. Cani. Smoothed particles: A new paradigm for animating highly deformable bodies. In *Comput. Anim. and Sim. '96 (Proc. of EG Workshop on Anim. and Sim.)*, pages 61–76, 1996.

[DeW05]   I. DeWolf. Divergence-free noise. 2005.

[DM89]   Iain Duff and Gerard Meurant. The effect of ordering on preconditioned conjugate gradients. *BIT*, 29:635–637, 1989.

[Doi91]   S. Doi. On parallelism and convergence of incomplete lu factorizations. *Appl. Numer. Math.*, 7(5):417–436, June 1991.

[Dür88]   M. J. Dürst. Additional reference to "marching cubes" (letters). *Comput. Graph*, 22(4):72–73, 1988.

[EB15]   Essex Edwards and Robert Bridson. The discretely-discontinuous Galerkin coarse grid for domain decomposition. Technical report, arXiv:1504.00907, 2015.

[Eij91]   Victor Eijkhout. Analysis of parallel incomplete point factorizations. *Lin. Alg. Appl.*, 154:154–156, 1991.

[EM90]   Herbert Edelsbrunner and Ernst Peter Mcke. Simulation of simplicity: A technique to cope with degenerate cases in geometric algorithms. *ACM Trans. Graph.*, 9(1):66–104, 1990.

[ETK+07]   S. Elcott, Y. Tong, E. Kanso, P. Schröder, and M. Desbrun. Stable, circulation-preserving, simplicial fluids. *ACM Trans. Graph.*, 26(1), 2007.

[FF01]   N. Foster and R. Fedkiw. Practical animation of liquids. In *Proc. SIGGRAPH*, pages 23–30, 2001.

[FL04]   R. Fattal and D. Lischinski. Target-driven smoke animation. *ACM Trans. Graph. (SIGGRAPH Proc.)*, 23(3):441–448, 2004.

[FM96]   N. Foster and D. Metaxas. Realistic animation of liquids. *Graph. Models and Image Processing*, 58:471–483, 1996.

[FM97]   N. Foster and D. Metaxas. Modeling the motion of a hot, turbulent gas. In *Proc. SIGGRAPH*, pages 181–188, 1997.

[FOA03]   B. E. Feldman, J. F. O'Brien, and O. Arikan. Animating suspended particle explosions. *ACM Trans. Graph. (Proc. SIGGRAPH)*, 22:708–715, 2003.

[FR86]   A. Fournier and W. T. Reeves. A simple model of ocean waves. In
            Proc. SIGGRAPH, pages 75–84, 1986.

[FSJ01]   R. Fedkiw, J. Stam, and H. W. Jensen. Visual simulation of smoke.
            In *Proc. SIGGRAPH*, pages 15–22, 2001.

[Gam95]   M. N. Gamito. Two dimensional Simulation of Gaseous Phenomena
            Using Vortex Particles. In *Proc. of the 6th Eurographics Workshop
            on Comput. Anim. and Sim.*, pages 3–15. Springer-Verlag, 1995.

[GBO04]   T. G. Goktekin, A. W. Bargteil, and J. F. O'Brien. A method for an-
            imating viscoelastic fluids. *ACM Trans. Graph. (Proc. SIGGRAPH)*,
            23:463–468, 2004.

[GFCK02]   F. Gibou, R. Fedkiw, L.-T. Cheng, and M. Kang. A second-order-
            accurate symmetric discretization of the Poisson equation on irreg-
            ular domains. *J. Comp. Phys.*, 176:205–227, 2002.

[GLG95]   M. N. Gamito, P. F. Lopes, and M. R. Gomes. Two-dimensional
            simulation of gaseous phenomena using vortex particles. In Dimitri
            Terzopoulos and Daniel Thalmann, editors, *Computer Animation
            and Simulation '95*, pages 2–15. Springer-Verlag, 1995.

[GR87]   L. Greengard and V. Rokhlin. A fast algorithm for particle simula-
            tions. *J. Comput. Phys.*, 73(2):325–348, 1987.

[GSLF05]   E. Guendelman, A. Selle, F. Losasso, and R. Fedkiw. Coupling water
            and smoke to thin deformable and rigid shells. *ACM Trans. Graph.
            (SIGGRAPH Proc.)*, 24(3):973–981, 2005.

[Har63]   F. H. Harlow. The particle-in-cell method for numerical solution of
            problems in fluid dynamics. In *Experimental arithmetic, high-speed
            computations and mathematics*, 1963.

[Har04]   F. H. Harlow. Fluid dynamics in group T-3 Los Alamos National
            Laboratory. *J. Comput. Phys.*, 195(2):414–433, 2004.

[Hor15]   Christopher Horvath. Empirical directional wave spectra for com-
            puter graphics. In *Proc. Digital Production Symposium*, 2015.

[HSF07]   J.-M. Hong, T. Shinar, and R. Fedkiw. Wrinkled flames and cellular
            patterns. *ACM Trans. Graph. (SIGGRAPH Proc.)*, 26(3), 2007.

[HW65]   F. Harlow and J. Welch. Numerical Calculation of Time-Dependent
            Viscous Incompressible Flow of Fluid with Free Surface. *Phys. Flu-
            ids*, 8:2182–2189, 1965.

[Irv07]   G. Irving. *Methods for the Physically Based Simulation of Solids and
            Fluids*. PhD thesis, Stanford University Dept. Computer Science,
            2007.

[JBS06]   M. Jones, A. Bærentzen, and M. Sramek. 3D distance fields: A sur-
            vey of techniques and applications. *IEEE Trans. Vis. Comp. Graph-
            ics*, 2006.

[JKSH13]   Alec Jacobson, Ladislav Kavan, , and Olga Sorkine-Hornung. Ro-
            bust inside-outside segmentation using generalized winding numbers.
            ACM Transactions on Graphics (proceedings of ACM SIGGRAPH),
            32(4):33:1–33:12, 2013.

[JL72]   W. P. Jones and B. E. Launder. The prediction of laminarization
            with a two-equation model of turbulence. *Int. J. Heat Mass Transfer*,
            15:301–314, 1972.

[Jon95]   Mark W. Jones. 3d distance from a point to a triangle. Technical
            report, Department of Computer Science, University of Wales, 1995.

[KCR08]   Petros Koumoutsakos, Georges-Henri Cottet, and Diego Rossinelli.
            Flow simulations using particles: Bridging computer graphics and
            cfd. In *ACM SIGGRAPH 2008 Classes*, SIGGRAPH '08, pages 25:1–
            25:73, 2008.

[KFL00]   M. Kang, R. Fedkiw, and X.-D. Liu. A boundary condition capturing
            method for multiphase incompressible flow. *J. Sci. Comput.*, 15:323–
            360, 2000.

[KH04]   J. Kniss and D. Hart.   Volume   effects: modeling
            smoke, fire, and clouds, 2004.   Section from ACM
            SIGGRAPH 2004 courses, *Real-Time Volume Graphics*,
            http://www.cs.unm.edu/ jmk/sig04_modeling.ppt.

[KLL+07]   B. Kim, Y. Liu, I. Llamas, X. Jiao, and J. Rossignac. Simulation
            of bubbles in foam with the volume control method. *ACM Trans.
            Graph. (SIGGRAPH Proc.)*, 26(3), 2007.

[KM90]   Michael Kass and Gavin Miller. Rapid, stable fluid dynamics for
            computer graphics. In *Proc. ACM SIGGRAPH*, pages 49–57, 1990.

[KTJG08]   Theodore Kim, Nils Thürey, Doug James, and Markus Gross.
            Wavelet turbulence for fluid simulation. *ACM Trans. Graph. (Proc.
            SIGGRAPH)*, 27(3):50:1–50:6, 2008.

[LC87]   William E. Lorensen and Harvey E. Cline. Marching cubes: A high
            resolution 3d surface construction algorithm. In *Proc. ACM SIG-
            GRAPH*, pages 163–169, 1987.

[LGF04]   F. Losasso, F. Gibou, and R. Fedkiw. Simulating water and smoke
            with an octree data structure. *ACM Trans. Graph. (Proc. SIG-
            GRAPH)*, 23:457–462, 2004.

[LIGF06]   F. Losasso, G. Irving, E. Guendelman, and R. Fedkiw. Melting and
            burning solids into liquids and gases. *IEEE Trans. Vis. Graph.*,
            12:343–352, 2006.

[LKHW03]   A.E. Lefohn, J.M. Kniss, C.D. Hansen, and R.T. Whitaker. Interac-
            tive deformation and visualization of level set surfaces using graphics
            hardware. In *IEEE Visualization 2003*, pages 75–82, October 2003.

[LS74]   B. E. Launder and B. I. Sharma. Application of the energy-
            dissipation model of turbulence to the calculation of flow near a
            spinning disc. *Lett. Heat Mass Trans.*, 1:131–138, 1974.

[LvdP02]   A. T. Layton and M. van de Panne. A numerically efficient and stable algorithm for animating water waves. *The Visual Computer*, 18(1):41–53, 2002.

[MÖ9]   Matthias Müller. Fast and robust tracking of fluid surfaces. In *Proc. ACM SIGGRAPH/Eurographics Symp. Comp. Anim.*, SCA '09, pages 237–245, 2009.

[MCG03]   M. Müller, D. Charypar, and M. Gross. Particle-based fluid simulation for interactive applications. In *Proc. ACM SIG-GRAPH/Eurographics Symp. Comp. Anim.*, pages 154–159, 2003.

[MCZ07]   Ken Museth, Michael Clive, and Nafees Bin Zafar. Blobtacular: surfacing particle system in "pirates of the caribbean 3". In *ACM SIGGRAPH 2007 sketches*, SIGGRAPH '07, 2007.

[MEB⁺12]   M. K. Misztal, K. Erleben, A. Bargteil, J. Fursund, B. Bunch Christensen, J. A. Bærentzen, and R. Bridson. Multiphase flow of immiscible fluids on unstructured moving meshes. In *Proc. ACM SIG-GRAPH/Eurographics Symp. Comp. Anim.*, SCA '12, pages 97–106, 2012.

[MK02]   Z. Melek and J. Keyser. Interactive simulation of fire. In *Proc. Pacific Graphics*, pages 431–432, 2002.

[MK03]   Z. Melek and J. Keyser. Interactive simulation of burning objects. In *Proc. Pacific Graphics*, pages 462–466, 2003.

[Mus11]   Ken Museth. Db+grid: a novel dynamic blocked grid for sparse high-resolution volumes and level sets. In *ACM SIGGRAPH 2011 Talks*, SIGGRAPH '11, pages 51:1–51:1, 2011.

[Mus13]   Ken Museth. Vdb: High-resolution sparse volumes with dynamic topology. *ACM Trans. Graph.*, 32(3):27:1–27:22, 2013.

[MW99]   Heinrich Müller and Michael Wehle. Visualization of implicit surfaces using adaptive tetrahedrizations. In *Dagstuhl '97, Scientific Visualization*, pages 243–250, 1999.

[NFJ02]   D. Q. Nguyen, R. Fedkiw, and H. W. Jensen. Physically based modeling and animation of fire. *ACM Trans. Graph. (Proc. SIGGRAPH)*, pages 721–728, 2002.

[NMG09]   Yen Ting Ng, Chohong Min, and Frédéric Gibou. An efficient fluidsolid coupling algorithm for single-phase flows. *J. Comp. Phys.*, 228(23):8807 – 8829, 2009.

[NSCL08]   Rahul Narain, Jason Sewall, Mark Carlson, and Ming C. Lin. Fast animation of turbulence using energy transport and procedural synthesis. *ACM Trans. Graph. (Proc. SIGGRAPH Asia)*, 27(5):166:1–166:8, 2008.

[OF02]   S. Osher and R. Fedkiw. *Level Set Methods and Dynamic Implicit Surfaces*. Springer-Verlag, 2002. New York, NY.

[OH95]   J. F. O'Brien and J. K. Hodgins. Dynamic simulation of splashing fluids. In *Proc. Computer Animation*, page 198, 1995.

[PAKF13]   Saket Patkar, Mridul Aanjaneya, Dmitriy Karpman, and Ronald
           Fedkiw. A hybrid lagrangian-eulerian formulation for bubble gener-
           ation and dynamics. In *Proc. ACM SIGGRAPH/Eurographics Symp.
           Comp. Anim.*, SCA '13, pages 105–114, 2013.

[Pes02]   C. S. Peskin. The immersed boundary method. *Acta Numerica*,
           11:479–517, 2002.

[PK05]   S. I. Park and M. J. Kim. Vortex fluid for gaseous phenomena. In
           Proc. ACM SIGGRAPH/Eurographics Symp. Comp. Anim., 2005.

[PN01]   K. Perlin and F. Neyret. Flow noise. In *ACM SIGGRAPH Tech-
           nical Sketches and Applications*, page 187, 2001. http://www-
           evasion.imag.fr/Publications/2001/PN01/.

[Pop00]   S. B. Pope. *Turbulent flows.* Cambridge University Press, 2000.

[PTB+03]   S. Premoze, T. Tasdizen, J. Bigler, A. Lefohn, and R. Whitaker.
           Particle–based simulation of fluids. In *Comp. Graph. Forum (Euro-
           graphics Proc.)*, volume 22, pages 401–410, 2003.

[PTC+10]   Tobias Pfaff, Nils Thuerey, Jonathan Cohen, Sarah Tariq, and
           Markus Gross. Scalable fluid simulation using anisotropic turbu-
           lence particles. *ACM Trans. Graph. (Proc. SIGGRAPH Asia)*,
           29(6):174:1–174:8, 2010.

[PTG12]   Tobias Pfaff, Nils Thuerey, and Markus Gross. Lagrangian vor-
           tex sheets for animating fluids. *ACM Trans. Graph. (Proc. SIG-
           GRAPH)*, 31(4):112:1–112:8, 2012.

[Ral62]   A. Ralston. Runge-Kutta methods with minimum error bounds.
           Mathematics of Computation, 16(80):431–437, 1962.

[RNGF03]   N. Rasmussen, D. Nguyen, W. Geiger, and R. Fedkiw. Smoke sim-
           ulation for large scale phenomena. *ACM Trans. Graph. (Proc. SIG-
           GRAPH)*, 22:703–707, 2003.

[SB08]   H. Schechter and R. Bridson. Evolving sub-grid turbulence for smoke
           animation. In *Proc. ACM SIGGRAPH/Eurographics Symp. Comp.
           Anim.*, SCA '08, pages 1–7, 2008.

[SBG04]   B. Smith, P. Bjorstad, and W. Gropp. *Domain Decomposition: Par-
           allel Multilevel Methods for Elliptic Partial Differential Equations.*
           Cambridge University Press, 2004.

[Set96]   J. Sethian. A fast marching level set method for monotonically ad-
           vancing fronts. *Proc. Natl. Acad. Sci.*, 93:1591–1595, 1996.

[SF92]   M. Shinya and A. Fournier. Stochastic motion: Motion under the
           influence of wind. In *Proc. Eurographics*, pages 119–128, 1992.

[SF93]   J. Stam and E. Fiume. Turbulent wind fields for gaseous phenomena.
           In *Proc. ACM SIGGRAPH*, pages 369–376, 1993.

[She97]   Jonathan Richard Shewchuk. Adaptive precision floating-point arith-
           metic and fast robust geometric predicates. *Discrete & Computa-
           tional Geometry*, 18:305–363, 1997.

[SO09]   Mark Sussman and Mitsuhiro Ohta. A stable and efficient method for treating surface tension in incompressible two-phase flow. *SIAM J. Sci. Comput.*, 31(4):2447–2471, 2009.

[SRF05]   A. Selle, N. Rasmussen, and R. Fedkiw. A vortex particle method for smoke, water and explosions. *ACM Trans. Graph. (Proc. SIGGRAPH)*, pages 910–914, 2005.

[Sta99]   J. Stam. Stable fluids. In *Proc. SIGGRAPH*, pages 121–128, 1999.

[Sto07]   Mark J. Stock. Summary of vortex methods literature. Technical report, 2007.

[SU94]   J. Steinhoff and D. Underhill. Modification of the Euler Equations for "Vorticity Confinement": Application to the Computation of Interacting Vortex Rings. *Phys. of Fluids*, 6(8):2738–2744, 1994.

[Tes04]   J. Tessendorf. Simulating ocean water. *SIGGRAPH Course Notes*, 1999–2004.

[THK02]   T. Takahashi, U. Heihachi, and A. Kunimatsu. The simulation of fluid-rigid body interaction. In *Proc. SIGGRAPH Sketches & applications*, 2002.

[TMSG07]   N. Thuerey, M. Müller, S. Schirm, and M. Gross. Real-time breaking waves for shallow water simulations. In *Proc. Pacific Graphics*, 2007.

[Tsa02]   Y.-H. R. Tsai. Rapid and accurate computation of the distance function using grids. *J. Comput. Phys.*, 178(1):175–195, 2002.

[Tsi95]   J. Tsitsiklis. Efficient algorithms for globally optimal trajectories. *IEEE Trans. on Automatic Control*, 40:1528–1538, 1995.

[Ü01]   Alper Üngör. Tiling 3D euclidean space with acute tetrahedra. In *Proc. 13th Canadian Conference on Computational Geometry (CCCG'01)*, pages 169–172, 2001.

[vFTS06]   W. von Funck, H. Theisel, and H.-P. Seidel. Vector field based shape deformations. *ACM Trans. Graph. (Proc. SIGGRAPH)*, 25(3):1118–1125, 2006.

[Wil08]   Brent Williams. Fluid surface reconstruction from particles. Master's thesis, University of British Columbia, 2008.

[WMFB11]   Chris Wojtan, Matthias Müller-Fischer, and Tyson Brochu. Liquid simulation with mesh-based surface tracking. In *ACM SIGGRAPH 2011 Courses*, SIGGRAPH '11, pages 8:1–8:84, 2011.

[WMT05]   H. Wang, P. J. Mucha, and G. Turk. Water drops on surfaces. *ACM Trans. Graph. (Proc. SIGGRAPH)*, pages 921–929, 2005.

[WMW86]   Geoff Wyvill, Craig McPheeters, and Brian Wyvill. Data Structure for Soft Objects. *The Visual Computer*, 2(4):227–234, February 1986.

[WP10]   Steffen Weißmann and Ulrich Pinkall. Filament-based smoke with vortex shedding and variational reconnection. *ACM Trans. Graph. (Proc. SIGGRAPH)*, 29(4):115:1–115:12, 2010.

[WTGT10]   Chris Wojtan, Nils Thürey, Markus Gross, and Greg Turk. Physics-inspired topology changes for thin fluid features. *ACM Trans. Graph. (Proc. SIGGRAPH)*, 29(4):50:1–50:8, 2010.

[YHK07]   Cem Yuksel, Donald H. House, and John Keyser. Wave particles. *ACM Trans. Graph. (Proc. SIGGRAPH)*, 26(3), 2007.

[YUM86]   L. Yaeger, C. Upson, and R. Myers. Combining physical and visual simulation—creation of the planet jupiter for the film 2010. In *Proc. ACM SIGGRAPH*, pages 85–93, 1986.

[ZB05]   Y. Zhu and R. Bridson. Animating sand as a fluid. *ACM Trans. Graph. (Proc. SIGGRAPH)*, pages 965–972, 2005.

[ZB14]   Xinxin Zhang and Robert Bridson. A pppm fast summation method for fluids and beyond. *ACM Trans. Graph. (Proc. SIGGRAPH Asia)*, 33(6):206:1–206:11, 2014.

[Zha05]   H. Zhao. A fast sweeping method for Eikonal equations. *Math. Comp.*, 74:603–627, 2005.

Index

Printed in the United States
by Baker & Taylor Publisher Services